# Other Books and Series by Jeff Bowen

*Applications for Enrollment of Chickasaw Newborn Act of 1905*
*Volumes I thru VII*

*Cherokee Intermarried White 1906 Volume I thru X*

*Applications for Enrollment of Creek Newborn Act of 1905*
*Volumes I thru XIV*

*Applications for Enrollment of Choctaw Newborn Act of 1905*
*Volume I, II, III, IV, V, VI, VII & VIII*

Visit our website at **www.nativestudy.com** to learn more about these and other books and series by Jeff Bowen

# APPLICATIONS FOR ENROLLMENT OF CHOCTAW NEWBORN ACT OF 1905

## VOLUME IX

### TRANSCRIBED BY
### JEFF BOWEN

NATIVE STUDY
Gallipolis, Ohio
USA

# Other Books and Series by Jeff Bowen

*1901-1907 Native American Census Seneca, Eastern Shawnee, Miami, Modoc, Ottawa, Peoria, Quapaw, and Wyandotte Indians (Under Seneca School, Indian Territory)*

*1932 Census of The Standing Rock Sioux Reservation with Births And Deaths 1924-1932*

*Census of The Blackfeet, Montana, 1897- 1901 Expanded Edition*

*Eastern Cherokee by Blood, 1906-1910, Volumes I thru XIII*

*Choctaw of Mississippi Indian Census 1929-1932 with Births and Deaths 1924-1931   Volume I*
*Choctaw of Mississippi Indian Census 1933, 1934 & 1937, Supplemental Rolls to 1934 & 1935 with Births and Deaths 1932-1938, and Marriages 1936-1938 Volume II*

*Eastern Cherokee Census Cherokee, North Carolina 1930-1939 Census 1930-1931 with Births And Deaths 1924-1931 Taken By Agent L. W. Page Volume I*
*Eastern Cherokee Census Cherokee, North Carolina 1930-1939 Census 1932-1933 with Births And Deaths 1930-1932 Taken By Agent R. L. Spalsbury   Volume II*
*Eastern Cherokee Census Cherokee, North Carolina 1930-1939 Census 1934-1937 with Births and Deaths 1925-1938 and Marriages 1936 & 1938 Taken by Agents R. L. Spalsbury And Harold W. Foght Volume III*

*Seminole of Florida Indian Census, 1930-1940 with Birth and Death Records, 1930-1938*

*Texas Cherokees 1820-1839 A Document For Litigation 1921*

*Choctaw By Blood Enrollment Cards 1898-1914 Volumes I thru XVII*

*Starr Roll 1894 (Cherokee Payment Rolls) Districts: Canadian, Cooweescoowee, and Delaware  Volume One*
*Starr Roll 1894 (Cherokee Payment Rolls) Districts: Flint, Going Snake, and Illinois   Volume Two*
*Starr Roll 1894 (Cherokee Payment Rolls) Districts: Saline, Sequoyah, and Tahlequah; Including Orphan Roll  Volume Three*

*Cherokee Intruder Cases Dockets of Hearings 1901-1909 Volumes I & II*

*Indian Wills, 1911-1921 Records of the Bureau of Indian Affairs Books One thru Seven;*
*Native American Wills & Probate Records 1911-1921*

# Other Books and Series by Jeff Bowen

*Turtle Mountain Reservation Chippewa Indians 1932 Census with Births & Deaths, 1924-1932*

*Chickasaw By Blood Enrollment Cards 1898-1914 Volume I thru V*

*Cherokee Descendants East An Index to the Guion Miller Applications Volume I*
*Cherokee Descendants West An Index to the Guion Miller Applications Volume II (A-M)*
*Cherokee Descendants West An Index to the Guion Miller Applications Volume III (N-Z)*

*Applications for Enrollment of Seminole Newborn Freedmen, Act of 1905*

*Eastern Cherokee Census, Cherokee, North Carolina, 1915-1922, Taken by Agent James E. Henderson*
    *Volume I (1915-1916)*
    *Volume II (1917-1918)*
    *Volume III (1919-1920)*
    *Volume IV (1921-1922)*

*Complete Delaware Roll of 1898*

*Eastern Cherokee Census, Cherokee, North Carolina, 1923-1929, Taken by Agent James E. Henderson*
    *Volume I (1923-1924)*
    *Volume II (1925-1926)*
    *Volume III (1927-1929)*

*Applications for Enrollment of Seminole Newborn Act of 1905 Volumes I & II*

*North Carolina Eastern Cherokee Indian Census 1898-1899, 1904, 1906, 1909-1912, 1914 Revised and Expanded Edition*

*1932 Hopi and Navajo Native American Census with Birth & Death Rolls (1925-1931) Volume 1 - Hopi*
*1932 Hopi and Navajo Native American Census with Birth & Death Rolls (1930-1932) Volume 2 - Navajo*

*Western Navajo Reservation Navajo, Hopi and Paiute 1933 Census with Birth & Death Rolls 1925-1933*

*Cherokee Citizenship Commission Dockets 1880-1884 and 1887-1889 Volumes I thru V*

Copyright © 2013
by Jeff Bowen

ALL RIGHTS RESERVED
No part of this publication may be reproduced
or used in any form or manner whatsoever
without previous written permission from the
copyright holder or publisher.

Originally published:
Baltimore, Maryland
2013

Reprinted by:

Native Study LLC
Gallipolis, OH
www.nativestudy.com
2020

Library of Congress Control Number: 2020918113

ISBN: 978-1-64968-102-7

Made in the United States of America.

This series is dedicated to the descendants of the Choctaw newborn listed in these applications.

This map of Indian Territory shows how large the Choctaw and Chickasaw Nations' land base was that contained huge deposits of asphalt and coal. Just the size and territory involved was flooded with the "Grafters".

DEPARTMENT OF THE INTERIOR.
Commissioner to the Five Civilized Tribes.

# NOTICE.

## Opening of Land Office at Wewoka,
### IN THE SEMINOLE NATION, INDIAN TERRITORY.

Notice is hereby given that on Monday, September 4, 1905, the Commissioner to the Five Civilized Tribes will establish a land office at Wewoka, in the Seminole Nation, Indian Territory, for the purpose of allowing citizens and freedmen of the Seminole Nation to select allotments of land for their minor children enrolled under the Act of Congress approved March 3, 1905 (33 Stat. L. 1060), and for the further purpose of allowing citizens and freedmen of the Seminole Nation, whose allotments are incomplete, to select additional land in order to bring the value of their allotments up to the standard of $309.09, as nearly as may be practicable.

Each child whose enrollment in accordance with the Act of March 3, 1905, has been duly approved by the Secretary of the Interior, is entitled to receive an alllotment of forty acres without regard to the character or value of the land selected.

Selection of allotments for minor children must be made by their citizen or freedmen parents or by a duly appointed guardian, or curator, or by a duly appointed administrator.

TAMS BIXBY,
Commissioner.

Muskogee, Indian Territory,
July 29, 1905.

*This particular notice for the Seminole and Creek Newborn makes mention of the Act of 1905. It is likely that a similar notice was posted in the Choctaw and Chickasaw Nations for the registration of newborn children.*

## DEPARTMENT OF THE INTERIOR,
## Commission to the Five Civilized Tribes.

### Rules and Regulations Governing the Selection of Allotments and the Designation of Homesteads in the Choctaw and Chickasaw Nations.

1. Selections of allotments and designations of homesteads for adult citizens and selections of allotments for adult freedmen must be made in person except as herein otherwise provided.

2. Applications to have land set apart and homesteads designated for duly identified Mississippi Choctaws must be made personally before the Commission to the Five Civilized Tribes. Fathers may apply for their minor children and if the father be dead the mother may apply. Husbands may apply for wives. Applications for orphans, insane persons and persons of unsound mind may be made by duly appointed guardian or curator, and for aged and infirm persons and prisoners by agents duly authorized thereunto by power of attorney, in the discretion of said Commission.

3. At the time of the selection of allotment each citizen and duly identified Mississippi Choctaw shall designate as a homestead out of said selection land equal in value to one hundred and sixty acres of the average allottable land of the Choctaw and Chickasaw Nations, as nearly as may be.

4. Each Choctaw and Chickasaw freedman, at the time of selection shall designate as his or her allotment of the lands of the Choctaw and Chickasaw Nations, land equal in value to forty acres of the average allottable land of the Choctaw and Chickasaw Nations.

5. Citizens, freedmen and identified Mississippi Choctaws who are married, whether they have attained their majority or not, will be regarded as of age for the purpose of making selections.

6. Selections may be made by citizen and freedman parents for unmarried male children under twenty-one years of age and for unmarried female children under eighteen years of age, and a male citizen or freedman may make selection for his wife, if she is entitled to make selection, unless she shall, at the time or previously thereto, protest in writing.

7. Where the father of an unmarried minor citizen, freedman or identified Mississippi Choctaw is a non-citizen, the citizen, freedman or identified Mississippi Choctaw mother of such children must make selection in person in behalf of said children.

8. Selections of allotments and designations of homesteads for minor citizens and selections of allotments for minor freedmen may be made by the citizen father or mother or freedman father or mother, as the case may be, or by a guardian, curator, or an administrator having charge of their estate, in the order named.

9. Selections of allotments and designations of homesteads for citizen, and selections of allotment for freedmen, prisoners, convicts, aged and infirm persons and soldiers and sailors of the United States on duty outside of Indian Territory, may be made by duly appointed agents under power of attorney, and for incompetents by guardians, curators, or other suitable person akin to them.

10. Selections of homes and homesteads designated by duly identified Mississippi Choctaws, who have, within one year after the date of their identification as such, made satisfactory proof of bona fide settlement within the Choctaw-Chickasaw country, at any time within six months after the date of their said identification.

11. Persons authorized to make selections by power of attorney, as provided in rules 2 and 9 hereof, must be the husband or wife, or a relative not further removed than a cousin of the first degree of the person for whom such selection is made.

12. It shall be the duty of the Commission to the Five Civilized Tribes to see that selections of allotments and designations of homesteads for the classes of persons mentioned in rules 2, 6, 7, 8 and 9 hereof, are made for the best interests of such persons.

13. Selections of allotments for citizens, freedmen and identified Mississippi Choctaws who have died subsequent to September 25, 1902, and before making a selection of allotment, shall be made by a duly appointed administrator or executor. If, however, such administrator or executor be not duly and expeditiously appointed, or fails to act promptly when appointed, or for any other cause such selections be not so made within a reasonable and practicable time, the Commission to the Five Civilized Tribes shall designate the lands thus to be allotted.

14. In determining the value of a selection the appraised value of the land selected shall be increased by the appraised value of such pine timber on such land as has heretofore been estimated by the Commission to the Five Civilized Tribes.

15. Selections of allotments may be made only by citizens and freedmen whose enrollment has been approved by the Secretary of the Interior, and by persons duly identified by the Commission to the Five Civilized Tribes as Mississippi Choctaws, and by none others.

16. When a selection of land has been made by a citizen, freedman or identified Mississippi Choctaw, and the land so selected is claimed by a person whose rights as a citizen or freedman have not been finally determined, contest for the land so selected may be instituted by the person claiming the land, formal application for the land being first made as is required by the Rules of Practice in Choctaw and Chickasaw allotment contest cases.

THE COMMISSION TO THE FIVE CIVILIZED TRIBES.
TAMS BIXBY, Chairman.

Muskogee, Indian Territory, March 24, 1903.

---

The above statement published prior to 1905, was established for what was supposed to be a set of guidelines when it came to allotments. But with supplemental agreements and Congressional legislation, time frames as well as rules and regulations often changed and were not the same for every tribe.

# INTRODUCTION

The *Applications for Enrollment of Choctaw Newborn Act of 1905*, National Archive film M-1301, Rolls 50-57, are found under the heading of Applications for Enrollment of the Commission to the Five Civilized Tribes. For this series, I have transcribed the application forms filled out by individuals applying for enrollment in the Five Civilized Tribes under the Dawes Commission. These applications contain considerably more information than stated on the census cards found in series M-1186. M-1301 possesses its own numerical sequence, separate from M-1186. To find each party's roll number you would have to reference M-1186.

The Choctaw as well as the Chickasaw allotments were likely some of the most sought after properties in Indian Territory. There was supposed to be a 25-year restriction on the sale or lease of any Indian lands so as to insure that the owners wouldn't be swindled, but that isn't what happened. This fact is borne out in the Dawes Commission General Allotment Act, of February 8, 1887, Section 5, which "Provides that after an Indian person is allotted land, the United States will hold the land 'in trust [1] for the sole use and benefit of the Indian' (or his heirs if the Indian landowner dies) for a period of 25 years. (Land held in trust by the United States government cannot be sold or in anyway alienated by the Indian landowner, since the United States government considers the underlying ownership of the land held by itself and not the tribe. After the period of trust ends, the Indian landowner is free to sell the land and is free from any encumbrance from the United States.)"[1] Instead, Native Americans were exploited by the devious. The Choctaw and Chickasaw Districts both had huge asphalt and coal deposits, so there was pressure from outsiders to acquire them from the minute they were discovered. After repeated attacks throughout the years and many legislative changes, President "Roosevelt finally signed the Five Tribes Bill at noon on April 26, 1906, the forces seeking to end all restrictions were disappointed. Section 19 removed restrictions from the sale of all inherited land but directed that no full-bloods could sell their land for twenty-five years. The Act also prohibited leases for more than one year without the approval of the Secretary of the Interior."[2]

Angie Debo described the opportunists that wanted these Native American allotments as, "Grafters". The parents of the newborns enumerated within this series would no sooner receive the approval for their child's allotment than there would be someone there with cash in hand holding a new deed or lease for the parents to sign their child's birthright away. Angie Debo said it best, "As the business incapacity of the allottees became apparent, a horde of despoilers fastened themselves upon their property." According to Debo, "The term 'grafter' was applied as a matter of course to dealers in Indian land, and was frankly accepted by them. The speculative fever also affected Government employees so that it was almost impossible to prevent them from making personal investments."[3]

---

[1] General Allotment Act, Act of Feb. 8, 1887 (24 Stat. 388, ch. 119, 25 USCA 331)
[2] The Dawes Commission and the Allotment of the Five Civilized Tribes, 1893-1914 by Kent Carter, pg. 173
[3] And Still the Waters Run, Angie Debo, p. 92.

# INTRODUCTION

According to the Department of Interior in 1905, "It is estimated that there will be added to the final rolls of the citizens and freedmen of the Choctaw and Chickasaw nations the names of 2,000 persons, including 1,500 new-born children to be enrolled under the provisions of the act of Congress approved March 3, 1905."[4]

The quote below explains, in detail, the requirements for qualifying as a newborn Choctaw, "By the act of Congress approved March 3, 1905 (H.R. 17474), entitled 'An act making appropriations for the current and contingent expenses of the Indian Department and for fulfilling treaty stipulations with various Indian tribes for the fiscal year ending June 30, 1906, and for other purposes,' it was provided as follows:

'That the Commission to the Five Civilized Tribes is hereby authorized for sixty days after the date of the approval of this act to receive and consider applications for enrollment of infant children born prior to September twenty-fifth, nineteen hundred and two, and who were living on said date, to citizens by blood of the Choctaw and Chickasaw tribes of Indians whose enrollment has been approved by the Secretary of the Interior prior to the date of the approval of this act; and to enroll and make allotments to such children.'

'That the Commission to the Five Civilized Tribes is authorized for sixty days after the date of the approval of this act to receive and consider applications for enrollment of children born subsequent to September twenty-fifth, nineteen hundred and two, and prior to March fourth, nineteen hundred and five, and who were living on said latter date, to citizens by blood of the Choctaw and Chickasaw tribes of Indians whose enrollment has been approved by the Secretary of the Interior prior to the date of the approval of this act; and to enroll and make allotments to such children.'

"Notice is hereby given that the Commission to the Five Civilized Tribes will, up to and inclusive of midnight, May 2, 1905, receive applications for the enrollment of infant children born prior to September 25, 1902, and who were living on said date, to citizens by blood of the Choctaw and Chickasaw tribes of Indians whose enrollment has been approved by the Secretary of the Interior prior to March 3, 1905."[5]

Following is the scope of these transcriptions: Besides the applications themselves, researchers will find the identities of other individuals within these applications -- doctors, lawyers, mid-wives, and other relatives -- that may help with you genealogical research.

Jeff Bowen
Gallipolis, Ohio
*NativeStudy.com*

---

[4] Annual Reports of the Department of the Interior For the Fiscal Year Ended June 30, 1905, p. 609.
[5] Annual Reports of the Department of the Interior For the Fiscal Year Ended June 30, 1905, p. 593.

# Applications for Enrollment of Choctaw Newborn
## Act of 1905  Volume IX

Choc New Born 520
    Jim Chilton  b. 12-13-04

7-441

Muskogee, Indian Territory, April 1, 1905.

Bond & Melton,
    Attorneys at Law,
        Chickasha, Indian Territory.

Gentlemen:

    Receipt is hereby acknowledged of the affidavits of Alma Lee Matthews (Chilton) and E. L. Dawson, to the birth of Jim Chilton, son of Blake and Alma Lee Mathews[sic] (Chilton), December 13, 1904, and the same have been filed with our records as an application for the enrollment of said child.

        Respectfully,

                Chairman.

**COPY**           7 N. B. 520

Muskogee, Indian Territory, April 11, 1905.

Blake Chilton,
    Chickasha, Indian Territory.

Dear Sir:

    There is inclosed you herewith for execution application for the enrollment of your infant child, Jim Chilton, born December 13, 1904.

    In having these affidavits executed care should be exercised to see that all names are written in full as they appear in the body of the affidavit, and in the event that either of the persons signing the affidavit are unable to write, signatures by mark must be attested by two witnesses. Each affidavit must be executed before a Notary Public and the notarial seal and signature of the officer must be attached to <u>each</u> <u>separate</u> affidavit.

        Respectfully,
        SIGNED

        *T. B. Needles.*
LM 11-25         Commissioner in Charge.

## Applications for Enrollment of Choctaw Newborn
## Act of 1905   Volume IX

**COPY**                                              7 NB 520

Muskogee, Indian Territory, April 26, 1905.

Blake Chilton,
    Chickasha, Indian Territory.

Dear Sir:

    Receipt is hereby acknowledged of the affidavits of Alma Lee (Mathews) Chilton and E. L. Dawson to the birth of Jim Chilton, son of Blake and Alma Lee (Mathews) Chilton, December 13, 1904, and the same have been filed with our records in the matter of the enrollment of said child.

        Respectfully,

        SIGNED  *Tams Bixby*
            Chairman.

---

**BIRTH AFFIDAVIT.**

## DEPARTMENT OF THE INTERIOR.
## COMMISSION TO THE FIVE CIVILIZED TRIBES.

---

    IN RE APPLICATION FOR ENROLLMENT, as a citizen of the Choctaw Nation of Jim Chilton, born on the 13th day of December, 1904

Name of Father: Blake Chilton     a citizen of the United States Nation.
Name of Mother: Alma Lee (Mathews[sic]) Chilton     a citizen of the Choctaw Nation.

        Postoffice     Chickasha, I.T.

---

### AFFIDAVIT OF MOTHER.

UNITED STATES OF AMERICA, INDIAN TERRITORY,
    Southern           DISTRICT.

    I, Alma Lee (Mathews) Chilton, on oath state that I am 18 years of age and a citizen by blood, of the Choctaw Nation; that I am the lawful wife of Blake Chilton, who is a citizen, ~~by~~ .......... of the United States ~~Nation~~; that a male child was born to me on 13th day of December, 1904, that said child has been named Jim Chilton, and is now living.

            Alma Lee (Matthews) Chilton

## Applications for Enrollment of Choctaw Newborn
## Act of 1905   Volume IX

WITNESSES TO MARK:

Subscribed and sworn to before me this  27th  day of  March  , 1905.

Alger Melton<br>Notary Public.

---

AFFIDAVIT OF ATTENDING PHYSICIAN OR MID-WIFE.

UNITED STATES OF AMERICA, INDIAN TERRITORY,
Southern           DISTRICT.

I,  E.L. Dawson  , a  physician  , on oath state that I attended on Mrs.  Alma Lee (Mathews) Chilton  , wife of  Blake Chilton  on the  13th  day of  December  , 190 4; that there was born to her on said date a  male  child; that said child is now living and is said to have been named  Jim Chilton

E.L. Dawson, M.D.

WITNESSES TO MARK:

Subscribed and sworn to before me this  27  day of  March  , 1905.

Ado Melton<br>Notary Public.

---

BIRTH AFFIDAVIT.

DEPARTMENT OF THE INTERIOR.<br>COMMISSION TO THE FIVE CIVILIZED TRIBES.

---

**IN RE APPLICATION FOR ENROLLMENT,** as a citizen of the  Choctaw  Nation, of  Jim Chilton  , born on the  13$^{th}$  day of  December  , 1904

Name of Father: Blake Chilton           a citizen of the United States Nation.
Name of Mother: Alma Lee (Mathews) Chilton   a citizen of the  Choctaw  Nation.

Postoffice   Chickasha I.T.

# Applications for Enrollment of Choctaw Newborn
## Act of 1905   Volume IX

**AFFIDAVIT OF MOTHER.**

UNITED STATES OF AMERICA, Indian Territory, }
  Southern           DISTRICT.

   I, Alma Lee (Mathews) Chilton , on oath state that I am 18 years of age and a citizen by blood , of the Choctaw Nation; that I am the lawful wife of Blake Chilton , who is a citizen, ~~by~~ ——— of the United States Nation; that a male child was born to me on 13th day of December , 1904; that said child has been named Jim Chilton , and was living March 4, 1905.

                                    Alma Lee (Mathews) Chilton
Witnesses To Mark:
  {

   Subscribed and sworn to before me this 21st day of April , 1905

                                    Ado Melton
                                         Notary Public.

---

**AFFIDAVIT OF ATTENDING PHYSICIAN OR MID-WIFE.**

UNITED STATES OF AMERICA, Indian Territory, }
  Southern           DISTRICT.

   I, E L Dawson , a Physician , on oath state that I attended on Mrs. Alma Lee (Mathews) Chilton , wife of Blake Chilton on the 13th day of December , 1904; that there was born to her on said date a male child; that said child was living March 4, 1905, and is said to have been named Jim Chilton

                                    E.L. Dawson, M.D.
Witnesses To Mark:
  {

   Subscribed and sworn to before me this 22nd day of April , 1905

                                    Ado Melton
                                         Notary Public.

## Applications for Enrollment of Choctaw Newborn
## Act of 1905   Volume IX

Choc New Born 521
   Jessie Jerome Gazaway   b. 10-24-03

7-235

Muskogee, Indian Territory, March 21, 1905.

Cornelia E. Gazaway,
   Ardmore, Indian Territory.

Dear Madam:

   Receipt is hereby acknowledged of the affidavits of Cornelia E. Gazaway and T. S. Booth to the birth of Jessie Jerome Gazaway, infant son of Samuel C. and Cornelia E. Gazaway, October 24, 1903, and the same have been filed with our records as an application for the enrollment of said child.

Respectfully,

Chairman.

**BIRTH AFFIDAVIT.**

### DEPARTMENT OF THE INTERIOR.
### COMMISSION TO THE FIVE CIVILIZED TRIBES.

   **IN RE APPLICATION FOR ENROLLMENT,** as a citizen of the   Choctaw   Nation, of Jessie Jerome Gazaway   , born on the   24   day of   October   , 1903

Name of Father: Samuel C Gazaway      ~~a citizen of the~~ non ~~Nation~~.
Name of Mother: Cornelia E Gazaway      a citizen of the   Choctaw   Nation.

Postoffice   Ardmore Ind Ter

**AFFIDAVIT OF MOTHER.**

UNITED STATES OF AMERICA, Indian Territory,
   Southern            DISTRICT.

   I,   Cornelia E. Gazaway   , on oath state that I am   Twenty   years of age and a citizen by   Blood   , of the   Choctaw Nation   Nation; that I am the lawful wife of   Samuel C Gazaway   , who is a non citizen, ~~by~~ _____ of the _____ ~~Nation~~; that a   male   child was born to me on   24   day of

5

## Applications for Enrollment of Choctaw Newborn
## Act of 1905   Volume IX

October     , 1904; that said child has been named   Jessie Jerome Gazaway    , and was living March 4, 1905.

Cornelia E Gazaway

Witnesses To Mark:
  { G L Lowery
  { Rosa *(Illegible)*

Subscribed and sworn to before me this  15  day of   March   , 1905

Sou Dist Ind Ter                                     U.T. Rexroat
                                                         Notary Public.

---

**AFFIDAVIT OF ATTENDING PHYSICIAN OR MID-WIFE.**

UNITED STATES OF AMERICA, Indian Territory, }
  Southern                  DISTRICT. }

I,   T S Booth   , a physician   , on oath state that I attended on Mrs.  Cornelia E Gazaway   , wife of  Samuel C Gazaway   on the  24  day of October    , 1904; that there was born to her on said date a   male   child; that said child was living March 4, 1905, and is said to have been named Jessie Jerome Gazaway

                                T S Booth MD
Witnesses To Mark:
  {
  {

Subscribed and sworn to before me this  17$^{th}$   day of   March    , 1905

                                J E Williams
                                    Notary Public.

---

Choc New Born 522
         Alvin H. Lowe   b.  7-30-03

## Applications for Enrollment of Choctaw Newborn
## Act of 1905  Volume IX

Choctaw-27.

Muskogee, Indian Territory, April 1, 1905.

B. M. Lowe,
    Fox, Indian Territory.

Dear Sir:

    Receipt is hereby acknowledged of the affidavits of Ella I. Lowe and D. M. Montgomery to the birth of Alvin H. Lowe, son of B. M. and Ella I. Lowe, July 30, 1903, and the same have been filed with our records as an application for the enrollment of said child.

Respectfully,

Chairman.

---

7-NB-522

Muskogee, Indian Territory, January 27, 1906.

Boyd M. Lowe,
    Marlow, Indian Territory.

Dear Sir:

    Receipt is hereby acknowledged of your letter of January 22, 1906, asking why application for the enrollment of your child Alvin H. Lowe has not yet been approved.

    In reply to your letter you are advised that on July 22, 1905, the Secretary of the Interior approved the enrollment of your child Alvin H. Lowe as a new born citizen of the Choctaw Nation and notice thereof was forwarded you to your former post office Fox, Indian Territory.

Respectfully,

Acting Commissioner.

## Applications for Enrollment of Choctaw Newborn
## Act of 1905   Volume IX

7-NB-522

Muskogee, Indian Territory, February 2, 1906.

B. M. Lowe,
    Marlow, Indian Territory.

Dear Sir:

    Your letter of January 22, 1906, addressed to the Secretary of the Interior has been by him referred to this office for consideration and appropriate action. Therein you[sic] the status of the enrollment of your child, Alvin H. Lowe.

    In reply to your letter you are advised that on July 22, 1905, the Secretary of the Interior approved the enrollment of your child, Alvin H. Lowe as a new born citizen of the Choctaw Nation, and notice thereof was forwarded you at your former postoffice, Fox, Indian Territory, and on January 27, 1906, a letter was addressed to you in response to your communication of January 22, 1906, advising you of the approval of our child, Alvin H. Lowe.

                    Respectfully,

                                     Acting Commissioner.

---

IN RE APPLICATION FOR ENROLLMENT, as a citizen of the Choctaw   Nation of   Alvin H. Lowe   born on the   30   day of   July   190 3

Name of Father   B.M. Lowe    citizen of   Choctaw   Nation
Name of Mother   Ella I. Lowe    citizen of   Choctaw   Nation

                    Post Office.

### AFFIDAVIT OF MOTHER
United States of America Southern District of the Indian Territory:

    I,   Ella I. Lowe   on oath state that I am   21   years of age and a citizen by Blood   of the   Choctaw   Nation that I am the lawful wife of   B.M. Lowe   who is a citizen by ~~blood~~ *intermarriage* of the Choctaw   Nation that a   male   Child was born to me on the   30   day of   July   190 3   that said Child has been named   Alvin H. Lowe   and was living March 4, 1905.

                                  Ella I Lowe

Subscribed and sworn to before me this   27   day of   March   A.D. 190 5

                            *(Name Illegible)*
                              Notary Public.

# Applications for Enrollment of Choctaw Newborn
## Act of 1905   Volume IX

AFFIDAVIT OF ATTENDING PHYSICIAN
United States of America Southern District of the Indian Territory:

I,   D. M. Montgomery   a   Physician   on oath state that I attend[sic] on Mrs. Ella I. Lowe   wife of   B.M. Lowe   on the   30   day of   July   190 3   and that there was born to her on that date a   male   child and that said child was living March 4 1905, and is said to have been named   Alvin H. Lowe

D.M. Montgomery M.D.

Subscribed and sworn to before me this the   27   day of   Mar   1905.

*(Name Illegible)*
Notary Public.

---

Choc New Born 523
    Sue Constance Farrill   b.   11-29-02
    Walter Edwin Farrill   b.   10-29-04

Choctaw-2833.

Muskogee, Indian Territory, April 1, 1905.

Walter Farrill,
    Whitefield, Indian Territory.

Dear Sir:

    Receipt is hereby acknowledged of the affidavits of Theodosia Farrill and A. B. Callaway to the birth of Sue Constance Farrill, daughter of Walter and Theodosia Farrill, November 29, 1902; also affidavits of Theodosia Farrill and James Culbertson to the birth of Walter Edwin Farrill, son of Walter and Theodosia Farrill, October 29, 1904, and the same have been filed with our records as an application for the enrollment of said children.

Respectfully,

Chairman.

## Applications for Enrollment of Choctaw Newborn
## Act of 1905 Volume IX

BIRTH AFFIDAVIT.

### DEPARTMENT OF THE INTERIOR.
### COMMISSION TO THE FIVE CIVILIZED TRIBES.

IN RE APPLICATION FOR ENROLLMENT, as a citizen of the Choctaw Nation, of Walter Edwin Farrill , born on the 29th day of Oct , 1904

Name of Father: Walter Farrill     a citizen of the United States Nation.
Name of Mother: Theodosia Farrill     a citizen of the Choctaw Nation.

Postoffice    Whitefield, I.T.

### AFFIDAVIT OF MOTHER.

UNITED STATES OF AMERICA, Indian Territory,
   Central      DISTRICT.

I, Theodosia Farrill , on oath state that I am 25 years of age and a citizen by blood of the Choctaw Nation; that I am the lawful wife of Walter Farrill , who is a citizen, ~~by~~ ............ of the United States ~~Nation~~; that a male child was born to me on 29th day of October , 1904; that said child has been named Walter Edwin Farrill , and was living March 4, 1905.

                          Theodosia Farrill

Witnesses To Mark:

Subscribed and sworn to before me this 21st day of March , 1905

                          Wirt Franklin
                                Notary Public.

### AFFIDAVIT OF ATTENDING PHYSICIAN OR MID-WIFE.

UNITED STATES OF AMERICA, Indian Territory,
   Western      DISTRICT.

I, James Culbertson , a Physician , on oath state that I attended on Mrs. Theodosia Farrill , wife of Walter Farrill on the 29" day of October , 1904; that there was born to her on said date a male child; that said child was living March 4, 1905, and is said to have been named Walter Edwin Farrill

                          James Culbertson

Witnesses To Mark:

## Applications for Enrollment of Choctaw Newborn
## Act of 1905 Volume IX

Subscribed and sworn to before me this 24" day of March, 1905

A.L. Bickers
Notary Public.

My Commission expires May 21" 1907

**NEW-BORN AFFIDAVIT.**

Number

...Choctaw Enrolling Commission...

IN THE MATTER OF THE APPLICATION FOR ENROLLMENT, as a citizen of the Choctaw Nation, of Sue Constance Farrill

born on the 29 day of November 190 2

Name of father  Walter Farrill          a citizen of   white
Nation final enrollment No.  —
Name of mother  Theodosia Farrill       a citizen of   Choctaw
Nation final enrollment No.  15666

Postoffice  Whitefield, I.T.

**AFFIDAVIT OF MOTHER.**

UNITED STATES OF AMERICA
INDIAN TERRITORY
~~Western~~         DISTRICT
Central

I  Theodosia Farrill , on oath state that I am 25 years of age and a citizen by blood of the Choctaw Nation, and as such have been placed upon the final roll of the Choctaw Nation, by the Honorable Secretary of the Interior my final enrollment number being 15666 ; that I am the lawful wife of Walter Farrill , who is a citizen of the white ~~Nation~~, and as such has been placed upon the final roll of said Nation by the Honorable Secretary of the Interior, his final enrollment number being —— and that a female child was born to me on the 29 day of November 190 2; that said child has been named Sue Constance Farrill , and is now living.

Theodosia Farrill

Witnesseth.
Must be two Witnesses who are Citizens.   John Taylor
                                          Charley King

## Applications for Enrollment of Choctaw Newborn
## Act of 1905   Volume IX

Subscribed and sworn to before me this  23   day of   Jan   190 5

E.M. Walton
Notary Public.

My commission expires:  Oct 20, 1908

**NEW-BORN AFFIDAVIT.**

Number

...Choctaw Enrolling Commission...

IN THE MATTER OF THE APPLICATION FOR ENROLLMENT, as a citizen of the Choctaw    Nation, of    Walter E. Farrill

born on the   29   day of   October   190 4

Name of father   Walter Farrill           a citizen of   white
Nation final enrollment No. ———
Name of mother   Theodosia Farrill       a citizen of   Choctaw
Nation final enrollment No.  15666

Postoffice   Whitefield, I.T.

**AFFIDAVIT OF MOTHER.**

UNITED STATES OF AMERICA
INDIAN TERRITORY
~~Western~~        DISTRICT
*Central*

I   Theodosia Farrill   , on oath state that I am 25 years of age and a citizen by  blood  of the  Choctaw  Nation, and as such have been placed upon the final roll of the  Choctaw  Nation, by the Honorable Secretary of the Interior my final enrollment number being  15666 ; that I am the lawful wife of  Walter Farrill  , who is a citizen of the  white  ~~Nation~~, and as such has been placed upon the final roll of said Nation by the Honorable Secretary of the Interior, his final enrollment number being ——— and that a  male  child was born to me on the  29  day of  October   190 4; that said child has been named  Walter E Farrill  , and is now living.

Theodosia Farrill

Witnesseth.
Must be two Witnesses who are Citizens.   } John Taylor
Charley King

12

## Applications for Enrollment of Choctaw Newborn
## Act of 1905   Volume IX

Subscribed and sworn to before me this   23   day of   Jan   190 5

          E.M. Walton
              Notary Public.

My commission expires:   Oct. 20 1908

---

### AFFIDAVIT OF ATTENDING PHYSICIAN OR MIDWIFE

UNITED STATES OF AMERICA
INDIAN TERRITORY
~~Western~~      DISTRICT
Central

 I,   J Culbertson   a   Practicing Physician on oath state that I attended on Mrs. Theodosia Farrill   wife of   Walter Farrill on the   29   day of   October  , 190 4, that there was born to her on said date a   male child, that said child is now living, and is said to have been named   Walter E Farrill

          J Culbertson   M.D.

    Subscribed and sworn to before me this, the   27   day of   Jan   190 5

WITNESSETH:        EM Walton   Notary Public.
         My commission expires Oct. 20, 1908

Must be two witnesses who are citizens { John Taylor
        Charley King

 We hereby certify that we are well acquainted with   J Culbertson   a physician   and know   him   to be reputable and of good standing in the community.

  John Taylor

  Charley King

---

### AFFIDAVIT OF ATTENDING PHYSICIAN OR MIDWIFE

UNITED STATES OF AMERICA
INDIAN TERRITORY
 Central      DISTRICT

 I,   A.B. Calloway   a   Practicing Physician on oath state that I attended on Mrs. Theodosia Farrill   wife of   Walter Farrill on the   29   day of   November  , 190 2, that there was born to her on said date a   female child, that said child is now living, and is said to have been named   Sue Constance Farrill

## Applications for Enrollment of Choctaw Newborn
## Act of 1905 Volume IX

A B Calloway  *M.D.*

Subscribed and sworn to before me this, the 9<sup>th</sup> day of January 190 5

W<sup>m</sup> O Carr   Notary Public.

WITNESSETH:
Must be two witnesses who are citizens { John Taylor

Charley King

We hereby certify that we are well acquainted with A.B. Calloway a physician and know him to be reputable and of good standing in the community.

John Taylor   _____

Charley King   _____

BIRTH AFFIDAVIT.

### DEPARTMENT OF THE INTERIOR.
### COMMISSION TO THE FIVE CIVILIZED TRIBES.

IN RE APPLICATION FOR ENROLLMENT, as a citizen of the Choctaw Nation, of Sue Constance Farrill, born on the 29th day of Nov, 1902

Name of Father: Walter Farrill    a citizen of the United States Nation.
Name of Mother: Theodosia Farrill    a citizen of the Choctaw Nation.

Postoffice  Whitefield, I.T.

### AFFIDAVIT OF MOTHER.

UNITED STATES OF AMERICA, Indian Territory,
Central    DISTRICT.

I, Theodosia Farrill, on oath state that I am 25 years of age and a citizen by blood of the Choctaw Nation; that I am the lawful wife of Walter Farrill, who is a citizen, ~~by~~ ............ of the United States ~~Nation~~; that a female child was born to me on 29th day of November, 1902; that said child has been named Sue Constance Farrill, and was living March 4, 1905.

Theodosia Farrill

Witnesses To Mark:
{

# Applications for Enrollment of Choctaw Newborn
## Act of 1905 Volume IX

Subscribed and sworn to before me this 21st day of March , 1905

Wirt Franklin
Notary Public.

---

### AFFIDAVIT OF ATTENDING PHYSICIAN OR MID-WIFE.

State of Missouri
UNITED STATES OF AMERICA, ~~Indian Territory~~,
City of St Louis            DISTRICT.

I, A.B. Calloway , a Physician , on oath state that I attended on Mrs. Theodosia Farrill , wife of Walter Farrill on the 29 day of November , 1902; that there was born to her on said date a female child; that said child was living March 4, 1905, and is said to have been named Sue Constance Farrill

A.B. Calloway

Witnesses To Mark:
    C. F. Brian
    C. B. Nichols

Subscribed and sworn to before me this 25th day of March , 1905

My Commission as Notary Public  
expires December 12$^{th}$ 1908

William Moore
Notary Public.
St Louis Mo.

---

Choc New Born 524
    Bernice Farrill b. 2-10-03

Choctaw-2860.

Muskogee, Indian Territory, April 1, 1905.

Emery Farrill,
    Whitefield, Indian Territory.

Dear Sir:

    Receipt is hereby acknowledged of the affidavits of Harriet Farrill and A. B. Calloway to the birth of Bernice Farrill, daughter of Emery and Harriet Farrill, February

## Applications for Enrollment of Choctaw Newborn
## Act of 1905   Volume IX

10, 1903, and the same have been filed with our records as an application for the enrollment of said child.

Respectfully,

Chairman.

---

BIRTH AFFIDAVIT.

## DEPARTMENT OF THE INTERIOR.
## COMMISSION TO THE FIVE CIVILIZED TRIBES.

---

IN RE APPLICATION FOR ENROLLMENT, as a citizen of the   Choctaw   Nation, of   Bernice Farrill   , born on the   10th day of   February   , 1903

Name of Father: Emery Farrill   a citizen of the United States ~~Nation~~.
Name of Mother: Harriet Farrill   a citizen of the   Choctaw   Nation.

Postoffice   Whitefield, I.T.

---

AFFIDAVIT OF MOTHER.

UNITED STATES OF AMERICA, Indian Territory,
Central   DISTRICT.

I,   Harriet Farrill   , on oath state that I am   29   years of age and a citizen by blood , of the   Choctaw   Nation; that I am the lawful wife of   Emery Farrill   , who is a citizen, ~~by~~ ............ of the   United States   ~~Nation~~; that a   female   child was born to me on 10th   day of   February   , 1903; that said child has been named   Bernice Farrill   , and was living March 4, 1905.

Harriet Farrill

Witnesses To Mark:

Subscribed and sworn to before me this  20th  day of   March   , 1905

Wirt Franklin
Notary Public.

# Applications for Enrollment of Choctaw Newborn
# Act of 1905  Volume IX

### AFFIDAVIT OF ATTENDING PHYSICIAN OR MID-WIFE.

UNITED STATES OF AMERICA, ~~Indian Territory~~,  
*State of Missouri*  
*City of St Louis*     DISTRICT.

I, A.B. Calloway, a Physician, on oath state that I attended on Mrs. Mrs Harriet Farrill, wife of Emery Farrill on the 10th day of February, 1903; that there was born to her on said date a female child; that said child was living March 4, 1905, and is said to have been named Bernice Farrill

            A.B. Calloway

Witnesses To Mark:
- C. W. Norris
- C. L. Sullivan

Subscribed and sworn to before me this 24th day of March, 1905

My Commission expires      William Moore  
December 12 1908         Notary Public.  
            *St Louis Mo.*

---

## AFFIDAVIT OF ATTENDING PHYSICIAN OR MIDWIFE

UNITED STATES OF AMERICA  
INDIAN TERRITORY  
 Central  DISTRICT

I, A.B. Calloway a Physician on oath state that I attended on Mrs. Harriet Farrill wife of Emery Farrill on the 10th day of February, 190 3, that there was born to her on said date a female child, that said child is now living, and is said to have been named Burnice[sic] Emery Farrill

          A B Calloway    *M.D.*

Subscribed and sworn to before me this, the 9th day of January 190 5

WITNESSETH:          W$^m$ O Carr   Notary Public.

Must be two witnesses who are citizens:
- John Taylor
- Charley King

We hereby certify that we are well acquainted with A.B. Calloway a physician and know him to be reputable and of good standing in the community.

  John Taylor     Interprise, Indian Territory

  Charley King    Interprise, Indian Territory

## Applications for Enrollment of Choctaw Newborn
## Act of 1905   Volume IX

**NEW-BORN AFFIDAVIT.**

Number..............

...Choctaw Enrolling Commission...

IN THE MATTER OF THE APPLICATION FOR ENROLLMENT, as a citizen of the Choctaw Nation, of   Bernice Emery Farrill

born on the 10 day of _February_ 190 3

Name of father   Emery Farrill     a citizen of   white
Nation final enrollment No. ———
Name of mother   Harriet Farrill    a citizen of   Choctaw
Nation final enrollment No. 15674

Postoffice   Whitefield I.T.

**AFFIDAVIT OF MOTHER.**

UNITED STATES OF AMERICA
INDIAN TERRITORY
_Central_   DISTRICT
~~Western~~

I   Harriet Farrill   , on oath state that I am 29 years of age and a citizen by blood of the Choctaw Nation, and as such have been placed upon the final roll of the Choctaw Nation, by the Honorable Secretary of the Interior my final enrollment number being 15674 ; that I am the lawful wife of Emery Farrill , who is a citizen of the White ~~Nation~~, and as such has been placed upon the final roll of said Nation by the Honorable Secretary of the Interior, his final enrollment number being ——— and that a Female child was born to me on the 10th day of February 190 3; that said child has been named Bernice Emery Farrill , and is now living.

Harriet Farrill

Witnesseth.
Must be two Witnesses who are Citizens.   } John Taylor
Charley King

Subscribed and sworn to before me this 23 day of Jan 190 5

EM Walton
Notary Public.

My commission expires: Oct 20 1908

# Applications for Enrollment of Choctaw Newborn
## Act of 1905   Volume IX

Choc New Born 525
    Arthur Bascom   b. 2-9-04

                              **COPY**                           N. B. 525.

                        Muskogee, Indian Territory, April 8, 1905.

John Bascom,
    Ironbridge, Indian Territory.

Dear Sir:

    There is inclosed you herewith for execution application for the enrollment of your infant child, Arthur Bascom, born February 9, 1904.

    In the application heretofore filed with the Commission, the affidavit of the physician or midwife was filled out by the father. If there was no physician or midwife in attendance at the birth of said child, it will be necessary that you secure the affidavits of two persons who have actual knowledge of the fact, that the child was born, was living on March 4, 1905, and that Alice Bascom was his mother.

    In having these affidavits executed care should be exercised to see that all names are written in full, as they appear in the body of the affidavit, and in the event that either of the persons signing the affidavit are unable to write, signatures by mark must be attested by two witnesses. Each affidavit must be executed before a Notary Public and the notarial seal and signature of the officer must be attached to each separate affidavit.

                        Respectfully,
                        SIGNED
                        *T. B. Needles.*
LM 8-28                Commissioner in Charge.

                            **COPY**                    Choctaw N.B. 525.

                        Muskogee, Indian Territory, April 26, 1905.

John Bascom,
    Ironbridge, Indian Territory.

Dear Sir:

    Receipt is hereby acknowledged of the affidavits of Joe McCann, Mike Jones, Alice Bascom and John Bascom to the birth of Arthur Bascom, son of John and Alice Bascom, February 9, 1904, and the same have been filed with our records in the matter of the enrollment of said child.

# Applications for Enrollment of Choctaw Newborn
# Act of 1905   Volume IX

Respectfully,

SIGNED   *Tams Bixby*
Chairman.

---

## *Affidavit of Attending Physician or Midwife*

UNITED STATES OF AMERICA,
INDIAN TERRITORY,
Central   DISTRICT

I, John Bascom   a ............

on oath state that I attended on Mrs. Allice[sic] Bascom   *my* wife ~~of~~ ..............

on the 9th day of Feb, 190 4, that there was born to her on said date a male child, that said child is now living, and is said to have been named Arthur Bascom

John Bascom   M. D.

Subscribed and sworn to before me this the  27  day of  March  1905

M.W. Newman
Notary Public.

WITNESSETH:
Must be two witnesses who are citizens and know the child.
{ Forbis Leflore
  Watson Wallis

We hereby certify that we are well acquainted with   John Bascom  *and Allice Bascom*   and know   them   to be reputable and of good standing in the community.

Must be two citizen witnesses.
{ Forbis Leflore
  Watson Wallis

Applications for Enrollment of Choctaw Newborn
Act of 1905 Volume IX

# NEW BORN AFFIDAVIT

No _____

## CHOCTAW ENROLLING COMMISSION

IN THE MATTER OF THE APPLICATION FOR ENROLLMENT as a citizen of the Choctaw Nation, of    Arthur Bascom    born on the 9$^{th}$ day of February 190 4

Name of father    John Bascom    a citizen of    Choctaw    Nation, final enrollment No.  8655
Name of mother    Allice Bascom    a citizen of    Choctaw    Nation, final enrollment No.  7272

Iron Bridge IT    Postoffice.

**AFFIDAVIT OF MOTHER**

UNITED STATES OF AMERICA  
INDIAN TERRITORY  
DISTRICT    Central

I    Allice Bascom    , on oath state that I am  22  years of age and a citizen by  Blood  of the  Choct  Nation, and as such have been placed upon the final roll of the  Choctaw  Nation, by the Honorable Secretary of the Interior my final enrollment number being  7272  ; that I am the lawful wife of  John Bascom  , who is a citizen of the  Choctaw  Nation, and as such has been placed upon the final roll of said Nation by the Honorable Secretary of the Interior, his final enrollment number being  8655  and that a  Male  child was born to me on the   9$^{th}$  day of  Feb  190 4; that said child has been named  Arthur Bascom  , and is now living.

                                                her  
WITNESSETH:    Allice x Bascom  
                                                mark

Must be two witnesses { Forbis Leflore  
who are citizens       { Watson Wallis

Subscribed and sworn to before me this, the 27" day of  March  , 190 5

                                              M.W. Newman  
                                                 Notary Public.

My Commission Expires:  
Jan the 17$^{th}$ 1909

## Applications for Enrollment of Choctaw Newborn
## Act of 1905   Volume IX

*(The affidavit below typed as given.)*

United States of America         }   In the Matter of the
Indian Teritory, Central Dist    }   Enrollment as a Citizen of

The Choctaw Nation of Arthur Bascom child of John and Alice Bascom  I  J.L. McCain state on oath that I am 35 years of age, that I am a citizen by Blood of the Choctaw Nation, that I now of my own knowledge that the above named child Arthur Bascom is the child of Alice Bascom who is a citizen by Blood of the Choctaw Nation and that said child is now living and was born on the $9^{th}$ day of February 1904 and that Alice Bascom is a citizen by Blood of the Choctaw Nation   Joe McCain

Sworn to subscribed before me this the $19^{th}$ day of April 1905

                         M.W. Newman
                         Notary Public.

---

*(The affidavit below typed as given.)*

United States of America         }   In the Matter of the
Indian Territory, Central Dist   }   Enrollment of as a Citizen of

The Choctaw Nation of Arthur Bascom child of John and Alice Bascom  I  Mike Jones state on oath that I am 22 years of age that I am a citizen of the Choctaw Nation by Blood That I know of my own knowledge that the above named child Arthur Bascom is the child of Alice Bascom and that said child was living on the 4" of March 1905 and is now living, and was born on the $9^{th}$ day of February 1904 and that Alice Bascom is a citizen by Blood of the Choctaw Nation    Mike Jones

Sworn to and subscribed before me this the 19" day of April 1905

                         M.W. Newman
                         Notary Public.

# Applications for Enrollment of Choctaw Newborn
# Act of 1905 Volume IX

**BIRTH AFFIDAVIT.**

## DEPARTMENT OF THE INTERIOR.
## COMMISSION TO THE FIVE CIVILIZED TRIBES.

---

IN RE APPLICATION FOR ENROLLMENT, as a citizen of the Choctaw Nation, of Arthur Bascom, born on the $9^{th}$ day of Feb, 1904

Name of Father: John Bascom     a citizen of the Choctaw Nation.
Name of Mother: Alice Bascom     a citizen of the Choctaw Nation.

Postoffice    Iron Bridge IT

---

**AFFIDAVIT OF MOTHER.**

UNITED STATES OF AMERICA, Indian Territory, }
Central     DISTRICT.

I, Alice Bascom, on oath state that I am 22 years of age and a citizen by Blood, of the Choctaw Nation; that I am the lawful wife of John Bascom, who is a citizen, by Blood of the Choctaw Nation; that a Male child was born to me on $9^{th}$ day of Feb, 1904; that said child has been named Arthur Bascom, and was living March 4, 1905.

                     her
                Alice x Bascom
Witnesses To Mark:         mark
   { Forbis Leflore
     Watson Wallis

Subscribed and sworn to before me this 27" day of March, 1905

                M.W. Newman
                    Notary Public.

---

**AFFIDAVIT OF ATTENDING PHYSICIAN OR MID-WIFE.**

UNITED STATES OF AMERICA, Indian Territory, }
Central     DISTRICT.

I, John Bascom, a ................., on oath state that I attended on Mrs. Alice Bascom My, wife of ................. on the $9^{th}$ day of Feb, 1904; that there was born to her on said date a Male child; that said child was living March 4, 1905, and is said to have been named Arthur Bascom

                 John Bascom

## Applications for Enrollment of Choctaw Newborn
## Act of 1905   Volume IX

Witnesses To Mark:
{ Forbis Leflore
{ Watson Wallis

Subscribed and sworn to before me this 27" day of March , 1905

M.W. Newman
Notary Public.

My Com Expires Jan 17" 1909

---

**BIRTH AFFIDAVIT.**

### DEPARTMENT OF THE INTERIOR.
### COMMISSION TO THE FIVE CIVILIZED TRIBES.

---

**IN RE APPLICATION FOR ENROLLMENT,** as a citizen of the Choctaw Nation, of Arthur Bascom , born on the 9" day of February , 1904

Name of Father: John Bascom          a citizen of the Choctaw Nation.
Name of Mother: Alice Bascom         a citizen of the Choctaw Nation.

Postoffice   Iron Bridge Ind Ter

---

### AFFIDAVIT OF MOTHER.

UNITED STATES OF AMERICA, Indian Territory, }
     Central         DISTRICT. }

I, Alice Bascom , on oath state that I am 22 years of age and a citizen by Blood , of the Choctaw Nation; that I am the lawful wife of John Bascom , who is a citizen, by Blood of the Choctaw Nation; that a Male child was born to me on 9" day of February , 1904; that said child has been named Arthur Bascom , and was living March 4, 1905.

                             her
                       Alice x Bascom
Witnesses To Mark:           mark
{ Joe McCain
{ Mike Jones

Subscribed and sworn to before me this 19th day of April , 1905

M.W. Newman
Notary Public.

# Applications for Enrollment of Choctaw Newborn
## Act of 1905   Volume IX

**AFFIDAVIT OF ATTENDING PHYSICIAN OR MID-WIFE.**

UNITED STATES OF AMERICA, Indian Territory,  
............................................... DISTRICT.

I,   John Bascom   , a ........................., on oath state that I attended on Mrs.   Alice Bascom  , wife of   John Bascom   on the 9" day of   February  , 1904; that there was born to her on said date a   Male   child; that said child was living March 4, 1905, and is said to have been named   Arthur Bascom

John Bascom

Witnesses To Mark:
{ Joe McCain
{ Mike Jones

Subscribed and sworn to before me this  19$^{th}$  day of   April   , 1905

M.W. Newman<br>Notary Public.

---

Choc New Born 526
    Maude Herndon   b. 4-4-03

## *Affidavit of Attending Physician or Midwife*

UNITED STATES OF AMERICA,  
   INDIAN TERRITORY,  
   Central    DISTRICT

I,   Mattie Buchanan   a   midwife on oath state that I attended on Mrs.  Lucy Herndon   wife of  Edgar B. Herndon on the   4$^{th}$   day of   April   , 190 3, that there was born to her on said date a   female   child, that said child is now living, and is said to have been named   Maude

...................... M. D.

Subscribed and sworn to before me this the  26   day of   Jan    1905

D.O. Spencer<br>Notary Public.

# Applications for Enrollment of Choctaw Newborn
## Act of 1905   Volume IX

WITNESSETH:
Must be two witnesses who are citizens and know the child. { W M Stanley
William W Swink

We hereby certify that we are well acquainted with  Mattie Buchanan a midwife  and know  her  to be reputable and of good standing in the community.

Must be two citizen witnesses. { W M Stanley
D A Fowler

## NEW-BORN AFFIDAVIT.

Number..............

## Choctaw Enrolling Commission.

IN THE MATTER OF THE APPLICATION FOR ENROLLMENT, as a citizen of the Choctaw  Nation, of  Maude Herndon

born on the  4th  day of  April  1903

Name of father  Edgar B Herndon     a citizen of  Choctaw  Nation final enrollment No  508
Name of mother  Lucy Herndon     a citizen of  Choctaw  Nation final enrollment No  2219

Postoffice  Parsons I. Ty.

## AFFIDAVIT OF MOTHER.

UNITED STATES OF AMERICA,
INDIAN TERRITORY,
.................... DISTRICT

I  Lucy Herndon  on oath state that I am  38  years of age and a citizen by  Blood  of the  Choctaw  Nation, and as such have been placed upon the final roll of the  Choctaw  Nation, by the Honorable Secretary of the Interior my final enrollment number being  2219 ; that I am the lawful wife of E B Herndon , who is a citizen of the  Choctaw  Nation, and as such has been placed upon the final roll of said Nation by the Honorable Secretary of the Interior, his final enrollment number being  508  and that a  Female  child was born to me on the 4th  day of  April  1903 ; that said child has been named  Maude , and is now living.

Lucy Herndon

## Applications for Enrollment of Choctaw Newborn
## Act of 1905    Volume IX

WITNESSETH:

Must be two Witnesses who are Citizens. } W M Stanley
D A Fowler

Subscribed and sworn to before me this  26  day of  Jan  190 5

D.O. Spencer
Notary Public.

My commission expires  Jan 30<sup>th</sup> 1905

---

BIRTH AFFIDAVIT.

### DEPARTMENT OF THE INTERIOR.
### COMMISSION TO THE FIVE CIVILIZED TRIBES.

IN RE APPLICATION FOR ENROLLMENT, as a citizen of the    Choctaw    Nation, of   Maude Herndon   , born on the  4<sup>th</sup>  day of  April  , 1903

Name of Father: Edgar B. Herndon         a citizen of the   Choctaw   Nation.
Name of Mother: Lucy Herndon             a citizen of the   Choctaw   Nation.

Postoffice    Parsons, I.T.

---

### AFFIDAVIT OF MOTHER.

UNITED STATES OF AMERICA, Indian Territory, }
  Central          DISTRICT.

I,   Lucy Herndon  , on oath state that I am  39  years of age and a citizen by   Blood  , of the   Choctaw   Nation; that I am the lawful wife of   Edgar B. Herndon  , who is a citizen, by   Marriage   of the   Choctaw   Nation; that a   female   child was born to me on  4<sup>th</sup>  day of  April  , 1903; that said child has been named   Maude Herndon  , and was living March 4, 1905.

                                    her
                              Lucy  x  Herndon
Witnesses To Mark:               mark
  { A.L. Nunnelly
  { J.L. Elder

Subscribed and sworn to before me this  27<sup>th</sup>  day of  March  , 1905

E.J. Gardner
Notary Public.

## Applications for Enrollment of Choctaw Newborn
## Act of 1905   Volume IX

**AFFIDAVIT OF ATTENDING PHYSICIAN OR MID-WIFE.**

UNITED STATES OF AMERICA, Indian Territory,  }
Central                    DISTRICT.

    I, Mattie Buchanan, a Midwife, on oath state that I attended on Mrs. Lucy Herndon, wife of Edgar B. Herndon on the 4$^{th}$ day of April, 1903; that there was born to her on said date a female child; that said child was living March 4, 1905, and is said to have been named Maude Herndon

                                        Mattie Buchanan

Witnesses To Mark:
{

    Subscribed and sworn to before me this 27$^{th}$ day of March, 1905

                                        E.J. Gardner
                                        Notary Public.

---

Choc New Born 527
    Ruthie LeFlore   b. 10-22-04

                                                  7-5342

                    Muskogee, Indian Territory, April 3, 1905.

Allen LeFlore,
    Boswell, Indian Territory.

Dear Sir:

    Receipt is hereby acknowledged of the affidavits of Ella Leflore and Babe Adair to the birth of Ruthie Leflore, daughter of Allen and Ella Leflore, October 22, 1904, and the same have been filed with our records as an application for the enrollment of said child.

                    Respectfully,

                                    Chairman.

# Applications for Enrollment of Choctaw Newborn
## Act of 1905  Volume IX

COPY                                                                N. B. 527

Muskogee, Indian Territory, April 8, 1905.

Allen LeFlore,
    Boswell, Indian Territory.

Dear Sir:

    There is inclosed you herewith for execution application for the enrollment of your infant child, Ruthie LeFlore, born October 22, 1904.

    In having these affidavits executed care should be exercised to see that all names are written in full, as they appear in the body of the affidavit, and in the event that either of the persons signing the affidavit are unable to write, signatures by mark must be attested by two witnesses. Each affidavit must be executed before a Notary Public and the notarial seal and signature of the officer must be attached to each separate affidavit.

    Respectfully,

SIGNED *T. B. Needles.*

LM 8029                                          Commissioner in Charge.

---

7-N B 527.

COPY

Muskogee, Indian Territory, April 26, 1905.

Allen LeFlore,
    Boswell, Indian Territory.

Dear Sir:

    Receipt is hereby acknowledged of the affidavits of Ella LeFlore and Chas. S. Lynch to the birth of Ruthie LeFlore, daughter of Allen and Ella LeFlore, October 22, 1904, and the same have been filed with our records in the matter of the enrollment of said child.

    Respectfully,

SIGNED

*Tams Bixby*
Chairman.

# Applications for Enrollment of Choctaw Newborn
## Act of 1905   Volume IX

7-NB-527.

Muskogee, Indian Territory, May 25, 1905.

Allen LeFlore,
    Boswell, Indian Territory.

Dear Sir:

    There is enclosed you herewith for execution application for the enrollment of your infant child.

    In the affidavits of January 18, 1905, the child's name is given as Luther LeFlore, while in the affidavits of April 17, 1905, it is given as Ruthie LeFlore. In the enclosed application the name of the child is left blank. Please insert the correct name of the applicant, and return the affidavits, when properly executed, to this office.

    In having these affidavits executed care should be exercised to see that all names are written in full, as they appear in the body of the affidavit, and in the event that either of the persons signing the affidavit are unable to write, signatures by mark must be attested by two witnesses. Each affidavit must be executed before a Notary Public and the notarial seal and signature of the officer must be attached to each separate affidavit.

        Respectfully,

VR 25-11.                                    Chairman.

---

7-N.B. 527.

Muskogee, Indian Territory, June 5, 1905.

Allen LeFlore,
    Boswell, Indian Territory.

Dear Sir:

    Receipt is hereby acknowledged of the affidavits of Ella LeFlore and Chas. S. Lynch to the birth of Ruthie LeFlore, daughter of Allen and Ella LeFlore, October 22, 1904, and the same have been filed with our records in the matter of the enrollment of said child.

        Respectfully,

                                Commissioner in Charge.

## Applications for Enrollment of Choctaw Newborn
## Act of 1905   Volume IX

7-NB-527.

Muskogee, Indian Territory, June 6, 1906.

Allen LeFlore,
    Boswell, Indian Territory.

Dear Sir:

    On April 3, 1905, there was filed in this office application for the enrollment of your infant child, Ruthie LeFlore, born October 22, 1904, while on May 3, 1905, an application for the enrollment of Luther Leflore, born on the same day, was filed in this office. You are requested to state whether Ruthie LeFlore and Luther LeFlore are names of the same person.

    This matter should receive your immediate attention, as no further action can be taken until these affidavits are filed in this office.

Respectfully,

Commissioner in Charge.

I never filed any affidavit giving name Luther Leflore. Look at it and you will see the error. My baby is Ruthie Leflore and I have no other to be enrolled.

Allen Leflore.

---

Choctaw N B 527

Muskogee, Indian Territory, June 29, 1905.

Allen LeFlore,
    Boswell, Indian Territory.

Dear Sir:

    Receipt is hereby acknowledged of your recent letter in which you state that your child is named Ruthie LeFlore and that you have never made affidavits to the birth of Luther LeFlore.

    In reply you are advised that affidavits filed with the Choctaw Commission give the name of your child as Luther LeFlore, and the date of her birth October 22, 1904, while those filed with this Commission give the same date of birth and state the name as Ruthie LeFlore.

    Your statement that the correct name of your child is Ruthie LeFlore has been made a matter of record in the enrollment of said child.

# Applications for Enrollment of Choctaw Newborn
# Act of 1905  Volume IX

Respectfully,

Chairman.

## *Affidavit of Attending Physician or Midwife*

UNITED STATES OF AMERICA,
INDIAN TERRITORY,
Central   DISTRICT

I,   C.S. Lynch   a   Practicing Physician on oath state that I attended on Mrs. Ellen Leflore   wife of   Allen Leflore on the 22   day of   October , 190 4, that there was born to her on said date a   Female child, that said child is now living, and is said to have been named Luther Leflore

Chas. S. Lynch   M. D.

Subscribed and sworn to before me this the   18   day of   Jan   1905

My commission exp 2/5/05   Perry M Clark
Notary Public.

WITNESSETH:
Must be two witnesses who are citizens and know the child.
{ Alex Wade
John T Brown

We hereby certify that we are well acquainted with   Chas S Lynch a   Physician   and know   him   to be reputable and of good standing in the community.

Must be two citizen witnesses.
{ Alex Wade
John T Brown

Applications for Enrollment of Choctaw Newborn
Act of 1905 Volume IX

**NEW-BORN AFFIDAVIT.**

Number..........

## Choctaw Enrolling Commission.

IN THE MATTER OF THE APPLICATION FOR ENROLLMENT, as a citizen of the Choctaw Nation, of Luther Leflore

born on the 22 day of October 190 4

Name of father   Allen Leflore           a citizen of   Choctaw
Nation final enrollment No  13532
Name of mother   Ellen Leflore           a citizen of   Choctaw
Nation final enrollment No    1039

Postoffice   Boswell

**AFFIDAVIT OF MOTHER.**

UNITED STATES OF AMERICA, }
INDIAN TERRITORY, }
Central   DISTRICT }

I   Ellen Leflore   on oath state that I am 21 years of age and a citizen by   marriage   of the   Choctaw   Nation, and as such have been placed upon the final roll of the   Choctaw   Nation, by the Honorable Secretary of the Interior my final enrollment number being   1039   ; that I am the lawful wife of   Allen Leflore   , who is a citizen of the   Choctaw   Nation, and as such has been placed upon the final roll of said Nation by the Honorable Secretary of the Interior, his final enrollment number being   13532   and that a   female   child was born to me on the   22   day of   October   190 4 ; that said child has been named   Luther Leflore   , and is now living.

Ellen Leflore

WITNESSETH:
Must be two  } Alex Wade
Witnesses who }
are Citizens.   John T Brown

Subscribed and sworn to before me this   18   day of   January   190 5

James Bower
Notary Public.

My commission expires   Sept 23 - 1907

## Applications for Enrollment of Choctaw Newborn
## Act of 1905   Volume IX

BIRTH AFFIDAVIT.

### DEPARTMENT OF THE INTERIOR.
### COMMISSION TO THE FIVE CIVILIZED TRIBES.

IN RE APPLICATION FOR ENROLLMENT, as a citizen of the Choctaw Nation, of Ruthie Leflore, born on the 22nd day of October, 1904

Name of Father: Allen Leflore     a citizen of the Choctaw Nation.
Name of Mother: Ella Leflore     a citizen of the Choctaw Nation.

Postoffice    Boswell, I.T.

### AFFIDAVIT OF MOTHER.

UNITED STATES OF AMERICA, Indian Territory,
Central     DISTRICT.

I, Ella Leflore, on oath state that I am 21 yrs years of age and a citizen by intermarriage, of the Choctaw Nation; that I am the lawful wife of Allen Leflore, who is a citizen, by blood of the Choctaw Nation; that a female child was born to me on 22nd day of October, 1904; that said child has been named Ruthie Leflore, and was living March 4, 1905.

                 Ella Leflore

Witnesses To Mark:

Subscribed and sworn to before me this 29th day of March, 1905

(Seal)           J R Armstrong
Commission expire March 11, 1907      Notary Public.

### AFFIDAVIT OF ATTENDING PHYSICIAN OR MID-WIFE.

UNITED STATES OF AMERICA, Indian Territory,
Central     DISTRICT.

I, Babe Adair, a midwife, on oath state that I attended on Mrs. Ella Leflore, wife of Allen Leflore on the 22nd day of Oct, 1904; that there was born to her on said date a female child; that said child was living March 4, 1905, and is said to have been named Ruthie Leflore

                 Babe Adair

Witnesses To Mark:

## Applications for Enrollment of Choctaw Newborn
## Act of 1905   Volume IX

Subscribed and sworn to before me this 29th day of March, 1905

(Seal)   Commission expire March 11, 1907

J R Armstrong
Notary Public.

BIRTH AFFIDAVIT.

### DEPARTMENT OF THE INTERIOR.
### COMMISSION TO THE FIVE CIVILIZED TRIBES.

IN RE APPLICATION FOR ENROLLMENT, as a citizen of the Choctaw Nation, of Ruthie LeFlore, born on the 22" day of October, 1904

Name of Father: Allen LeFlore        a citizen of the Choctaw Nation.
Name of Mother: Ella LeFlore         a citizen of the Choctaw Nation.

Postoffice   Boswell, Ind. Ter.

### AFFIDAVIT OF MOTHER.

UNITED STATES OF AMERICA, Indian Territory, }
................................................ DISTRICT. }

I, Ella LeFlore, on oath state that I am 21 years of age and a citizen by Intermarriage, of the Choctaw Nation; that I am the lawful wife of Allen LeFlore, who is a citizen, by Blood of the Choctaw Nation; that a Female child was born to me on 22" day of October, 1904; that said child has been named Ruthie Leflore, and was living March 4, 1905.

Ella Leflore

Witnesses To Mark:
{

Subscribed and sworn to before me this 17th day of April, 1905

J R Armstrong
Notary Public.

### AFFIDAVIT OF ATTENDING PHYSICIAN OR MID-WIFE.

UNITED STATES OF AMERICA, Indian Territory, }
................................................ DISTRICT. }

I, ................................., a ........................., on oath state that I attended on Mrs. Ella LeFlore, wife of Allen LeFlore on the 22" day of October,

# Applications for Enrollment of Choctaw Newborn
## Act of 1905   Volume IX

1904; that there was born to her on said date a   Female   child; that said child was living March 4, 1905, and is said to have been named   Ruthie Leflore

            Chas. S. Lynch MD

Witnesses To Mark:

 { Subscribed and sworn to before me this   24   day of   April   , 1905

            Thos. W. Hunter
            Notary Public.

---

**BIRTH AFFIDAVIT.**

### DEPARTMENT OF THE INTERIOR.
### COMMISSION TO THE FIVE CIVILIZED TRIBES.

**IN RE APPLICATION FOR ENROLLMENT,** as a citizen of the   Choctaw   Nation, of ........................................, born on the   22   day of   October   , 1904

Name of Father: Allen LeFlore    a citizen of the   Choctaw   Nation.
Name of Mother: Ella LeFlore    a citizen of the   Choctaw   Nation.

        Postoffice   Boswell, Ind. Ter.

---

### AFFIDAVIT OF MOTHER.

UNITED STATES OF AMERICA, Indian Territory, }
........................................ DISTRICT.

 I,   Ella LeFlore   , on oath state that I am   21   years of age and a citizen by intermarriage   , of the   Choctaw   Nation; that I am the lawful wife of   Allen LeFlore   , who is a citizen, by   blood   of the   Choctaw   Nation; that a   female   child was born to me on   22"   day of   October   , 1904; that said child has been named   Ruthie LeFlore   , and was living March 4, 1905.

            Ella LeFlore

Witnesses To Mark:
 {

 Subscribed and sworn to before me this   29"   day of   May   , 1905

            J R Armstrong
            Notary Public.

## Applications for Enrollment of Choctaw Newborn
## Act of 1905  Volume IX

**AFFIDAVIT OF ATTENDING PHYSICIAN OR MID-WIFE.**

UNITED STATES OF AMERICA, Indian Territory,
................................................. DISTRICT.

I, Chas S Lynch , a M.D. , on oath state that I attended on Mrs. Ella LeFlore , wife of Allen LeFlore on the 22" day of October , 1904; that there was born to her on said date a female child; that said child was living March 4, 1905, and is said to have been named Ruthie LeFlore

Chas S Lynch
Witnesses To Mark:

Subscribed and sworn to before me this 29" day of May , 1905

J R Armstrong
Notary Public.

---

Choc New Born 528
   Richard S. Bond  b. 11-14-03
   Alice Bond  b. 3-2-05

7-3829

Muskogee, Indian Territory, April 3, 1905.
Redmond Bond,
   Duncan, Indian Territory.

Dear Sir:

Receipt is hereby acknowledged of the affidavits of Sallie Bond and Winnie Frazier to the birth of Richard S. Bond, son of Redmond and Sallie Bond, November 14, 1903, and the same have been filed with our records as an application for the enrollment of said child.

As you do not state the address of the Mrs. Miriam Frazier for whom you request a blank birth certificate it is impracticable to send the same to her and blank of this description is inclosed herewith for her use.

Respectfully,

B.C.                                                                                            Chairman.

## Applications for Enrollment of Choctaw Newborn
## Act of 1905   Volume IX

7-3829

Muskogee, Indian Territory, May 8, 1905.

Redmond Bond,
    Duncan, Indian Territory.

Dear Sir:

    Receipt is hereby acknowledged of your letter of April 27, 1905, addressed to the United States Indian Agent which has been by him referred to this Commission for appropriate action. Therewith you inclose affidavits of Sallie Bond and Susan Charleston to the birth of Alice Bond, daughter of Readmond[sic] and Sallie Bond, March 2, 1905, and the same have been filed with our records as an application for the enrollment of said child.

Respectfully,

Commissioner in Charge.

---

**BIRTH AFFIDAVIT.**

### DEPARTMENT OF THE INTERIOR.
### COMMISSION TO THE FIVE CIVILIZED TRIBES.

---

**IN RE APPLICATION FOR ENROLLMENT,** as a citizen of the Choctaw Nation, of Richard S. Bond, born on the 14 day of November, 1903

Name of Father: Redmond Bond     a citizen of the Choctaw Nation.
Name of Mother: Sallie Bond     a citizen of the Choctaw Nation.

Postoffice   Duncan, Ind. Ter.

---

**AFFIDAVIT OF MOTHER.**

UNITED STATES OF AMERICA, Indian Territory, }
    Southern      DISTRICT. }

    I, Sallie Bond, on oath state that I am 36 years of age and a citizen by blood, of the Choctaw Nation; that I am the lawful wife of Redmond Bond, who is a citizen, by blood of the Choctaw Nation; that a boy child was born to me on 14 day of November, 1903; that said child has been named Richard S. Bond, and was living March 4, 1905.

Sallie Bond

# Applications for Enrollment of Choctaw Newborn
# Act of 1905   Volume IX

Witnesses To Mark:
{ (Name Illegible)
{ Miriam Frazier

Subscribed and sworn to before me this 29 day of March , 1905

Edie A Bowerman
Notary Public.

---

**AFFIDAVIT OF ATTENDING PHYSICIAN OR MID-WIFE.**

UNITED STATES OF AMERICA, Indian Territory,
Southern    DISTRICT.

I, Winnie Frazier , a mid-wife , on oath state that I attended on Mrs. Sallie Bond , wife of Redmond Bond on the 14th day of November , 1903; that there was born to her on said date a male child; that said child was living March 4, 1905, and is said to have been named Richard S. Bond

Winnie Frazier

Witnesses To Mark:
{

Subscribed and sworn to before me this 29 day of March , 1905

Edie A Bowerman
Notary Public.

---

BIRTH AFFIDAVIT.

## DEPARTMENT OF THE INTERIOR.
## COMMISSION TO THE FIVE CIVILIZED TRIBES.

---

IN RE APPLICATION FOR ENROLLMENT, as a citizen of the  Choctaw  Nation, of Alice Bond , born on the 2 day of March , 1905

Name of Father: Readmond[sic] Bond     a citizen of the  Choctaw  Nation.
Name of Mother: Sallie Bond             a citizen of the  Choctaw  Nation.

Postoffice   Duncan, Ind. Ter.

## Applications for Enrollment of Choctaw Newborn
## Act of 1905   Volume IX

### AFFIDAVIT OF MOTHER.

UNITED STATES OF AMERICA, Indian Territory, }
Southern          DISTRICT.

I,   Sallie Bond   , on oath state that I am   38   years of age and a citizen by blood   , of the   Choctaw   Nation; that I am the lawful wife of   Readmond Bond   , who is a citizen, by blood   of the   Choctaw   Nation; that a   female   child was born to me on   2   day of   March   , 1905; that said child has been named   Alice Bond   , and was living March 4, 1905.

Sallie Bond

Witnesses To Mark:
{ L. T. Weaver
{ J.R. Priddy

Subscribed and sworn to before me this  27   day of   April   , 1905

E H Bond
Notary Public.

### AFFIDAVIT OF ATTENDING PHYSICIAN OR MID-WIFE.

UNITED STATES OF AMERICA, Indian Territory, }
Southern          DISTRICT.

I,   Susan Charleston   , a   midwife   , on oath state that I attended on Mrs.   Sallie Bond   , wife of   Readmond Bond   on the   2 day of   March   , 1905; that there was born to her on said date a   female   child; that said child was living March 4, 1905, and is said to have been named Alice Bond

her
Susan x Charleston
mark

Witnesses To Mark:
{ L.T. Weaver
{ J R Priddy

Subscribed and sworn to before me this  27   day of   April   , 1905

E H Bond
Notary Public.

## Applications for Enrollment of Choctaw Newborn
## Act of 1905   Volume IX

Choc New Born 529
    Levy Willis  b. 3-6-03

BIRTH AFFIDAVIT.

**DEPARTMENT OF THE INTERIOR.**
**COMMISSION TO THE FIVE CIVILIZED TRIBES.**

IN RE APPLICATION FOR ENROLLMENT, as a citizen of the   Choctaw   Nation, of Levy Willis  , born on the  6  day of  March  , 1903

Name of Father: James Willis        a citizen of the   Choctaw   Nation.
Name of Mother: Alin[sic] Willis    a citizen of the   Choctaw   Nation.

                        Postoffice   Talihina I.T.

*James Willis Interpreter*

**AFFIDAVIT OF MOTHER.**

UNITED STATES OF AMERICA, Indian Territory, }
    Central        DISTRICT.               }

    I,  Alin Willis  , on oath state that I am  35  years of age and a citizen by Blood  , of the   Choctaw   Nation; that I am the lawful wife of   James Willis  , who is a citizen, by Blood   of the    Choctaw   Nation; that a   Male   child was born to me on  6  day of  March  , 1903; that said child has been named Levy Willis  , and was living March 4, 1905.

                                her
                            Alin x Willis
Witnesses To Mark:        mark
  { Willard N Everett
  { Jno J Thomas

    Subscribed and sworn to before me this  29  day of  March  , 1905

My commission expires Feb. 4, 1908
Commission from U.S. Court at So. McAlester I.T.        Sam T. Roberts Jr
MY OFFICE TALIHINA, I. T.                                Notary Public.

**AFFIDAVIT OF ATTENDING PHYSICIAN OR MID-WIFE.**

UNITED STATES OF AMERICA, Indian Territory, }
    Central        DISTRICT.               }

    I,   James Willis   , a  ———  , on oath state that I attended on Mrs. Alin Willis  , wife of   my wife   on the  6  day of  March  , 1903; that

## Applications for Enrollment of Choctaw Newborn
## Act of 1905   Volume IX

there was born to her on said date a   Male   child; that said child was living March 4, 1905, and is said to have been named Levy Willis

James Willis

Witnesses To Mark:
{

Subscribed and sworn to before me this  29  day of  March  , 1905

My commission expires Feb. 4, 1908
Commission from U.S. Court at So. McAlester I.T.
MY OFFICE TALIHINA, I. T.

Sam T. Roberts Jr
Notary Public.

---

**BIRTH AFFIDAVIT.**

### DEPARTMENT OF THE INTERIOR.
### COMMISSION TO THE FIVE CIVILIZED TRIBES.

IN RE APPLICATION FOR ENROLLMENT, as a citizen of the   Choctaw   Nation, of Levy Willis  , born on the  6"  day of  March  , 1903

Name of Father: James Willis         a citizen of the   Choctaw   Nation.
Name of Mother: Cillen Willis        a citizen of the   Choctaw   Nation.

Postoffice   Talihina I.T.

---

**AFFIDAVIT OF MOTHER.**

UNITED STATES OF AMERICA, Indian Territory, }
        Central         DISTRICT.

I,  Cillen Willis  , on oath state that I am  35  years of age and a citizen by Blood  , of the   Choctaw   Nation; that I am the lawful wife of   James Willis  , who is a citizen, by Blood   of the    Choctaw   Nation; that a   Male   child was born to me on   6"  day of   March  , 1903; that said child has been named Levy Willis  , and was living March 4, 1905.

                                her
                        Cillen x Willis
Witnesses To Mark:              mark
{ Sam T Roberts Jr
{ Joseph Williams

Subscribed and sworn to before me this  30  day of  May  , 1905

My Com expires                  T.B. Lunsford
Feb 1-1908                      Notary Public.

# Applications for Enrollment of Choctaw Newborn
## Act of 1905 Volume IX

### AFFIDAVIT OF ATTENDING PHYSICIAN OR MID-WIFE.

UNITED STATES OF AMERICA, Indian Territory,  
Central DISTRICT.

I, James Willis  husband of Cillin[sic] Willis , on oath state that I attended on Mrs. Cillen Willis , wife of  James Willis  on the 6" day of March , 1903; that there was born to her on said date a  Male  child; that said child was living March 4, 1905, and is said to have been named Levy Willis

                                     James Willis  
Witnesses To Mark:

      Subscribed and sworn to before me this  30 day of  May  , 1905

                                     T.B. Lunsford  
                                         Notary Public.

---

Central District,  
Indian Territory.

I, John Durant  on oath state that I am  57  years of age, my post-office is  Talihina  Indian Territory.

That I know James Willis who is a Choctaw by blood, and I also know his wife Cillin Willis, who is also a Choctaw by blood.

I know that on or about the 6th day of March 1903 there was born to Cillin Willis a male child, who was said to be named Levy Willis, that said child was living on the 4th day of March 1905. And that said child is still living. *I am not kin to any of the parties and am a disinterested party.*  
I am a citizen of the Choctaw Nation by blood.

                                   John Durant  
Witnesses.  
   Eli Paxton  
   M. K. M<sup>c</sup>Elhannan

Subscribed and sworn to before me this the 30th day of May 1905.

My commission expires Feb. 4, 1908  
Commission from U.S. Court, So. McAlester I.T.      T.B. Lunsford  
MY OFFICE TALIHINA, I. T.                         Notary Public.

# Applications for Enrollment of Choctaw Newborn
## Act of 1905 Volume IX

Central District,
Indian Territory.

I, Watkin[sic] Robert[sic] on oath state that I am 21 years of age, my post-office is Muse Indian Territory.

That I know James Willis who is a Choctaw by blood, and I also know his wife Cillin Willis, who is also a Choctaw by blood.

I know that on or about the 6th day of March 1903 there was born to Cillin Willis a male child, who was said to be named Levy Willis, that said child was living on the 4th day of March 1905. And that said child is still living. *I am not kin to any of the parties and am a disinterested party.*
I am a citizen of the Choctaw Nation by blood.

                                      Watkin Robert

Witnesses.
    Eli Paxton
    M. K. M$^c$Elhannan

Subscribed and sworn to before me this the 30th day of May 1905.

My commission expires Feb. 4, 1908
Commission from U.S. Court, So. McAlester I.T.
MY OFFICE TALIHINA, I. T.
                            T.B. Lunsford
                                  Notary Public.

---

                                              7-2125

Muskogee, Indian Territory, April 3, 1905.

James Willis,
    Talihina, Indian Territory.

Dear Sir:

    Receipt is hereby acknowledged of the affidavits of Alin[sic] Willis and James Willis to the birth of Levy Willis, son of James and Alin Willis, March 6, 1903, and the same have been filed with our records as an application for the enrollment of said child.

                                Respectfully,

                                                  Chairman.

## Applications for Enrollment of Choctaw Newborn
## Act of 1905   Volume IX

**COPY**  N. B. 529

Muskogee, Indian Territory, April 8, 1905.

James Willis,
    Talihina, Indian Territory.

Dear Sir:

    There is inclosed you herewith for execution application for the enrollment of your infant child, Levy Willis, born March 3, 1903.

    It appears from the application heretofore filed with the Commission that the affidavit of the physician or midwife was filled out by the father. If there was no physician or midwife in attendance at the birth of said child, it will be necessary for you to furnish the affidavits of two persons who have actual knowledge of the fact, that the child was born, was living on March 4, 1905, and that Cillen Willis was his mother.

    In having these affidavits executed care should be exercised to see that all names are written in full, as they appear in the body of the affidavit, and in the event that either of the persons signing the affidavit are unable to write, signatures by mark must be attested by two witnesses. Each affidavit must be executed before a Notary Public and the notarial seal and signature of the officer must be attached to each separate affidavit.

                                    Respectfully,
                                      SIGNED
                                    *T. B. Needles.*
LM 8-37                               Commissioner in Charge.

---

                                              7-N.B. 529.

                      Muskogee, Indian Territory, June 1, 1905.

James Willis,
    Talihina, Indian Territory.

Dear Sir:

    Receipt is hereby acknowledged of the affidavits of Cillen Willis, James Willis, Watkin Roberts[sic] and John Durant to the birth of Levy Willis, son of James and Cillen Willis, March 6, 1903, and the same have been filed with our records in the matter of the enrollment of said child.

                                Respectfully,

                                        Commissioner in Charge.

# Applications for Enrollment of Choctaw Newborn
## Act of 1905   Volume IX

Choc New Born 530
   Martha Williams   b. 1-14-04

7-3481

Muskogee, Indian Territory, April 3, 1905.

Mary Frazier,
   Bokchito, Indian Territory.

Dear Madam:

Receipt is hereby acknowledged of your affidavit and the affidavit of Francis Williams to the birth of Martha Williams, daughter of Daniel Williams and Mary Frazier, January 14, 1904, and the same have been filed with our records as an application for the enrollment of said child.

Respectfully,

Chairman.

**BIRTH AFFIDAVIT.**

**DEPARTMENT OF THE INTERIOR.**
**COMMISSION TO THE FIVE CIVILIZED TRIBES.**

IN RE APPLICATION FOR ENROLLMENT, as a citizen of the   Choctaw   Nation, of Martha Williams   , born on the 14$^{th}$   day of   January   , 1904

Name of Father: Daniel Williams      a citizen of the   Choctaw   Nation.
Name of Mother: Mary Frazier         a citizen of the   Choctaw   Nation.

Postoffice   Bokchito, I.T.

**AFFIDAVIT OF MOTHER.**

UNITED STATES OF AMERICA, Indian Territory,
   Central          DISTRICT.

I, Mary Frazier  , on oath state that I am  19  years of age and a citizen by Blood  , of the  Choctaw  Nation; that I am the lawful wife of  un married  , who is a citizen, by ............ of the  Choctaw  Nation; that a  Female  child was born to me on  14$^{th}$  day of  January  , 1904; that said child has been named  Martha Williams  , and was living March 4, 1905.

Mary Frazier

# Applications for Enrollment of Choctaw Newborn
## Act of 1905   Volume IX

Witnesses To Mark:
{

Subscribed and sworn to before me this 29th   day of   March   , 1905

W C Caudill
Notary Public.

---

**AFFIDAVIT OF ATTENDING PHYSICIAN OR MID-WIFE.**

UNITED STATES OF AMERICA, Indian Territory, }
Central           DISTRICT. }

I,   Francis Williams   , a   Mid-wife   , on oath state that I attended on Mrs.   Miss Mary Frazier   , wife of ........................................ on the 14th   day of   January   , 1904; that there was born to her on said date a   Female   child; that said child was living March 4, 1905, and is said to have been named Martha Williams

Francis Williams

Witnesses To Mark:
{

Subscribed and sworn to before me this 29th   day of   March   , 1905

W C Caudill
Notary Public.

---

Choc New Born 531
       Samuel Arnold Farmer   b. 1-27-03

7-2524

Muskogee, Indian Territory, April 3, 1905.

B. F. Farmer,
       Durant, Indian Territory.

Dear Sir:

Receipt is hereby acknowledged of the affidavits of Fannie L. Farmer and Nancy Farmer to the birth of Samuel Arnold Farmer, son of B. F. and Fannie L. Farmer, January

# Applications for Enrollment of Choctaw Newborn
## Act of 1905  Volume IX

27, 1903, and the same have been filed with our records as an application for the enrollment of said child.

Respectfully,

Chairman.

**COPY**

N. B. 531

Muskogee, Indian Territory, April 8, 1905.

B. F. Farmer,
 Durant, Indian Territory.

Dear Sir:

There is inclosed you herewith for execution application for the enrollment of your infant child, Samuel Arnold Farmer, born January 27, 1903.

In having these affidavits executed care should be exercised to see that all names are written in full, as they appear in the body of the affidavit, and in the event that either of the persons signing the affidavit are unable to write, signatures by mark must be attested by two witnesses. Each affidavit must be executed before a Notary Public and the notarial seal and signature of the officer must be attached to each separate affidavit.

Respectfully,
SIGNED
*T. B. Needles.*

LM 8-35.  Commissioner in Charge.

**COPY**  Choctaw N.B. 531.

Muskogee, Indian Territory, April 18, 1905.

B. F. Farmer,
 Durant, Indian Territory.

Dear Sir:

Receipt is hereby acknowledged of your letter of April 12, enclosing the affidavits of Fannie Farmer and Nannie Farmer to the birth of Samuel Arnold Farmer, son of B. F. and Fannie Farmer, January 27, 1903, and the same have been filed with our records in the matter of the enrollment of said child.

## Applications for Enrollment of Choctaw Newborn
## Act of 1905 Volume IX

Respectfully,
SIGNED

*Tams Bixby*
Chairman.

---

## AFFIDAVIT OF ATTENDING PHYSICIAN OR MIDWIFE

UNITED STATES OF AMERICA
INDIAN TERRITORY
Central DISTRICT

I, Mrs Nannie Farmer a Midwife on oath state that I attended on Mrs. Fannie L Farmer wife of Benj. F. Farmer on the 27 day of January , 190 3, that there was born to her on said date a Male child, that said child is now living, and is said to have been named Samuel Arnold

(Seal) Mrs Nannie Farmer

Subscribed and sworn to before me this, the 28 day of February 190 5

My commission expires June 16$^{th}$ 1907  J. L. Farmer
Notary Public.

WITNESSETH:
Must be two witnesses who are citizens and know the child.
- F E Buck
- W.H. Stanton

We hereby certify that we are well acquainted with Mrs Nannie Farmer a Midwife and know her to be reputable and of good standing in the community.

- F C Buck
- *(Name Illegible)*

# Applications for Enrollment of Choctaw Newborn
## Act of 1905   Volume IX

**NEW-BORN AFFIDAVIT.**

Number..................

## Choctaw Enrolling Commission.

IN THE MATTER OF THE APPLICATION FOR ENROLLMENT, as a citizen of the Choctaw Nation, of  Samuel Arnold Farmer

born on the 27 day of January 190 3

Name of father   Benj. F. Farmer   a citizen of   the U.S. Nation final enrollment No ———
Name of mother   Fannie L. Farmer   a citizen of   Choctaw Nation final enrollment No   7325

Postoffice   Durant I.T.

**AFFIDAVIT OF MOTHER.**

UNITED STATES OF AMERICA,
INDIAN TERRITORY,
.................................DISTRICT

I   Fannie L. Farmer   on oath state that I am 27 years of age and a citizen by  blood   of the  Choctaw   Nation, and as such have been placed upon the final roll of the   Choctaw   Nation, by the Honorable Secretary of the Interior my final enrollment number being   7325   ; that I am the lawful wife of   Benj. F. Farmer   , who is a citizen of the   U.S.   Nation, and as such has been placed upon the final roll of said Nation by the Honorable Secretary of the Interior, his final enrollment number being — and that a   male   child was born to me on the   27   day of   January   190 3; that said child has been named   Samuel Arnold   , and is now living.

Fannie L Farmer

WITNESSETH:
Must be two Witnesses who are Citizens.   Green Thompson
M. M$^c$Daniel

Subscribed and sworn to before me this   18   day of   Jany AD   190 5

J H Downing
Notary Public.

My commission expires Nov 28$^{th}$ 1908

## Applications for Enrollment of Choctaw Newborn
## Act of 1905   Volume IX

BIRTH AFFIDAVIT.

### DEPARTMENT OF THE INTERIOR.
## COMMISSION TO THE FIVE CIVILIZED TRIBES.

IN RE APPLICATION FOR ENROLLMENT, as a citizen of the    Choctaw    Nation, of Samuel Arnold Farmer    , born on the   27   day of   January  , 1903

Name of Father: B.F. Farmer         a citizen of the    U.S.    Nation.
Name of Mother: Fannie L Farmer     a citizen of the    Choctaw    Nation.

Postoffice    Durant Ind. Ter

### AFFIDAVIT OF MOTHER.

UNITED STATES OF AMERICA, Indian Territory, }
Central Dist.        DISTRICT.

I,   Fannie L Farmer   , on oath state that I am   28   years of age and a citizen by   blood  , of the   Choctaw   Nation; that I am the lawful wife of   B.F. Farmer  , who is a citizen, by blood   of the   U.S.   Nation; that a   male   child was born to me on   27   day of   January   , 1903; that said child has been named Samuel Arnold   , and was living March 4, 1905.

Fannie L Farmer

Witnesses To Mark:
{

Subscribed and sworn to before me this 29th   day of   March AD    , 1905
My commission expires
on Nov 27-1908        J H Downing
            Notary Public.

### AFFIDAVIT OF ATTENDING PHYSICIAN OR MID-WIFE.

UNITED STATES OF AMERICA, Indian Territory, }
Central        DISTRICT.

I,   Nancy Farmer    , a   Midwife   , on oath state that I attended on Mrs.   Fannie L Farmer   , wife of   B F Farmer   on the 27 day of   January  , 1903; that there was born to her on said date a   male   child; that said child was living March 4, 1905, and is said to have been named Samuel Arnold

Nancy Farmer

Witnesses To Mark:
{

## Applications for Enrollment of Choctaw Newborn
## Act of 1905   Volume IX

Subscribed and sworn to before me this  28  day of   March   , 1905

(Seal)                                    J L Farmer
                                                      Notary Public.
My commission expires June 16<sup>th</sup> 1907

---

**BIRTH AFFIDAVIT.**

## DEPARTMENT OF THE INTERIOR.
## COMMISSION TO THE FIVE CIVILIZED TRIBES.

---

**IN RE APPLICATION FOR ENROLLMENT,** as a citizen of the   Choctaw   Nation, of Samuel Arnold Farmer   , born on the  27"  day of   January , 1903

Name of Father: B.F. Farmer            a citizen of the    U.S.    Nation.
Name of Mother: Fannie Farmer          a citizen of the   Choctaw   Nation.

                        Postoffice    Durant Ind. Ter

---

### AFFIDAVIT OF MOTHER.

UNITED STATES OF AMERICA, Indian Territory, }
  Central Dist.        **DISTRICT.** }

I,  Fannie Farmer  , on oath state that I am  28   years of age and a citizen by   Blood  , of the   Choctaw   Nation; that I am the lawful wife of   B.F. Farmer  , who is a citizen, ~~by~~ ———  of the    United States    Nation; that a   male   child was born to me on   27"   day of   January    , 1903; that said child has been named   Samuel Arnold Farmer   , and was living March 4, 1905.

                                Fannie Farmer
Witnesses To Mark:
  {

Subscribed and sworn to before me this  11<sup>th</sup>   day of   April   , 1905
My commission
expires Nov 27<sup>th</sup> 1908           J H Downing
                                                Notary Public.

---

# Applications for Enrollment of Choctaw Newborn
## Act of 1905   Volume IX

**AFFIDAVIT OF ATTENDING PHYSICIAN OR MID-WIFE.**

UNITED STATES OF AMERICA, Indian Territory,  
Central                    DISTRICT.

I,   Nannie Farmer   , a   Midwife   , on oath state that I attended on Mrs.   Fannie Farmer   , wife of   B F Farmer   on the 27" day of   January   , 1903; that there was born to her on said date a   male   child; that said child was living March 4, 1905, and is said to have been named Samuel Arnold Farmer

                                                   Nannie Farmer
Witnesses To Mark:

   Subscribed and sworn to before me this   12$^{th}$   day of   April   , 1905

                                                   T. R. Dean
My commission expires                              Notary Public.
October 10, 1905

---

Choc New Born 532
   Dellar Walker   b. 12-29-02
   Hortey Walker   b. 1-9-05

**BIRTH AFFIDAVIT.**
## DEPARTMENT OF THE INTERIOR.
## COMMISSION TO THE FIVE CIVILIZED TRIBES.

**IN RE APPLICATION FOR ENROLLMENT,** as a citizen of the   Choctaw   Nation, of Dellar Walker  , born on the   29   day of   Dec  , 1902

Name of Father:  Willie Walker          a citizen of the   Choctaw   Nation.
Name of Mother:  May Walker             a citizen of the   intermarried   Nation.

                    Postoffice    Wayne I.T.

# Applications for Enrollment of Choctaw Newborn
## Act of 1905   Volume IX

### AFFIDAVIT OF MOTHER.

UNITED STATES OF AMERICA, Indian Territory, }
  Southern        DISTRICT.

    I, May Walker, on oath state that I am 28 years of age and a citizen by intermarriage, of the Choctaw Nation; that I am the lawful wife of Willie Walker, who is a citizen, by Birth of the Choctaw Nation; that a Female child was born to me on 29 day of Dec, 1902; that said child has been named Dellar Walker, and was living March 4, 1905.

                        her mark
                        May x Walker

Witnesses To Mark:
  { J M Garland
    M.J. Box

    Subscribed and sworn to before me this 28 day of March, 1905

                        Geo Box
                        Notary Public.

---

### AFFIDAVIT OF ATTENDING PHYSICIAN OR MID-WIFE.

UNITED STATES OF AMERICA, Indian Territory, }
  Southern        DISTRICT.

    I, Sarah Garland, a midwife, on oath state that I attended on Mrs. May Walker, wife of Willie Walker on the 29 day of Dec, 1902; that there was born to her on said date a Female child; that said child was living March 4, 1905, and is said to have been named Dellar Walker

                        Sarah Garland

Witnesses To Mark:
  {

    Subscribed and sworn to before me this 28 day of March, 1905

                        Geo Box
                        Notary Public.

## Applications for Enrollment of Choctaw Newborn
## Act of 1905   Volume IX

BIRTH AFFIDAVIT.

## DEPARTMENT OF THE INTERIOR.
## COMMISSION TO THE FIVE CIVILIZED TRIBES.

IN RE APPLICATION FOR ENROLLMENT, as a citizen of the   Choctaw   Nation, of Hortey Walker  , born on the  9th  day of  January , 1905

Name of Father: Willie Walker          a citizen of the   Choctaw    Nation.
Name of Mother: Mary[sic] Walker  intermarried  a citizen of the .................... Nation.

Postoffice   Wayne Ind Territory

### AFFIDAVIT OF MOTHER.

UNITED STATES OF AMERICA, Indian Territory,
Southern         DISTRICT.

I, Mary Walker , on oath state that I am  28  years of age and a citizen by ................, of the ................. Nation; that I am the lawful wife of Willie Walker , who is a citizen, by birth of the  Choctaw  Nation; that a  Female  child was born to me on  the 9th  day of  January  , 1905; that said child has been named  Hortey Walker , and was living March 4, 1905.

                                                     her
                                            Mary  x  Walker
Witnesses To Mark:               mark
  { *(Name Illegible)*
    *(Name Illegible)*

Subscribed and sworn to before me this  29th  day of  March  , 1905

My Com expires July 22-1907         M.S. Edwards
                                               Notary Public.

### AFFIDAVIT OF ATTENDING PHYSICIAN OR MID-WIFE.

UNITED STATES OF AMERICA, Indian Territory,
Southern         DISTRICT.

I, Mary Powell  , a  Mid wife  , on oath state that I attended on Mrs. Mary Walker , wife of  Willie Walker  on the 9th  day of  January , 1905; that there was born to her on said date a  Female  child; that said child was living March 4, 1905, and is said to have been named  Hortey Walker

                                               Mary Powell

# Applications for Enrollment of Choctaw Newborn
## Act of 1905   Volume IX

Witnesses To Mark:

   Subscribed and sworn to before me this   29th   day of   March   , 1905

M.S. Edwards
Notary Public.

---

Choc New Born 533
   Ray Berry  b. 2-18-04

**BIRTH AFFIDAVIT.**

## DEPARTMENT OF THE INTERIOR,
### COMMISSION TO THE FIVE CIVILIZED TRIBES.

   *IN RE Application for Enrollment,* as a citizen of the   Choctaw   Nation, of   Ray Berry  , born on the   18   day of   Feb   , 1904

Name of Father:  John Berry           a citizen of the   Choctaw   Nation.
Name of Mother:  Dena Berry           a citizen of the   Choctaw   Nation.

Post-Office:   McGee IT

**AFFIDAVIT OF MOTHER.**

UNITED STATES OF AMERICA,
   **INDIAN TERRITORY.**
   Southern      District.

   I,   Dena Berry  , on oath state that I am   25   years of age and a citizen by blood  , of the   Choctaw   Nation; that I am the lawful wife of   John Berry  , who is a citizen, by   Inttermarrage[sic]   of the   Choctaw   Nation; that a   male   child was born to me on   18   day of   Feb  , 1904 , that said child has been named   Ray Berry  , and is now living.

Dena Berry

**WITNESSES TO MARK:**

# Applications for Enrollment of Choctaw Newborn
## Act of 1905  Volume IX

*Subscribed and sworn to before me this*  27  *day of*  Mch  , 1905.

J J Copeland
**NOTARY PUBLIC.**

---

### AFFIDAVIT OF ATTENDING PHYSICIAN OR MID-WIFE.

UNITED STATES OF AMERICA, }
INDIAN TERRITORY.
Southern        District.

I,  J R Craig  , a  Physician  , on oath state that I attended on Mrs.  Dena Berry  , wife of  John Berry  on the  18  day of  Feb  , 1904 ; that there was born to her on said date a  male  child; that said child is now living and is said to have been named  Ray Berry

J.R. Craig M.D.

**WITNESSES TO MARK:**
{

*Subscribed and sworn to before me this*  27  *day of*  Mch  , 1905.

J J Copeland
**NOTARY PUBLIC.**

---

7-303

Muskogee, Indian Territory, April 3, 1905.

John Berry,
    McGee, Indian Territory.

Dear Sir:

Receipt is hereby acknowledged of your letter of March 28, 1905, enclosing the affidavits of Dena Berry and J. R. Craig to the birth of Ray Berry, son of John and Dena Berry, February 18, 1904, and the same have been filed with our records as an application for the enrollment of said child.

Respectfully,

Chairman.

## Applications for Enrollment of Choctaw Newborn
## Act of 1905   Volume IX

**COPY**

Choctaw N.B.
533.

Muskogee, Indian Territory, April 18, 1905.

John Berry,
    McGee, Indian Territory.

Dear Sir:

    Receipt is hereby acknowledged of your letter of April 10, stating that on March 28 you forwarded affidavits to the birth of Ray Berry, and asking if the same had been received

    In reply to your letter you are advised that the affidavits of Dena Berry and J. R. Craig to the birth of Ray Berry, son of John and Dena Berry, February 18, 1904, have been received and filed with our records in the matter of the enrollment of said child.

Respectfully,

SIGNED    *Tams Bixby*
Chairman.

---

7 NB 533

**COPY**

Muskogee, Indian Territory, April 25, 1905.

John Berry,
    McGee, Indian Territory.

Dear Sir:

    Receipt is hereby acknowledged of your letter of April 18, 1905, stating that you forwarded affidavits for the enrollment of your child sometime ago, and ask if same have been received.

    In reply to your letter you are advised that, as you were informed on April 18, 1905, the affidavits heretofore forwarded to the birth of your son, Ray Berry, have been filed with our records as an application for the enrollment of said child.

Respectfully,
SIGNED    *Tams Bixby*
Chairman.

## Applications for Enrollment of Choctaw Newborn
## Act of 1905    Volume IX

7-NB-533

Muskogee, Indian Territory, July 7, 1905.

John Berry,
    McGee, Indian Territory.

Dear Sir:

    Receipt is hereby acknowledged of your letter of June 29, 1905, asking if your child Ray Berry has been approved and if you will be notified of the approval of his enrollment.

    In reply to your letter you are advised that the name of your child Ray Berry has been placed upon a schedule of citizens by blood of the Choctaw Nation prepared for forwarding to the Secretary of the Interior, but this office has not yet been notified of Departmental action thereon.

    You will be advised when the enrollment of this child is approved by the Secretary of the Interior.

                                       Respectfully,

                                                          Commissioner.

---

Choc New Born 534
        Laura Winnie Stowers   b. 2-28-03
        Wesley Stowers   b. 9-6-04

Applications for Enrollment of Choctaw Newborn
Act of 1905 Volume IX

534

## NEW BORN
### CHOCTAW ENROLLMENT

LAURA WINNIE STOWERS
(BORN FEBRUARY 28, 1903)

WESLEY STOWERS
(BORN SEPTEMBER 6, 1904)

As Citizen of the
CHOCTAW NATION
Act of Congress
Approved March 3, 1905

NO 2.............HEREON DISMISSED UNDER ORDER OF THE COMMISSIONER OF THE FIVE CIVILIZED TRIBES OF JULY 18, 1905.

NOTICE OF DECISION FORWARDED APPLICANT'S FATHER AUGUST 23, 1905

534

7-NB-534

Muskogee, Indian Territory, August 4, 1905.

William M. Stowers,
Tyler, Indian Territory.

Dear Sir:

There is inclosed herewith blank for proof of death of your son Wesley Stowers, which please have executed and returned to this office as early as practicable.

In having the same executed be careful to see that all blanks are properly filled, all names written in full and that the Notary Public before whom the same are executed,

## Applications for Enrollment of Choctaw Newborn
## Act of 1905   Volume IX

affixes his name and seal to each affidavit. Signatures by mark must be attested by two disinterested witnesses.

Respectfully,

Commissioner.

D C

---

7-NB-534

Muskogee, Indian Territory, August 12, 1905.

Frances Stowers,
    Tyler, Indian Territory.

Dear Madam:

    Receipt is hereby acknowledged of your affidavit and the affidavit of Sue Holt to the death of Wesley Stowers which occurred October 20, 1904, and the same have been filed as evidence of the death of the above named child.

Respectfully,

Acting Commissioner.

---

7-NB-534      **COPY**

Muskogee, Indian Territory, August 23, 1905.

William Monroe Stowers,
    Tyler, Indian Territory.

Dear Sir:

    You are hereby advised that it appearing from the records of this office that your child, Wesley Stowers, died prior to March 4, 1905, the Commissioner to the Five Civilized Tribes, on August 23, 1905, dismissed the application for the enrollment of said child as a citizen by blood of the Choctaw Nation.

Respectfully,<br>SIGNED<br>*Tams Bixby*<br>Commissioner.

## Applications for Enrollment of Choctaw Newborn
## Act of 1905   Volume IX

7-NB-534                                                                              **COPY**

Muskogee, Indian Territory, August 23, 1905.

Mansfield, McMurray & Cornish,
    Attorneys for Choctaw and Chickasaw Nations,
        South McAlester, Indian Territory.

Gentlemen:

    You are hereby advised that it appearing from the records of this office that Wesley Stowers died prior to March 4, 1905, the Commissioner to the Five Civilized Tribes, on August 23, 1905, dismissed the application for the enrollment of this child as a citizen by blood of the Choctaw Nation.

                      Respectfully,
                      SIGNED

                      *Tams Bixby*
                      Commissioner.

---

### DEPARTMENT OF THE INTERIOR.
## COMMISSION TO THE FIVE CIVILIZED TRIBES.

In the matter of the death of   Wesley Stowers   a citizen of the   Choctaw   Nation, who formerly resided at or near   Tyler   , Ind. Ter., and died on the   20th   day of   October   , 1904

**AFFIDAVIT OF RELATIVE.**

UNITED STATES OF AMERICA, Indian Territory,
    Southern                    **DISTRICT.**

    I,   Laura Frances Stowers   , on oath state that I am   Thirty Six   years of age and a citizen by blood   , of the   Choctaw   Nation; that my postoffice address is   Tyler   , Ind. Ter.; that I am   the Mother   of   Wesley Stowers   who was a citizen, by blood   , of the   Choctaw   Nation and that said   Wesley Stowers   died on the   20th   day of   October   , 1904

                                    her
                      Laura Frances x Stowers
Witnesses To Mark:                   mark
    { J.Y. Lynn
      Geo. A. Henshaw

# Applications for Enrollment of Choctaw Newborn
## Act of 1905   Volume IX

Subscribed and sworn to before me this  9<sup>th</sup>  day of  August  , 1905.

J.W. Falkner
Notary Public.

---

**AFFIDAVIT OF ACQUAINTANCE.**

UNITED STATES OF AMERICA, Indian Territory, }
Southern        DISTRICT.  }

I,  Sue Holt  , on oath state that I am  fifty  years of age, and a citizen ~~by~~ of the United States  Nation; that my postoffice address is  Tyler  , Ind. Ter.; that I was personally acquainted with  Wesley Stowers  who was a citizen, by  blood  , of the  Choctaw  Nation; and that said  Wesley Stowers  died on the  20<sup>th</sup>  day of  October  , 1904

Sue Holt

Witnesses To Mark:
{

Subscribed and sworn to before me this  9<sup>th</sup>  day of  August  , 1905.

J.W. Falkner
Notary Public.

---

**BIRTH AFFIDAVIT.**

**DEPARTMENT OF THE INTERIOR.**
**COMMISSION TO THE FIVE CIVILIZED TRIBES.**

---

IN RE APPLICATION FOR ENROLLMENT, as a citizen of the  Choctaw  Nation, of  Laura Winnie Stowers  , born on the  28  day of  February  , 1903

Name of Father: William Monroe Stowers     a citizen of the  Choctaw  Nation.
Name of Mother: Laura Francis Stowers     a citizen of the  Choctaw  Nation.

Postoffice    Tyler, Ind. Ter.

---

**AFFIDAVIT OF MOTHER.**

UNITED STATES OF AMERICA, Indian Territory, }
22<sup>nd</sup>           DISTRICT. }

I,  Laura Francis Stowers  , on oath state that I am  36  years of age and a citizen by  blood  , of the  Choctaw  Nation; that I am the lawful wife of  William Monroe Stowers  , who is a citizen, by  Marriage  of the  Choctaw

## Applications for Enrollment of Choctaw Newborn
## Act of 1905   Volume IX

Nation; that a   female   child was born to me on   28   day of   February   , 1903; that said child has been named   Laura Winnie Stowers   , and was living March 4, 1905.

              her
          Laura Francis x Stowers
Witnesses To Mark:         mark
 { Dollie Willingham
   M.C. Simpson

  Subscribed and sworn to before me this   24   day of   March   , 1905

            Joe Simpson
            Notary Public.

---

**AFFIDAVIT OF ATTENDING PHYSICIAN OR MID-WIFE.**

UNITED STATES OF AMERICA, Indian Territory,
 22$^{nd}$      DISTRICT.

  I,   R.A. Gardner   , a   practicing physician   , on oath state that I attended on Mrs.   Laura Francis Stowers   , wife of   William Monroe Stowers   on the 28$^{th}$ day of   Feb.   , 1903; that there was born to her on said date a   female   child; that said child was living March 4, 1905, and is said to have been named Laura Winnie Stowers

          R.A. Gardner
Witnesses To Mark:
 {

  Subscribed and sworn to before me this   30$^{th}$   day of   Mar.   , 1905

          Dayton B. Steed
          Notary Public.

---

BIRTH AFFIDAVIT.
       DEPARTMENT OF THE INTERIOR.
    **COMMISSION TO THE FIVE CIVILIZED TRIBES.**

  IN RE APPLICATION FOR ENROLLMENT, as a citizen of the   Choctaw   Nation, of   Wesley Stowers   , born on the   6   day of   Sept   , 1904

Name of Father:   William Monroe Stowers  a citizen of the   Choctaw   Nation.
Name of Mother:   Laura Francis Stowers  a citizen of the   Choctaw   Nation.

       Postoffice  Tyler, Ind. Ter.

# Applications for Enrollment of Choctaw Newborn
## Act of 1905 Volume IX

**AFFIDAVIT OF MOTHER.**

UNITED STATES OF AMERICA, Indian Territory, }
22<sup>nd</sup> DISTRICT. }

I, Laura Francis Stowers, on oath state that I am 36 years of age and a citizen by blood, of the Choctaw Nation; that I am the lawful wife of William Monroe Stowers, who is a citizen, by Marriage of the Choctaw Nation; that a male child was born to me on 6 day of Sept, 1904; that said child has been named Wesley Stowers, and was living ~~March 4, 1905~~. *on 19 day of October 1904*

                        her
                Laura Francis x Stowers

Witnesses To Mark:              mark
   { Dollie Willingham
     Mary Simpson

Subscribed and sworn to before me this 24 day of March, 1905

                Joe Simpson
                Notary Public.

---

**AFFIDAVIT OF ATTENDING PHYSICIAN OR MID-WIFE.**

UNITED STATES OF AMERICA, Indian Territory, }
.................................................DISTRICT. }

I, R.A. Gardner, a practicing physician, on oath state that I attended on Mrs. Laura Francis Stowers, wife of William Monroe Stowers on the 6<sup>th</sup> day of Sept., 1904; that there was born to her on said date a male child; that said child was living March 4, 1905, and is said to have been named Wesley Stowers

              R.A. Gardner

Witnesses To Mark:
{

Subscribed and sworn to before me this 30<sup>th</sup> day of Mar., 1905

              Dayton B. Steed
              Notary Public.

# Applications for Enrollment of Choctaw Newborn
## Act of 1905   Volume IX

Choc New Born 535
Denver Madison Robinson   b. 2-12-05

**BIRTH AFFIDAVIT.**

### DEPARTMENT OF THE INTERIOR.
### COMMISSION TO THE FIVE CIVILIZED TRIBES.

IN RE APPLICATION FOR ENROLLMENT, as a citizen of the   Choctaw   Nation, of   Denver Madison Robinson   , born on the   $12^{th}$   day of   Feb   , 1905

Name of Father: Samuel P Robinson        a citizen of the   Choctaw   Nation.
Name of Mother: Cora Robinson            a citizen of the   Choctaw   Nation.

Postoffice ...........................................................................

### AFFIDAVIT OF MOTHER.

UNITED STATES OF AMERICA, Indian Territory,
Southern                   DISTRICT.

I,   Cora Robinson   , on oath state that I am   36   years of age and a citizen by   Blood   , of the   Choctaw   Nation; that I am the lawful wife of   Samuel P Robinson   , who is a citizen, by   Intermarriage   of the   Choctaw   Nation; that a   male   child was born to me on   $12^{th}$   day of   February   , 1905; that said child has been named   Denver Madison Robinson   , and was living March 4, 1905.

Cora Robinson

Witnesses To Mark:

Subscribed and sworn to before me this   29   day of   March   , 1905

(Name Illegible)<br>Notary Public.

### AFFIDAVIT OF ATTENDING PHYSICIAN OR MID-WIFE.

UNITED STATES OF AMERICA, Indian Territory,
Southern                   DISTRICT.

I,   Mrs. R.E. Albright   , a   midwife   , on oath state that I attended on Mrs.   Cora Robinson   , wife of   Samuel P Robinson   on the   12"   day of   February   , 1905; that there was born to her on said date a   male   child; that said

## Applications for Enrollment of Choctaw Newborn
## Act of 1905   Volume IX

child was living March 4, 1905, and is said to have been named Denver Madison Robinson

R E Albright

Witnesses To Mark:
{

Subscribed and sworn to before me this 29 day of March , 1905

*(Name Illegible)*
Notary Public.

---

Choc New Born 536
William Ira Sanner   b. 8-8-03
Charlie Sanner   b. 1-16-05

7-409

Muskogee, Indian Territory, March 14, 1905.

J. J. Sanner,
Harrisburg, Indian Territory.

Dear Sir:

Receipt is hereby acknowledged of the affidavits of Eva Broadway Sanner and W. S. spears to the birth of William Ira Sanner and Charley[sic] Sanner, children of J. J. and Eva Broadway Sanner, August 8, 1903, and January 16, 1905, respectively.

It is stated in the affidavits of the mother that you are a citizen by blood of the Choctaw Nation and for the purpose of identifying you upon our records you are requested to state your age, your full name, and the names of your parents as well as the time and place application was made for your enrollment. The matter of the affidavits referred to will then receive further consideration.

Respectfully,

Chairman.

## Applications for Enrollment of Choctaw Newborn
## Act of 1905 Volume IX

*(The letter below typed as given.)*

Velma, I. T.

March 22, 1905.

Commission of the Five Civilized Tribes,
Muskogee, I.T.

Gentlemen:

In reply to letter enclosed will state that I am 21 years of age, will be Twenty Two the 20 day of June, 1905. My full name is Jessie James Sanner. My father name William A. Sanner My Mother name Maggie F. Sanner . My mother after my father death remarried and is now Maggie F. Richerson. My Roll No. 14390.

(Signed) Jessie James Sanner.

---

**COPY**      N. B. 536

Muskogee, Indian Territory, April 8, 1905.

J. J. Sanner,
Harrisburg, Indian Territory.

Dear Sir:

You are hereby advised that before the application for the enrollment of Charlie Sanner, can be finally disposed of, it will be necessary for you to furnish the Commission with either the original or a certified copy of the license and certificate of your marriage to Eva Broadway Sanner.

Please attend to this matter at once.

Respectfully,
SIGNED
*T. B. Needles.*
Commissioner in Charge.

## Applications for Enrollment of Choctaw Newborn
## Act of 1905 Volume IX

COPY  Choctaw N.B. 536

Muskogee, Indian Territory, April 19, 1905.

J. J. Sanner,
    Harrisburg, Indian Territory.

Dear Sir:

    Receipt is hereby acknowledged of the marriage license and certificate between yourself and Eva Broadway which you offer in support of the application for the enrollment of your children, William,[sic] Ira and Charley Sanner, and the same have been filed with our records in the matter of the enrollment of said children.

    Respectfully,
    SIGNED   *Tams Bixby*
    Chairman.

---

**BIRTH AFFIDAVIT.**

## DEPARTMENT OF THE INTERIOR,
### COMMISSION TO THE FIVE CIVILIZED TRIBES.

*IN RE Application for Enrollment,* as a citizen of the Choctaw Nation, of Charlie Sanner, born on the 16 day of January, 1905

Name of Father: J J Sonner[sic]     a citizen of the Chockataw[sic] Nation.
Name of Mother: Eva Broadway Sonner     a citizen of the Chockataw Nation.

Post-Office:     Harrisburg I.T.

---

**AFFIDAVIT OF MOTHER.**

UNITED STATES OF AMERICA,
  INDIAN TERRITORY.
  Southern     District.

    I, Eva Broadway Sonner, on oath state that I am 20 years of age and a citizen by Intermarriage, of the Choctaw Nation; that I am the lawful wife of J J Sonner, who is a citizen, by Blood of the Choctaw Nation; that a male child was born to me on 16 day of January, 1905, that said child has been named Charlie Sonner, and is now living.

    Eva Broadway Sanner

# Applications for Enrollment of Choctaw Newborn
## Act of 1905   Volume IX

**WITNESSES TO MARK:**

*Subscribed and sworn to before me this*  8  *day of*  March  , 1905.

                          T.J. Nichols
                                 NOTARY PUBLIC.

---

### AFFIDAVIT OF ATTENDING PHYSICIAN OR MID-WIFE.

UNITED STATES OF AMERICA,
    INDIAN TERRITORY.
Southern       District.

I,  W.S. Spears  , a   phisicion[sic]  , on oath state that I attended on Mrs.  Sonner  , wife of   J J Sonner   on the  16   day of   January  , 1905 ; that there was born to her on said date a   male   child; that said child is now living and is said to have been named    Charlie Sonner

                        W S Spears MD

**WITNESSES TO MARK:**

*Subscribed and sworn to before me this*  8  *day of*  March  , 1905.

                        T.J. Nichols
                             NOTARY PUBLIC.

---

BIRTH AFFIDAVIT.

# DEPARTMENT OF THE INTERIOR,
### COMMISSION TO THE FIVE CIVILIZED TRIBES.

---

*IN RE Application for Enrollment,* as a citizen of the    Choctaw    Nation, of   William Ira Sanner  , born on the   8   day of   August   , 1903

Name of Father:  J J Sonner[sic]          a citizen of the Chockataw[sic] Nation.
Name of Mother:  Eva Broadway Sonner     a citizen of the  Chockataw    Nation.

                  Post-Office:     Harrisburg I.T.

## Applications for Enrollment of Choctaw Newborn
## Act of 1905 Volume IX

**AFFIDAVIT OF MOTHER.**

UNITED STATES OF AMERICA,
    **INDIAN TERRITORY.**
Southern     District.

    I, Eva Broadway Sonner , on oath state that I am 20 years of age and a citizen by Intermarriage , of the Choctaw Nation; that I am the lawful wife of J J Sonner , who is a citizen, by Blood of the Choctaw Nation; that a male child was born to me on 8 day of August , 1903 , that said child has been named William Ira Sonner , and is now living.

                                    Eva Broadway Sanner
**WITNESSES TO MARK:**

{

    Subscribed and sworn to before me this 8 day of March , 1905.

                                    T.J. Nichols
                                    **NOTARY PUBLIC.**

**AFFIDAVIT OF ATTENDING PHYSICIAN OR MID-WIFE.**

UNITED STATES OF AMERICA,
    **INDIAN TERRITORY.**
Southern     District.

    I, W.S. Spears , a phisicion[sic] , on oath state that I attended on Mrs. Sonner , wife of J J Sonner on the 8 day of August , 1903 ; that there was born to her on said date a male child; that said child is now living and is said to have been named William Ira Sonner

                                    W S Spears MD
**WITNESSES TO MARK:**

{

    Subscribed and sworn to before me this 8 day of March , 1905.

                                    T.J. Nichols
                                    **NOTARY PUBLIC.**

# Applications for Enrollment of Choctaw Newborn
## Act of 1905 Volume IX

Choc New Born 537
    Harold Stidham b. 4-22-03
    Granted 2-18-07

DEPARTMENT OF THE INTERIOR,
COMMISSIONER TO THE FIVE CIVILIZED TRIBES.

-----

In the matter of the application for the enrollment as a citizen by blood of the Choctaw Nation . . . . .

                HAROLD STIDHAM...................7-NB-537.

### Certificate of Record of Marriage

United States of America,
    Indian Territory,    } sct.
    Southern District.

    I, C. M. CAMPBELL, Clerk of the United States Court, in the Territory and District aforesaid DO HEREBY CERTIFY, that the License for and Certificate of Marriage of

MR     Marion Stidham     and

M     Hattie Mitchell

were filed in my office in said Territory and District the 14" day of February A.D., 1903 and duly recorded in Book   G of Marriage Record, Page   164

        WITNESS my hand and Seal of said Court, at Ardmore, this   14"   day of February   A.D. 190 3

        C. M. Campbell
                CLERK.

Return this License to the United States Clerk at Ardmore, that it may be recorded, when it will be mailed to the proper address.

Ardmoreite Steam Print.

DEPARTMENT OF THE INTERIOR,
Commission to the Five Civilized Tribes.
**FILED**
APR 25 1905
Tams Bixby CHAIRMAN.

**FILED**

FEB 14 1903 8 AM

*C. M. CAMPBELL, Clerk.*
Southern Dist. Ind. Ter.

Applications for Enrollment of Choctaw Newborn
Act of 1905  Volume IX

## MARRIAGE LICENSE

No. 271

UNITED STATES OF AMERICA,
INDIAN TERRITORY,  ss:   To Any Person Authorized by Law to Solemnize Marriage, Greeting:
SOUTHERN DISTRICT.

You are hereby commanded to solemnize the Rite and publish the Banns of Matrimony between Mr. Marion Stidham of Attie in the Indian Territory, aged 22 years, and Miss Hattie Mitchell of Spanish Fort Texas in the Indian Territory, aged 19 years, according to law; and do you officially sign and return this License to the parties therein named.

Witness my hand and official Seal, this 14 day of February A. D. 1903

C.M. Campbell
Clerk of the United States Court.

## Certificate of Marriage.

UNITED STATES OF AMERICA,
INDIAN TERRITORY,  ss:
SOUTHERN DISTRICT.         I, C.M. Campbell

a Clerk U.S. Court do hereby certify that on the 14 day of Feby, A. D. 1903, I did duly according to law, as commanded in the foregoing License, solemnize the Rite and publish the Banns of Matrimony between the parties therein named.

Witness my hand this 14 day of Feby A. D. 1903

My credentials are recorded in the office of the Clerk of the United States Court, Indian Territory, Southern District, at Ardmore, Book........., Page.........

(NOTE-The person officiating should fill in the spaces for book and page and sign here.)

CM Campbell
a Clerk U.S. Court

NSC M<sup>c</sup>Coy Deputy Clerk

## Applications for Enrollment of Choctaw Newborn
## Act of 1905   Volume IX

NOTE (a)-The License and Certificate of Marriage must be returned to the office of the Clerk of the United States Court in the Indian Territory, at Ardmore, within sixty days from the date thereof, or the party to whom the License was issued will be liable in the amount of One Hundred Dollars ($100).

NOTE (b)-No person is authorized to perform the Marriage Ceremony in the Southern District unless the proper credentials have first been recorded in the Clerk's office.

# DECREE OF DIVORCE.

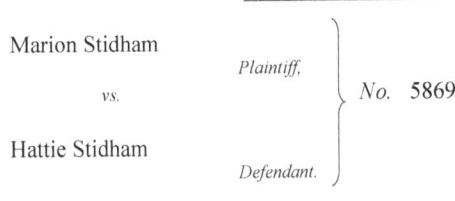

Marion Stidham
    *Plaintiff,*
  vs.                    No. 5869
Hattie Stidham
    *Defendant.*

    Now on this  4th  day of  July, 1904 , this cause comes on to be heard upon the report of the Master in Chancery, filed herein, which said report is by the Court confirmed and approved, and exhibits filed therewith; and the plaintiff appearing by h is attorney  Brown & Marsh , and it appearing that the defendant had been legally summoned and failed to appear and make answer; and it appearing from said Master's report that the allegations in the plaintiff's complaint are true, and the Court being fully advised in the premises;

    **It is therefore ordered, adjudged and decreed,** That the Bonds of Matrimony existing between the Plaintiff and the Defendant be, and the same are hereby, set aside and held for naught.

**United States of America,**
**INDIAN TERRITORY,**  } ss.
**SOUTHERN DISTRICT.**

    I, C. M. CAMPBELL, Clerk of the United States Court for the Southern District of the Indian Territory, do hereby certify that the above and foregoing is a true and correct copy of the original decree as appears from the records of this Court.

WITNESS my hand and seal of office, at   Ardmore  , this the  25th  day of  March  190 5

C. M. Campbell
*Clerk U. S. Court, Southern District, Indian Territory.*

By  N.H. M<sup>c</sup>Coy   *Deputy Clerk.*

# Applications for Enrollment of Choctaw Newborn
# Act of 1905   Volume IX

In the United States of America, Southern Judicial District of the
Indian Territory, at Ardmore.

---

Now comes M. L. Mitchell, and upon oath states that his name is M. L. Mitchell; that his age is fifty-eight years, and his post-office is Spanish Fort, Texas. That he is the father of Hattie M. Stidham, and the grand-father of Harold Stidham, the son of Hattie M. Stidham and Marion Stidham. That his daughter, Hattie M. Stidham and said Marion Stidham were married on the 14th day of February, 1903, and said Harold Stidham was born on the 22nd day of April, 1903. That said Marion Stidham was a member of the Choctaw Tribe of Indians. And that said Marion Stidham had been coming to the home of said Hattie M. Stidham quite often and two years prior to their marriage, he had been courting her. That it became evident that said Marion Stidham had seduced Hattie M. Stidham, whereupon, a warrant was issued and said Marion Stidham was arrested and brought to the United States Court, at Ardmore, Indian Territory, charged with seduction, and the said Hattie M. Stidham, affiant's daughter, whose maiden name was Hattie M. Mitchell, and said Marion Stidham, were married, and said charge of seduction was dismissed. That during two years prior to the time of their marriage the said Hattie M. Stidham and Marion Stidham had been engaged and he was keeping company with her, and that during said time, she never kept company with any-other man, only the said Marion Stidham. That during the time since they have been divorced the said Hattie M. Stidham has been living with this affiant, her father, and she has supported said child, with his assistance, that is the assistance of this affiant, who is the grandfather of said Harold Stidham.

Witness to mark  
Lee L Gyer

his  
M. L. x Mitchell  
mark

Subscribed and sworn to before me this the 13th day of November, A. D. 1905.

Lee L Gyer  
Notary Public, So. Dis., Ind. Ter.

---

In the United States of America, Southern Judicial District of the
Indian Territory, at Ardmore.

---

In re the Application for Enrollment of Harold Stidham, minor child of Marion Stidham and Hattie M. Stidham, to be enrolled as a new born Choctaw; same being docketed, 7-NB-537 ::::::::::::::::::::::::::::::::

---

# Applications for Enrollment of Choctaw Newborn
## Act of 1905   Volume IX

    Now comes Mrs. Hattie M. Stidham, and upon oath states that her name is Hattie M. Stidham; that she is twenty-one years of age; that her post-office address, at this time is Spanish Fort, Texas. Affiant further states that she is the mother of Harold Stidham, a minor, who was born on the 22nd day of April, 1903; she further states that at the time she was lawfully married to the said Marion Stidham and at the time she has been his lawful wife, he was a member of the Choctaw Tribe of Indians, by blood; that she has since been divorced from the said Marion Stidham. That the said Harold Stidham their minor son, was born during wed-lock, but that the affiant and said Marion Stidham were not married until the 13th day of February, 1903. That the affiant and said Marion Stidham had been engaged for two years prior to the time of their marriage, and she had been under marriage contract with him for two years prior to the time they were married and he would call at her home to see her quite often; that by virtue of the promise of marriage the said Marion Stidham seduced her and at the time she married him she was pregnant. That prior to the birth of said child she had not had intercourse with any-other man other than the said Marion Stidham, who is the father of said child and said child is the son of Marion Stidham. That prior to their marriage the said Marion Stidham became careless and was failing to carry out his marriage contract with her, whereupon he was arrested, charged with seduction and brought to the United States Court room, at Ardmore, Indian Territory and he there married her and said charge of seduction was dismissed against him. That since the birth of said child he has recognized the child as his child and has repeatedly stated that he intended to manage and control the property of said child, which it might have by virtue of being a member of said Tribe of Indians, and affiant further states that since their separation said child has lived with this affiant, and she has supported said child, together with the help of her father.

                                                    Hattie M Stidham

    Subscribed and sworn to before me this the 13th day of November, A. D. 1905.

                                                       Lee L Gyer
                                          Notary Public, So. Dis., Ind. Ter.

---

*(The letter below typed as given. Extremely difficult to read.)*

*Exhibit*
*"A"*

Maysville I.T.
H H Brown
    *(Illegible)*

Dear Sir  as I *(illegible)* not yet to *(illegible)* last week I will rite you a line or 2  I will say I have lurned that you tould Hattie Stidham to move over on this side off the River if she wanted to enroll that Baby  well if you did that it all right the thing I want to know is

# Applications for Enrollment of Choctaw Newborn
## Act of 1905  Volume IX

whather she can enroll the child withaugh me *(illegible)* not for you know and you must have some off that money back that she maid me spend
 So let me know soon   Yours truly

                                                  Marion Stidham

---

*(The letter below typed as given.  Extremely difficult to read.)*

                                                  *Exhibit "B"*

**COOK & CO.,**

Dealer in Drugs and Medicines

                        Maysville, Ind. Ter.,   Apr 26   190 5
                        H.H. Brown
                              Ardmore I.T.

dear Sur  I just resived your letter.  and I think I will bee redy for the 24  say I wnt and seen Hattie Stidham about enrolling Harld Stidham and if I can work thing a little smath and when the child is enrolld I can file it withaug any truble  I maid a traid with Hattie the thing I want is to let me know when the cild is enrolled and I will get in my bugie and go and get Haz and the Boy that a part off my traid with hur so dont let thime know when the ciled is en enrolll.  that is if Comish sends you the papers before they do me

I dont think I will have any truble withaug frank Driskill gives one truble

                                    Yours truly

                                          Marian Stidham

---

**Dr. M. C. High,**
Office with Cook Drug Company.

                                        *Exhibit "C"*

                              Maysville, I. T.   Nov- 21   190 5

H.H. Brown
                    Ardmore I.T.

Dear Sir:

Before I sign the papers sent me I want to know who will be Guardian for the child If myself alright- if the othr parties it all off.
I will get the $50 down there soon

                              Respt

                                    Marion Stidham

# Applications for Enrollment of Choctaw Newborn
## Act of 1905   Volume IX

In the United States of America, Southern District of the Indian Territory, at Ardmore.

----------

In Re The Enrollment of Harold Stidham.

Now comes H. H. Brown, and upon oath states that he is thirty-four years of age, and his post-office is Ardmore, Indian Territory; that he is a practicing attorney, and is well acquainted with Marion Stidham and his wife Hattie Stidham, father and mother of Harold Stidham. That he has been acquainted with Marion Stidham for ten years last past; that he was acquainted with him at the time he married Hattie Stidham. Affiant further states that he represented Marion Stidham in the suit which he filed to obtain a divorce from Hattie Stidham, and knows that after said suit was filed that Hattie Stidham came in and employed a lawyer and threatened to contest the right of Marion Stidham to procure a divorce, and said suit was settled by said Marion Stidham agreeing to pay said Hattie Stidham the sum of $250.00 as alimony and as support for said Hattie Stidham and their only child Harold Stidham. At no time while the evidence was being taken or while the controversy was pending relative to said divorce did Marion Stidham in his conversations with his wife Hattie Stidham and this affiant deny the fact that he was the father of Harold Stidham, but repeatedly said it was his child and would like to have the custody of it; he seemed very anxious about said child. That in the Spring of 1905, when the law passed giving members of the Chickasaw and Choctaw Tribes the right to enroll their children which were born after the closing of the rolls and prior to March 5$^{th}$, 1905, Marion Stidham talked to this affiant relative to having said child enrolled and desired this affiant to place an application before the Commissioner to the Five Civilized Tribes for the enrollment of said child. That about the first of April, 1905, this affiant received a letter from said Marion Stidham, which is hereto attached, Marked Exhibit "A"; again on or about the 26th day of April, 1905, this affiant received another letter from Marion Stidham, which is hereto attached, Marked Exhibit "B"; by reading both of said letters the Commissioner, can see that said Marion Stidham did not deny that said child was his' he was then seeking to be enabled to get the child's estate or the land which said child would be entitled to allot, if enrolled. That after the said Marion Stidham ascertained that Hattie Stidham, the mother of said Harold Stidham, would have the preferred right, to the custody and control of said child by reason of having the custody of said child after the divorce was granted and by reason of having cared for said child, he did nothing more to have said child enrolled; this affiant then prepared a statement for said Marion Stidham to sign, so as to show that this was his child; said statement was sent to Marion Stidham, and in reply to same, this affiant receive a letter, which is hereto attached, Marked Exhibit "C", which letter does not seem to be in his hand-writing, but was written in reply to the letter addressed to him at his request; all of which letters are made a part of this affidavit. The last mentioned letter does not deny the fact that said child is his. This affiant states that at no time when talking to affiant has Marion Stidham ever denied the fact that said Harold Stidham was his child.

HH Brown

## Applications for Enrollment of Choctaw Newborn
## Act of 1905   Volume IX

Subscribed and sworn to before me on this the 18 day of January, A. D. 1906.

LLGyer<br>Notary Public, So. Dis., I.Ter.

---

In the United States of America, Southern District of the Indian Territory, at Ardmore.

------

On this <u>18th</u> day of January, 1906, S. H. Butler, who after first being duly sworn, deposes and says:

My name is S. H. Butler; my age is thirty-one years; my post-office is Ardmore, Indian Territory; I am a practicing attorney, and know and am acquainted with both Marion Stidham and his wife Hattie Stidham. I represented his wife, Hattie Stidham, in a divorce suit filed by said Marion Stidham, in which case judgment was entered on the *4th* day of ___*July*___, 190_*4*_. The defendant, Hattie Stidham in said suit employed me to represent her and we prepared an answer in said case, and after the answer was filed the plaintiff Marion Stidham agreed to give $250.00, *and know he paid $125.00 of same* by way of alimony and support for said Hattie Stidham and their minor son, Harold Stidham; that we settled said case without making any record of this fact. Marion Stidham did not deny the child being his. In conversation which I have heard between them and from the facts I know about it, I do not think there is any question but what said child is the child of Marion Stidham. I am not related to either of said parties and not interested in the enrollment of said child, Harold Stidham in any way, what-ever.

S.H. Butler

Subscribed and sworn to before me this the 18th day of January, 1906.

LeeLGyer<br>Notary Public, So.Dis., Ind.T.

# Applications for Enrollment of Choctaw Newborn
# Act of 1905   Volume IX

7-NB-537.                                                                                          O.L.J.

### DEPARTMENT OF THE INTERIOR,
### COMMISSIONER TO THE FIVE CIVILIZED TRIBES.
-------

In the matter of the application for the enrollment of Harold Stidham as a citizen by blood of the Choctaw Nation.

### DECISION.

It appears from the record herein that on March 30, 1905, application was made to the Commission to the Five Civilized Tribes for the enrollment of Harold Stidham as a citizen by blood of the Choctaw Nation under the provisions of the Act of Congress approved March 3, 1905 (33 Stats., 1060).

It further appears from the record herein and from the records in the possession of this office that applicant was born on April 22, 1903, and is the son of Marion Stidham, whose name appears opposite No. 532 upon the final roll of citizens by blood of the Choctaw Nation approved by the Secretary of the Interior December 12, 1902, and Hattie Stidham, a non-citizen; and that said applicant was living on March 4, 1905.

I am, therefore, of the opinion that Harold Stidham should be enrolled as a citizen by blood of the Choctaw Nation under the provisions of the Act of Congress approved March 3, 1905 (33 Stats., 1060), and it is so ordered.

Tams Bixby   Commissioner.

Muskogee, Indian Territory.
FEB 18 1907

7-NB-537

7-NB-537
**COPY**
Muskogee, Indian Territory, February 23, 1907.

Marion Stidham,
　　Atlee, Indian Territory.

Dear Sir:-

Inclosed herewith you will find a copy of the decision of the Commissioner to the Five Civilized Tribes, rendered February 18,1907, granting the application for the enrollment of Harold Stidham as a citizen by blood of the Choctaw Nation.

You are further advised that the name of Harold Stidham has been placed upon a schedule of citizens by blood of the Choctaw Nation to be submitted to the Secretary of the Interior for his approval. You will be notified of Departmental action thereon.

## Applications for Enrollment of Choctaw Newborn
## Act of 1905 Volume IX

Respectfully,
SIGNED  *Tams Bixby*
Commissioner.

Registered.
Incl. 7-NB-537

---

7-NB-537.

**COPY**

Muskogee, Indian Territory, February 23, 1907.

Hattie Stidham,
    Ardmore, Indian Territory.

Dear Madam:-

    Inclosed herewith you will find a copy of the decision of the Commissioner to the Five Civilized Tribes, rendered February 18, 1907, granting the application for the enrollment of Harold Stidham as a citizen by blood of the Choctaw Nation.

    You are hereby advised that the name of Harold Stidham has been placed upon a schedule of citizens by blood of the Choctaw Nation to be submitted to the Secretary of the Interior for his approval. You will be notified of Departmental action thereon.

Respectfully,

SIGNED  *Tams Bixby*
Commissioner.

Registered.
Incl. 7-NB-537

---

7-NB-537.

**COPY**

Muskogee, Indian Territory, February 23, 1907.

Chilion[sic] Riley,
    Attorney-al-law;[sic]
        Ardmore, Indian Territory.

Dear Sir:-

    You are hereby notified that the Commissioner to the Five Civilized Tribes on February 18, 1907, rendered his decision granting the application for the enrollment of Harold Stidham as a citizen by blood of the Choctaw Nation.

# Applications for Enrollment of Choctaw Newborn
## Act of 1905   Volume IX

    You are further advised that the name of Harold Stidham has been placed upon a schedule of citizens by blood of the Choctaw Nation to be submitted to the Secretary of the Interior for his approval. You will be notified of Departmental action thereon.

                                        Respectfully,

                              SIGNED    *Tams Bixby*
                                                    Commissioner.

Registered.
Incl. 7-NB-537

---

7-NB-537.

                                        **COPY**

                            Muskogee, Indian Territory, February 23, 1907.

H. H. Brown,
        Attorney at law;
                Ardmore, Indian Territory.

Dear Sir:-

    You are hereby notified that the Commissioner to the Five Civilized Tribes on February 18, 1907, rendered his decision granting the application for the enrollment of Harold Stidham as a citizen by blood of the Choctaw Nation.
    You are further advised that the name of Harold Stidham has been placed upon a schedule of citizens by blood of the Choctaw Nation to be submitted to the Secretary of the Interior for his approval. You will be notified of Departmental action thereon.

                                        Respectfully,

                              SIGNED    *Tams Bixby*
                                                    Commissioner.

Registered.
Incl. 7-NB-537

# Applications for Enrollment of Choctaw Newborn
## Act of 1905 Volume IX

7-NB-537.

Muskogee, Indian Territory, February 23, 1907.

Mansfield, McMurray & Cornish,
    Attorneys for the Choctaw and Chickasaw Nations,
        South McAlester, Indian Territory.

Gentlemen:

    Inclosed herewith you will find a copy of the decision of the Commissioner to the Five Civilized Tribes, rendered February 18, 1907, granting the application for the enrollment of Harold Stidham as a citizen by blood of the Choctaw Nation.

    You are hereby advised that the name of Harold Stidham has been placed upon a schedule of citizens by blood of the Choctaw Nation to be submitted to the Secretary of the Interior for his approval. You will be notified of Departmental action thereon.

                Respectfully,

                Commissioner.

Registered.
Incl. 7-NB-537.

---

**BIRTH AFFIDAVIT.**

## DEPARTMENT OF THE INTERIOR.
## COMMISSION TO THE FIVE CIVILIZED TRIBES.

---

    **IN RE APPLICATION FOR ENROLLMENT,** as a citizen of the Choctaw Nation, of Harold Stidham, born on the 22 day of April, 1903

Name of Father: Marion Stidham      a citizen of the Choctaw Nation.
Name of Mother: Hattie Stidham      a citizen of the United States Nation.

            Postoffice    Atlee, I.T.

---

**AFFIDAVIT OF MOTHER.**

UNITED STATES OF AMERICA, Indian Territory, }
    Southern          DISTRICT. }

    I, Hattie Stidham, on oath state that I am 21 years of age and a citizen ~~by~~ of the United, ~~of the~~ States ~~Nation~~; that I ~~am~~ *was* the lawful wife of Marion Stidham, who is a citizen, by Blood of the Choctaw Nation;

# Applications for Enrollment of Choctaw Newborn
## Act of 1905    Volume IX

that a    male    child was born to me on    22$^{nd}$    day of    April    , 1903; that said child has been named    Harold Stidham    , and was living March 4, 1905.

                                        Hattie Stidham

Witnesses To Mark:
{

    Subscribed and sworn to before me this    21$^{st}$    day of    March    , 1905

                                        W A Wilson
                                        Notary Public.

---

**AFFIDAVIT OF ATTENDING PHYSICIAN OR MID-WIFE.**

UNITED STATES OF AMERICA, ~~Indian Territory~~,
    *State of Texas*    ~~DISTRICT~~.
*County of Montague*

    I,    L.A. Winstead    , a    Physician    , on oath state that I attended on Mrs.    Hattie Stidham    , wife of    Marion Stidham    on the    22$^{nd}$    day of April, 1903; that there was born to her on said date a    male    child; that said child was living March 4, 1905, and is said to have been named Harold Stidham

                                        L.A. Winstead M.D.

Witnesses To Mark:
{ L A Kuykendall
  A T Blackwell

    Subscribed and sworn to before me this    17    day of    March    , 1905

                                        J.T. Cooper J.P. &
                                          Notary Public.
                                        *for Montague Co Texas*

---

**COPY**

                                                  N. B. 537

                Muskogee, Indian Territory, April 8, 1905.

Marion Stidham,
    Atlee, Indian Territory.

Dear Sir:

    You are hereby advised that before the application for the enrollment of Harold Stidham, as a citizen of the Choctaw Nation, can be finally disposed of, it will be

# Applications for Enrollment of Choctaw Newborn
# Act of 1905  Volume IX

necessary that you furnish the Commission with either the original or a certified copy of the license and certificate of your marriage to Hattie Stidham.

Prompt attention should be given this matter.

Respectfully,<br>
SIGNED<br>
*T. B. Needles.*<br>
Commissioner in Charge.

---

7 NB 537

**COPY**

Muskogee, Indian Territory, April 27, 1905.

Brown & Turner,
    Attorneys at Law,
        Ardmore, Indian Territory.

Gentlemen:

Receipt is hereby acknowledged of your letter of April 21, 1905, inclosing the marriage license and certificate between Marion Stidham and Hattie Mitchell which is offered in support of the application for the enrollment of Harold Stidham, and the same has been filed with the record in this case.

Respectfully,<br>
SIGNED<br>
*Tams Bixby*<br>
Chairman.

---

*(The letter below typed as given.)*

(Copy)

Atlee, I. T.  5/ 13--- 05.

the Daws Comishian Of  the Five Sinlized Tribs
    Ardmore, I. T.

Gents

    it has bin som Time Since I filed aplication for inrollement of My Child Harold Stidham the son of my devorsed husband Merron Stidham who is a citizon by Blood. and up til now i havnt Bin able to here anything in regard to the matter and I also have the Custoda of the Child which was Granted mee by him (Stidham) in Settlement in divors

## Applications for Enrollment of Choctaw Newborn
## Act of 1905   Volume IX

Sute in the Cort at Ardmore I. T. and i also warn the Comishion to not Let any one and a Speceealy Meron Stidham file any Land for my child herold Stidham ecept My Self as hee has no custido of the Child and i have worked & Surported My Self and Child and have got Land i Want him to be filed on whin hee is admited to the Roll.

  hoping to here from yew Soon.

                   Hattie Stidham.

---

                   7-N.B. 537.

           Muskogee, Indian Territory, May 24, 1905.

Hattie Stidham,
  Atlee, Indian Territory.

Dear Sir[sic]:

  Receipt is hereby acknowledged of your letter of May 13, asking in regard to the application heretofore filed for the enrollment of your child, Harold Stidham, and protesting against anyone but yourself filing on his allotment.

  In reply to your letter you are advised that the affidavits heretofore forwarded have been filed with our records as an application for the enrollment of said child. No selection of allotment can be permitted in his behalf until his enrollment has been approved by the Secretary of the Interior.

              Respectfully,

                    Chairman.

---

7-NB-537

          Muskogee, Indian Territory, October 31, 1905.

Chilion Riley,
  Attorney at Law,
    Ardmore, Indian Territory.

Dear Sir:

  Receipt is hereby acknowledged of your letter of October 25, 1905, asking the status of the enrollment of Harold Stidham, child of Marion Z. and Hattie M. Stidham as a new born citizen of the Choctaw Nation.

# Applications for Enrollment of Choctaw Newborn
## Act of 1905   Volume IX

In reply to your letter you are advised that it appears from the record in this case that Marion Stidham a citizen by blood of the Choctaw Nation, and Hattie Mitchell a non citizen, were married February 14, 1903, and Harold Stidham was born April 22, 1903. It further appears that on July 4, 1904, the said Marion and Hattie Stidham were divorced.

Before further consideration can be given the application for the enrollment of Harold Stidham as a citizen by blood it will be necessary that testimony be introduced showing that Harold Stidham is the child of Marion Stidham.

If you desire to introduce testimony on this point the same will be heard upon the personal appearance of the witnesses at this office.

Respectfully,

Commissioner.

---

7-NB-537

Muskogee, Indian Territory, January 29, 1906.

Brown & Turner,
    Attorneys at Law,
        Ardmore, Indian Territory.

Gentlemen:

Receipt is hereby acknowledged of your letter of January 17, 1906, inclosing affidavits of S. H. Butler and H. H. Brown and letters of Marion Stidham of April 1, April 26, and November 21, 1905, and the same have been filed with the record in the matter of the application for the enrollment of Harold Stidham as a new born citizen of the Choctaw Nation.

Respectfully,

Acting Commissioner.

# Applications for Enrollment of Choctaw Newborn
## Act of 1905 Volume IX

7-NB-537

Muskogee, Indian Territory, February 5, 1906.

Chilion Riley,
    Attorney at Law,
        Ardmore, Indian Territory.

Dear Sir:

In the matter of the enrollment of Harold Stidham, son of Marion Stidham a citizen by blood of the Choctaw Nation, and Hattie Stidham, a non citizen, you are advised that it appears from the records in this case that Marion and Hattie Stidham were married February 14, 1903, while Harold Stidham was born April 22, 1903. It will therefore be necessary that both Marion and Hattie Stidham appear at this office to testify relative to the enrollment of this child.

This matter should receive immediate attention and notice of the time of taking such testimony must be served upon the attorneys for the Choctaw and Chickasaw Nations.

                          Respectfully,

                          Acting Commissioner.

---

7-NB-537

Muskogee, Indian Territory, August 31, 1906.

H. H. Brown,
    Attorney at Law,
        Ardmore, Indian Territory.

Dear Sir:

Receipt is hereby acknowledged of your letter of August 20, 1906, asking what disposition has been made of the application of Harold Stidham for enrollment as a citizen of the Choctaw Nation under the act of Congress approved March 3, 1905.

In reply to your letter you are advised that it appears from the record in this case that Marion Stidham, a citizen by blood of the Choctaw Nation, and Hattie Mitchell a non citizen, were married February 14, 1903, and Harold Stidham was born April 22, 1903. It further appears that on July 4, 1904, the said Marion and Hattie Stidham were divorced.

Before further consideration can be given the application for the enrollment of Harold Stidham as a citizen by blood it will be necessary that testimony be introduced showing that Harold Stidham is the child of Marion Stidham.

# Applications for Enrollment of Choctaw Newborn
## Act of 1905   Volume IX

If you desire to introduce testimony on this point the same will be heard upon the personal appearance of the witnesses at this office, notice of the time of such appearance having been served upon the attorneys for the Choctaw and Chickasaw Nations.

Respectfully,

Acting Commissioner.

---

7-NB-537

Muskogee, Indian Territory, March 9, 1907.

Chief Clerk,
    Choctaw Land Office,
        Atoka, Indian Territory.

Dear Sir:

    Referring to Choctaw New born[sic] roll card 537, Harold Stidham, you are advised that the mother Hattie Stidham has protested against any person but herself selecting an allotment for said child and her letter is inclosed herewith for your information and for investigation when an attempt is made to select allotment for said child.

Respectfully,

Commissioner.

---

7-NB-537

Muskogee, Indian Territory, March 9, 1907.

Chief Clerk,
    Chickasaw Land Office,
        Ardmore, Indian Territory.

Dear Sir:

    Referring to Choctaw New Born roll card 537, Harold Stidham, you are advised that the mother Hattie Stidham has protested against any person but herself selecting an allotment for said child and her letter is inclosed herewith for your information and for investigation when an attempt is made to select allotment for said child.

# Applications for Enrollment of Choctaw Newborn
# Act of 1905   Volume IX

Respectfully,

EB 4-9.

Commissioner.

𝑎𝐵

REFER IN REPLY TO THE FOLLOWING:

7-NB-537

**DEPARTMENT OF THE INTERIOR,**
**COMMISSIONER TO THE FIVE CIVILIZED TRIBES.**

Muskogee, Indian Territory, March 28, 1907.

Hattie Stidham,
    Ardmore, Indian Territory.

Dear Madam:

    You are hereby advised that on March 2, 1907, the Secretary of the Interior approved the enrollment of Harold Stidham as a new born citizen of the Choctaw Nation, under the Act of Congress approved March 3, 1905, and his name appears upon the final roll of such citizens opposite No. 1581.

    He is now entitled to an allotment and application therefor should be made without delay at the Land Office for the Nation in which the prospective allotment is located.

Respectfully,

Geo. D. Rogers
Acting Commissioner.

7-NB-537

Muskogee, Indian Territory, April 9, 1907.

Marion Sitdham[sic],
    Wallville, Indian Territory.

Dear Sir:

    Receipt is hereby acknowledged of your letter of March 25, 1907, relative to the enrollment of Harold Stidham in which you state that this is not your child.

    In reply to your letter you are advised that it appears from the records of this office that you were married to Hattie Stidham, the mother of Harold Stidham February 14, 1903 and this child was born April 22, 1903.

## Applications for Enrollment of Choctaw Newborn
## Act of 1905 Volume IX

It appears from the records of this office that Harold Stidham has been enrolled as a new born citizen of the Choctaw Nation under the Act of Congress approved March 3, 1905, and his enrollment as such approved by the Secretary of the Interior March 2, 1907.

Respectfully,

Acting Commissioner.

---

Choc New Born 538
 Dwight C. Rogers   b. 9-5-03

## AFFIDAVIT OF ATTENDING PHYSICIAN OR MIDWIFE

UNITED STATES OF AMERICA
INDIAN TERRITORY
 Central     DISTRICT

I,   J. S. Fulton     a     Physician on oath state that I attended on Mrs. Kittie D. Rogers  wife of  William F. Rogers on the  5$^{th}$  day of  September , 190 3, that there was born to her on said date a   male child, that said child is now living, and is said to have been named   Dwight Charles Rogers

J.S. Fulton     M.D.

WITNESSETH:
Must be two witnesses who are citizens and know the child.
{ J H M$^c$Gahey
  A.J. M$^c$Gahey

Subscribed and sworn to before me this, the   21$^{st}$   day of  February   190 5

AE Folsom     Notary Public.

We hereby certify that we are well acquainted with   Dr. J S Fulton   a   Practicing Physician    and know him    to be reputable and of good standing in the community.

{ J.H. M$^c$Gahey
  B F Rogers

# Applications for Enrollment of Choctaw Newborn
## Act of 1905  Volume IX

**NEW-BORN AFFIDAVIT.**

Number..................

**...Choctaw Enrolling Commission...**

IN THE MATTER OF THE APPLICATION FOR ENROLLMENT, as a citizen of the Choctaw Nation, of  Dwight Charles Rogers

born on the  $5^{th}$  day of  September  190 3

Name of father   William F Rogers       a citizen of   Choctaw
Nation final enrollment No.  5030
Name of mother   Kittie D. Rogers       a citizen of   Choctaw
Nation final enrollment No.  94

Postoffice   Atoka Ind. Ty.

**AFFIDAVIT OF MOTHER.**

UNITED STATES OF AMERICA
INDIAN TERRITORY
  Central    DISTRICT

I   Kittie D. Rogers   , on oath state that I am  24  years of age and a citizen by  Inter. M.  of the  Choctaw  Nation, and as such have been placed upon the final roll of the  Choctaw  Nation, by the Honorable Secretary of the Interior my final enrollment number being  Ninety Four ; that I am the lawful wife of  William F Rogers  , who is a citizen of the  Choctaw  Nation, and as such has been placed upon the final roll of said Nation by the Honorable Secretary of the Interior, his final enrollment number being  5030  and that a  Male  child was born to me on the  $5^{th}$  day of  Sept.  190 3; that said child has been named  Dwight Charles Rogers  , and is now living.

Kittie D. Rogers

Witnesseth.
  Must be two  ⎫  A.J. M$^c$Gahey
  Witnesses who ⎬
  are Citizens. ⎭  J.H. M$^c$Gahey

Subscribed and sworn to before me this  $4^{th}$  day of  Feb  190 5

W F Rogers
Notary Public.

My commission expires: February 24$^{th}$ 1906

## Applications for Enrollment of Choctaw Newborn
## Act of 1905 Volume IX

BIRTH AFFIDAVIT.

### DEPARTMENT OF THE INTERIOR.
### COMMISSION TO THE FIVE CIVILIZED TRIBES.

IN RE APPLICATION FOR ENROLLMENT, as a citizen of the Choctaw Nation, of Dwight C Rogers, born on the $5^{th}$ day of September, 1903

Name of Father: William F. Rogers     a citizen of the Choctaw Nation.
Name of Mother: Kittie D. Rogers     a citizen of the Choctaw Nation.

Postoffice    Atoka, I.T.

### AFFIDAVIT OF MOTHER.

UNITED STATES OF AMERICA, Indian Territory,
Central      DISTRICT.

I, Kittie D. Rogers, on oath state that I am 24 years of age and a citizen by intermarriage, of the Choctaw Nation; that I am the lawful wife of William F Rogers, who is a citizen, by blood of the Choctaw Nation; that a male child was born to me on $5^{th}$ day of September, 1903; that said child has been named Dwight C. Rogers, and was living March 4, 1905.

                                 Kittie D. Rogers

Witnesses To Mark:

{

Subscribed and sworn to before me this $30^{th}$ day of March, 1905

                                 W.H. Angell
                                 Notary Public.

### AFFIDAVIT OF ATTENDING PHYSICIAN OR MID-WIFE.

UNITED STATES OF AMERICA, Indian Territory,
Central      DISTRICT.

I, J.S. Fulton, a physician, on oath state that I attended on Mrs. Kittie D. Rogers, wife of William F Rogers on the $5^{th}$ day of September, 1903; that there was born to her on said date a male child; that said child was living March 4, 1905, and is said to have been named Dwight C Rogers

                                 J.S. Fulton

Witnesses To Mark:

{

## Applications for Enrollment of Choctaw Newborn
## Act of 1905   Volume IX

Subscribed and sworn to before me this  30  day of    March        , 1905

                                            A.J. Cline
                                                              Notary Public.
My commission expires Jan 15-1907

---

Choc New Born 539
        Saler Homer   (b. 2-16-04)

                                                           Choctaw 5502.

                       Muskogee, Indian Territory, April 4, 1905.

Enoch Homer,
      Non, Indian Territory.

Dear Sir:

       Receipt is hereby acknowledged of the affidavits of Ellen Homer and Hallicha Lewis to the birth of Saler Homer, daughter of Enoch and Ellen Homer, February 16, 1904, and the same have been filed with our records as an application for the enrollment of said child.
                                    Respectfully,

                                                  Commissioner in Charge.

---

7-NB-539

                       Muskogee, Indian Territory, July 21, 1905.

Enoch Homer,
      Non, Indian Territory.

Dear Sir:

       Receipt is hereby acknowledged of your letter of July 13, 1905, asking the status of the enrollment of your child, Saler Homer.

       In reply to your letter you are advised that the name of Saler Homer has been placed upon a schedule of citizens by blood of the Choctaw Nation, which has been

## Applications for Enrollment of Choctaw Newborn
## Act of 1905   Volume IX

forwarded to the Secretary of the Interior, and you will be notified when her enrollment has been approved.

Respectfully,

Commissioner.

**BIRTH AFFIDAVIT.**

### DEPARTMENT OF THE INTERIOR.
### COMMISSION TO THE FIVE CIVILIZED TRIBES.

IN RE APPLICATION FOR ENROLLMENT, as a citizen of the   Choctaw   Nation, of Saler Homer   , born on the   16   day of   feb[sic]   , 1904

Name of Father: Enoch Homer         a citizen of the   Choctaw   Nation.
Name of Mother: Ellen Homer         a citizen of the   Choctaw   Nation.

Postoffice   Non Ind Ter

AFFIDAVIT OF MOTHER.

UNITED STATES OF AMERICA, Indian Territory,  }
Central                 DISTRICT.

I,   Ellen Homer   , on oath state that I am   26   years of age and a citizen by Blood   , of the   Choctaw   Nation; that I am the lawful wife of   Enoch Homer   , who is a citizen, by Blood   of the   Choctaw   Nation; that a   female   child was born to me on   16   day of   feb[sic]   , 1904; that said child has been named Saler Homer   , and was living March 4, 1905.

her<br>
Ellen x Homer<br>
mark

Witnesses To Mark:
{ S.W. Wenner
{ S M Dilbeck

Subscribed and sworn to before me this   28   day of   March   , 1905

C.E. McCain<br>
Notary Public.

# Applications for Enrollment of Choctaw Newborn
## Act of 1905   Volume IX

**AFFIDAVIT OF ATTENDING PHYSICIAN OR MID-WIFE.**

UNITED STATES OF AMERICA, Indian Territory,  
Central DISTRICT.

I, Hallisha Lewis, a mid wife, on oath state that I attended on Mrs. Ellen Homer, wife of Enoch Homer on the 16 day of feb, 1904; that there was born to her on said date a female child; that said child was living March 4, 1905, and is said to have been named Saler Homer

            her  
          Hallisha x Lewis  
Witnesses To Mark:     mark  
 S.W. Wenner  
 S M Dilbeck

Subscribed and sworn to before me this 28 day of March, 1905

        C.E. McCain  
         Notary Public.

---

Choc New Born 540  
 Lawrence W Nicholson b. 12-18-03

             Choctaw 3678.

      Muskogee, Indian Territory, April 4, 1905.

Omer R. Nicholson,  
 Caddo, Indian Territory.

Dear Sir:

 Receipt is hereby acknowledged of your letter of March 25th, enclosing the affidavits of Minnie E. Nicholson and Le Roy Long to the birth of Lawrence W. Nicholson, son of Omer R. and Minnie E. Nicholson, December 18, 1903, and the same have been filed with our records as an application for the enrollment of said child.

 Replying to that portion of your letter in which you ask if it will be necessary for you to make personal application for the enrollment of your child herein named, you are advised that it will not be necessary for you to make a personal appearance in the matter of the enrollment of this child unless you so desire.

Applications for Enrollment of Choctaw Newborn
Act of 1905   Volume IX

Respectfully,

Commissioner in Charge.

7-NB 540

Muskogee, Indian Territory, April 7, 1905.

Omer R. Nicholson,
    Caddo, Indian Territory.

Dear Sir:

    Receipt is hereby acknowledged of your letter of April 2, 1905, stating that you have recently filed with the Commission an application for the enrollment of your infant child Lawrence W. Nicholson and you ask if the same has been received.

    In reply to your letter you are informed that the affidavits heretofore forwarded to the birth of your child have been filed with our records as an application for the enrollment of said child and receipt has heretofore been acknowledged to you of such affidavits.

Respectfully,

Commissioner in Charge.

# NEW BORN AFFIDAVIT

No _____

## CHOCTAW ENROLLING COMMISSION

IN THE MATTER OF THE APPLICATION FOR ENROLLMENT as a citizen of the Choctaw Nation, of Lawrence W. Nicholson born on the 18$^{th}$ day of December 190 3

Name of father Omer R Nicholson a citizen of Choctaw Nation, final enrollment No. 7-d-793

Name of mother Mamie E Nicholson a citizen of Choctaw Nation, final enrollment No. 10399

Postoffice.

# Applications for Enrollment of Choctaw Newborn
## Act of 1905 Volume IX

**AFFIDAVIT OF MOTHER**

UNITED STATES OF AMERICA  
INDIAN TERRITORY  
DISTRICT   Central

I   Mamie E Nicholson   , on oath state that I am   26   years of age and a citizen by   blood   of the   Choctaw   Nation, and as such have been placed upon the final roll of the   Choctaw   Nation, by the Honorable Secretary of the Interior my final enrollment number being   10399   ; that I am the lawful wife of Omer R. Nicholson , who is a citizen of the   Choctaw   Nation, and as such has been placed upon the final roll of said Nation by the Honorable Secretary of the Interior, his final enrollment number being   7-D-793   and that a   Male   child was born to me on the   18$^{th}$   day of   December   190 3; that said child has been named   Lawrence W Nicholson   , and is now living.

WITNESSETH:   Mayme E Nicholson

Must be two witnesses who are citizens { Henry Byington
Miss Daisy Baxter

Subscribed and sworn to before me this, the   8$^{th}$   day of   February   , 190 5

A.E. Folsom  
Notary Public.

My Commission Expires:  
Jan. 9-1909

---

## *Affidavit of Attending Physician or Midwife*

UNITED STATES OF AMERICA,  
INDIAN TERRITORY,  
Central   DISTRICT

I,   Le Roy Long   a   Practicing Physician   on oath state that I attended on Mrs. Mamie E. Nicholson   wife of   Omer R Nicholson   on the   18"   day of   December   , 190 3, that there was born to her on said date a   Male   child, that said child is now living, and is said to have been named   Lawrence W Nicholson

LeRoy Long   M. D.

Subscribed and sworn to before me this the   16$^{th}$   day of   Feby   1905

Com Ex 3/6/09   Brooks Fort  
Notary Public.

WITNESSETH:

Must be two witnesses who are citizens and know the child. { Henry Byington
Miss Daisy Baxter

## Applications for Enrollment of Choctaw Newborn
## Act of 1905   Volume IX

We hereby certify that we are well acquainted with   Le Roy Long   a   Physician   and know   him   to be reputable and of good standing in the community.

Must be two citizen witnesses. { Henry Byington
Miss Daisy Baxter

BIRTH AFFIDAVIT.

### DEPARTMENT OF THE INTERIOR.
### COMMISSION TO THE FIVE CIVILIZED TRIBES.

IN RE APPLICATION FOR ENROLLMENT, as a citizen of the   Choctaw   Nation, of Lawrence W. Nicholson   , born on the 18th day of December , 1903

Name of Father: Omer R. Nicholson   a citizen of the CHOCTAW   Nation.
Name of Mother: Mamie E. Nicholson   a citizen of the CHOCTAW   Nation.

Postoffice Caddo, Choctaw Nation, Indian Territory.

**AFFIDAVIT OF MOTHER.**

UNITED STATES OF AMERICA, Indian Territory,
Central Judicial   DISTRICT.

I,   Mamie E. Nicholson   , on oath state that I am   25   years of age and a citizen by   blood   , of the   CHOCTAW   Nation; that I am the lawful wife of Omer R. Nicholson   , who is a citizen, by Intermarriage   of the CHOCTAW   Nation; that a   male   child was born to me on   18th   day of DECEMBER   , 1903; that said child has been named   Lawrence W. Nicholson   , and was living March 4, 1905.

Mamie E. Nicholson
Witnesses To Mark:
{

Subscribed and sworn to before me this   20th day of   March   , 1905

My Com Exp 12/1/05   C. H. Ewing
Notary Public.

## Applications for Enrollment of Choctaw Newborn
## Act of 1905   Volume IX

**AFFIDAVIT OF ATTENDING PHYSICIAN OR MID-WIFE.**

UNITED STATES OF AMERICA, Indian Territory,  
Central Judicial       DISTRICT.

  I, LeRoy Long , a   Physician , on oath state that I attended on Mrs.  Mamie E. Nicholson , wife of   Omer R. Nicholson on the  18th  day of December , 1903; that there was born to her on said date a MALE child; that said child was living March 4, 1905, and is said to have been named Lawrence W. Nicholson

             LeRoy Long

Witnesses To Mark:

  Subscribed and sworn to before me this  24$^{th}$  day of   March   , 1905

           Brooks Fort
             Notary Public.

My Com Ex 3/6/07.

---

Choc New Born 541
  Evalina Allen  b. 2-25-04

                       7-159

**COPY**

      Muskogee, Indian Territory, March 31, 1905.

Rufus Allen,
  Rush Springs, Indian Territory.

Dear Sir:

  Referring to the affidavits recently forwarded of Laura Gray Allen and R. J. Gordon to the birth of Evalina Allen, daughter of Rufus and Laura Gray Allen, February 25, 1904, you are advised that on August 8, 1904, there were received at this office the affidavits of Laura Gray Allen and R. J. Gordon to the birth of Eva Lena Allen, child of Rufus and Laura Gray Allen, February 25, 1904.

  You are therefore requested to state which is the correct name of this child and under which name you desire to have her enrolled.

## Applications for Enrollment of Choctaw Newborn
## Act of 1905   Volume IX

Respectfully,

SIGNED   *Tams Bixby*
Chairman.

---

The ~~motte~~ mother of this child is enrolled as Lawla Gray and has heretofore made application to the Commission for it.

W<sup>ms</sup>

---

**BIRTH AFFIDAVIT.**

## DEPARTMENT OF THE INTERIOR,
### COMMISSION TO THE FIVE CIVILIZED TRIBES.

---

**In Re Application for Enrollment,** as a citizen of the Choctaw Nation, of  Eva Lena Allen , born on the  25  day of  February , 1904

Name of Father: Rufus Allen             a citizen of the   US.    Nation.
Name of Mother: Laura Gray Allen    a citizen of the   Choctaw   Nation.

Post-office    Rush Springs Ind. Ter.

---

**AFFIDAVIT OF MOTHER.**

---

UNITED STATES OF AMERICA, ⎫
  INDIAN TERRITORY, ⎬
  Southern       District. ⎭

I, Laura Gray-Allen , on oath state that I am  19  years of age and a citizen by  Blood , of the  Choctaw  Nation; that I am the lawful wife of  Rufus Allen , who is a citizen, by —— of the  US  Nation; that a  Female  child was born to me on  25th  day of  February , 1904 , that said child has been named  Eva Lena Allen , and is now living.

Laura Gray-Allen

WITNESSES TO MARK:
  { RB. Shannon
    F.C. Blakely

Subscribed and sworn to before me this 30th  day of  July  , 1904

*(Illegible)* Brown
NOTARY PUBLIC.

# Applications for Enrollment of Choctaw Newborn
## Act of 1905   Volume IX

**AFFIDAVIT OF ATTENDING PHYSICIAN OR MID-WIFE.**

UNITED STATES OF AMERICA,  
   INDIAN TERRITORY,  
Southern District.

I, R.J. Gordon, a Phistian[sic], on oath state that I attended on Mrs. Laura Gray Allen, wife of Rufus Allen on the 25 day of February, 1904; that there was born to her on said date a Female child; that said child is now living and is said to have been named Eva Lena Allen

R.J. Gordon M.D.

WITNESSES TO MARK:  
  R.A. Thompson  
  *(Name Illegible)*

Subscribed and sworn to before me this 4 day of August, 1904

*(Name Illegible)*  
**NOTARY PUBLIC.**

BIRTH AFFIDAVIT.

### DEPARTMENT OF THE INTERIOR.
### COMMISSION TO THE FIVE CIVILIZED TRIBES.

IN RE APPLICATION FOR ENROLLMENT, as a citizen of the Choctaw Nation, of Lena Allen, born on the 25 day of February, 1904

Name of Father: Rufus Allen     a citizen of the US Nation.  
Name of Mother: Laura Allen nee Laura Gray     a citizen of the Choctaw Nation.

Postoffice     Rush Springs IT

**AFFIDAVIT OF MOTHER.**

UNITED STATES OF AMERICA, Indian Territory,  
   Southern DISTRICT.

I, Laura Allen, on oath state that I am 20 years of age and a citizen by blood, of the Choctaw Nation; that I am the lawful wife of Rufus Allen, who is a citizen, ~~by~~ of the United States Nation; that a female child was born to me on 25 day of February, 1904; that said child has been named Lena Allen, and was living March 4, 1905.

Laura Allen

## Applications for Enrollment of Choctaw Newborn
## Act of 1905 Volume IX

Witnesses To Mark:

{

Subscribed and sworn to before me this 5<sup>th</sup> day of April , 1905

JE Williams
Notary Public.

---

**AFFIDAVIT OF ATTENDING PHYSICIAN OR MID-WIFE.**

UNITED STATES OF AMERICA, Indian Territory, }
Southern DISTRICT. }

I, R.J. Gordon , a physician , on oath state that I attended on Mrs. Laura Allen , wife of Rufus Allen on the 25 day of February , 1904; that there was born to her on said date a female child; that said child was living March 4, 1905, and is said to have been named Lena Allen

R.J. Gordon M.D.

Witnesses To Mark:

{

Subscribed and sworn to before me this Seventh day of April , 1905

Henry Lunts
Notary Public.

---

BIRTH AFFIDAVIT.

## DEPARTMENT OF THE INTERIOR,
### COMMISSION TO THE FIVE CIVILIZED TRIBES.

**In Re Application for Enrollment,** as a citizen of the Choctaw Nation, of Evalina Allen , born on the 25 day of February , 1904

Name of Father: Rufus Allen a citizen of the US. Nation.
Name of Mother: Laura Gray-Allen a citizen of the Choctaw Nation.

Post-office Rush Springs Indian Ter.

# Applications for Enrollment of Choctaw Newborn
## Act of 1905   Volume IX

**AFFIDAVIT OF MOTHER.**

UNITED STATES OF AMERICA,  
INDIAN TERRITORY,  
Southern        District.

I, Laura Gray-Allen , on oath state that I am  19  years of age and a citizen by Blood , of the Choctaw Nation; that I am the lawful wife of Rufus Allen , who is a citizen, by —— of the US Nation; that a Female child was born to me on 25 day of February , 1904 , that said child has been named Evalina Allen , and is now living.

Laura Gray-Allen

**WITNESSES TO MARK:**

Subscribed and sworn to before me this 20th day of March , 1905

My Commission Expires Jan 13-08        *(Illegible)* Brown  
                                        NOTARY PUBLIC.

**AFFIDAVIT OF ATTENDING PHYSICIAN OR MID-WIFE.**

UNITED STATES OF AMERICA,  
INDIAN TERRITORY,  
Southern        District.

I, R.J. Gordon M.D. , a Physician , on oath state that I attended on Mrs. Laura Gray-Allen , wife of Rufus Allen on the 25 day of February , 1904 ; that there was born to her on said date a Female child; that said child is now living and is said to have been named Evalina Allen

R.J. Gordon M.D.

**WITNESSES TO MARK:**

Subscribed and sworn to before me this 21 day of March , 1905

Henry Lunts  
NOTARY PUBLIC.

# Applications for Enrollment of Choctaw Newborn
# Act of 1905   Volume IX

Choc New Born 542
    Juston H. Morgan   b  9-16-04

~~J. M. Morgan~~
~~PHYSICIAN AND SURGEON~~

                              EGO. IND. TER.,........................................................190

Affidavit of Attending Physician or Midwife
United States of America Indian Territory
Central District

I. J.M. Morgan, a physician on oath state that I attended on Mrs. Lenora M. Jones wife of H. N. Morgan on the 16th day of September 1904 That there was born to her on said date a male child that said child ~~is now~~ was living March the 4th 1905 and is said to have been named Juston H Morgan

                              J.M. Morgan M.D.

Witness to mark
must be two           Francis M Jones
  witnesses           Ida M Jones

Subscribed and sworn to before me this the 18th day of March 1905

                              J.T. Hoover
                                  Notary Public

                                              7 NB 542

                Muskogee, Indian Territory, June 16, 1905.

Hiram M[sic]. Morgan,
    Ego, Indian Territory.

Dear Sir:

    Receipt is hereby acknowledged of your letter of June 9, 1905, asking the status of the enrollment of your son Justin H. Morgan.

    In reply to your letter you are informed that the name of your son Juston H. Morgan is being placed upon a schedule of citizens by blood of the Choctaw Nation prepared for forwarding to the Secretary of the Interior and you will be notified when his enrollment is approved but pending his approval no selection of allotment can be made for said child.

                    Respectfully,

                                        Chairman.

# Applications for Enrollment of Choctaw Newborn
## Act of 1905   Volume IX

7-NB-542

Muskogee, Indian Territory, August 3, 1905.

Hiram M[sic]. Morgan,
　　Ego, Indian Territory.

Dear Sir:

　　Receipt is hereby acknowledged of your letter of July 24, 1905, asking if the enrollment of you son Juston H. Morgan has been approved.

　　In reply to your letter you are advised that on July 22, 1905, the Secretary of the Interior approved the enrollment of your son Juston H. Morgan as a citizen by blood of the Choctaw Nation.

Respectfully,

Commissioner.

---

7-NB-542

Muskogee, Indian Territory, August 3, 1905.

Lenora M. Morgan,
　　Ego, Indian Territory.

Dear Madam:

　　Receipt is hereby acknowledged of your letter of July 23, 1905, asking when you can file for your child Juston H. Morgan.

　　In reply to your letter you are advised that on July 22, 1905, the Secretary of the Interior approved the enrollment of Juston H. Morgan as a citizen by blood of the Choctaw Nation and selection of allotment may now be made in his behalf in accordance with the rules and regulations governing the selection of allotments and the designation of homesteads in the Choctaw and Chickasaw Nations.

Respectfully,

Commissioner.

# Applications for Enrollment of Choctaw Newborn
## Act of 1905   Volume IX

BIRTH AFFIDAVIT.

### DEPARTMENT OF THE INTERIOR.
### COMMISSION TO THE FIVE CIVILIZED TRIBES.

---

IN RE APPLICATION FOR ENROLLMENT, as a citizen of the    Choctaw    Nation, of Juston H. Morgan    , born on the 16$^{th}$   day of  Sept   , 1904

Name of Father:  Hiram N. Morgan    a citizen of the United States  Nation.
Name of Mother:  Lenora M. Jones    a citizen of the   Choctaw   Nation.

Postoffice    Ego, I.T.

---

### AFFIDAVIT OF MOTHER.

UNITED STATES OF AMERICA, Indian Territory,
Central    DISTRICT.

I,  Lenora M. Morgan (nee Lenora M. Jones)  , on oath state that I am  18   years of age and a citizen by   blood   , of the   Choctaw   Nation; that I am the lawful wife of    Hiram N Morgan    , who is a ~~citizen, by~~   non citizen   ~~of the~~ ──────────── Nation; that a    male    child was born to me on    16$^{th}$    day of September   , 1904; that said child has been named    Juston H. Morgan   , and was living March 4, 1905.

Lenora M Morgan
Witnesses To Mark:    nee Lenora M Jones

{

Subscribed and sworn to before me this  20$^{th}$   day of   March    , 1905

W.H. Angell
Notary Public.

---

*Affidavit of Attending Physician or Midwife*

UNITED STATES OF AMERICA,
INDIAN TERRITORY,
Central    DISTRICT

I,   Thos M. Morgan    a    Physician on oath state that I attended on  Mrs. Lenora M Jones now Morgan  wife of   Hiram N Morgan  on the   16th   day of  Sept   , 190 4, that there was born to her on said date a  male   child, that said child is now living, and is said to have been named   Juston H Morgan

Thos. M. Morgan    M. D.

Applications for Enrollment of Choctaw Newborn
Act of 1905   Volume IX

Subscribed and sworn to before me this the   2   day of   February   1905

J.T. Hoover
Notary Public.

WITNESSETH:
Must be two witnesses
who are citizens and
know the child.
{ D S. Moran
  S B Izard

We hereby certify that we are well acquainted with   Thos M Morgan   a   Physician   and know   him   to be reputable and of good standing in the community.

Must be two citizen witnesses. { D S Moran
                                 S B Izard

# NEW BORN AFFIDAVIT

No

## CHOCTAW ENROLLING COMMISSION

IN THE MATTER OF THE APPLICATION FOR ENROLLMENT as a citizen of the Choctaw Nation, of   Justin H Morgan   born on the   16th   day of   Sept   190 4

Name of father   Hiram N Morgan   a citizen of ............ Nation, final enrollment No. .............   Morgan
Name of mother   Lenora M Jones   now   a citizen of   Choctaw   Nation, final enrollment No.   15249

Ego Ind.T.   Postoffice.

### AFFIDAVIT OF MOTHER

UNITED STATES OF AMERICA
  INDIAN TERRITORY
DISTRICT   Central

I   Lenora M Jones now Morgan   , on oath state that I am   18   years of age and a citizen by   Blood   of the   Choctaw   Nation, and as such have been placed upon the final roll of the   Choctaw   Nation, by the Honorable Secretary of the Interior my final enrollment number being   15249   ; that I am the lawful wife of

## Applications for Enrollment of Choctaw Newborn
## Act of 1905 Volume IX

Hiram N Morgan, who is a citizen of the ............................. Nation, and as such has been placed upon the final roll of said Nation by the Honorable Secretary of the Interior, his final enrollment number being ............ and that a Male child was born to me on the 16th day of September 190 4; that said child has been named Justin H Morgan, and is now living.

                                              Lenora M Jones now Morgan

WITNESSETH:
Must be two witnesses who are citizens { D S Moran
S B Izard

Subscribed and sworn to before me this, the 2 day of February, 190 5

                                               J. T. Hoover
                                                      Notary Public.

My Commission Expires: Feb 26-1906

---

Choc New Born 543
    Roy K. Payte  b. 5-17-03

                                                                        Choctaw 4113.

                        Muskogee, Indian Territory, April 4, 1905.

Nettie W. Payte,
    Nixon, Indian Territory.

Dear Madam:

    Receipt is hereby acknowledged of your letter of March 29th, enclosing your affidavit and the affidavit of N. L. Linker to the birth of Roy K. Payte, son on A. J. and Nettie W. Payte, May 17, 1903, and the same have been filed with our records as an application for the enrollment of said child.

                                               Respectfully,

                                                            Commissioner in Charge.

## Applications for Enrollment of Choctaw Newborn
## Act of 1905 Volume IX

7-NB-543.

Muskogee, Indian Territory, May 25, 1905.

A. J. Payte,
    Nixon, Indian Territory.

Dear Sir:

    There is enclosed you herewith for execution application for the enrollment of your infant child, Roy K. Payte.

    In the affidavits filed in this office on April 4, 1905, the mother gives the date of the applicant's birth as May 17, 1903, while the midwife, N. L. Linker, gives it as May 17, 1905. In the enclosed application the date of the applicant's birth is left blank. Please insert the correct date and, when the affidavits are properly executed, return them to this office.

    In having these affidavits executed care should be exercised to see that all names are written in full, as they appear in the body of the affidavit, and in the event that either of the persons signing the affidavit are unable to write, signatures by mark must be attested by two witnesses. Each affidavit must be executed before a Notary Public and the notarial seal and signature of the officer must be attached to each separate affidavit.

                  Respectfully,

VR 25-12.                                                                        Chairman.

7 NB 543

Muskogee, Indian Territory, June 13, 1905.

A. J. Payte,
    Nixon, Indian Territory.

Dear Sir:

    Receipt is hereby acknowledged of your letter of June 9, 1905, transmitting the affidavits of Nettie W. Payte and N. L. Linker to the birth of Roy T. Payte, son of A. J. and Nettie W. Payte, May 17, 1903, and the same have been filed in the matter of the enrollment of said child.

                    Respectfully,

                              Chairman.

## Applications for Enrollment of Choctaw Newborn
## Act of 1905   Volume IX

**BIRTH AFFIDAVIT.**

### DEPARTMENT OF THE INTERIOR.
### COMMISSION TO THE FIVE CIVILIZED TRIBES.

IN RE APPLICATION FOR ENROLLMENT, as a citizen of the   Choctaw   Nation, of Roy K. Payte   , born on the   17 day of   May   , 1903

Name of Father: A. J. Payte   a citizen of the   U. S.   Nation.
Name of Mother: Nettie W. Payte   a citizen of the   Choctaw   Nation.

Postoffice   Nixon I.T.

### AFFIDAVIT OF MOTHER.

UNITED STATES OF AMERICA, Indian Territory, }
Central   DISTRICT. }

I,   Nettie W. Payte   , on oath state that I am   19   years of age and a citizen by   Blood   , of the   Choctaw   Nation; that I am the lawful wife of   A.J. Payte   , who is a citizen, by ............... of the   U.S.   Nation; that a   male   child was born to me on   17   day of   May   , 1903; that said child has been named   Roy K Payte   , and was living March 4, 1905.

Nettie W Payte

Witnesses To Mark:
{

Subscribed and sworn to before me this 21   day of   March   , 1905

John H Cross
Notary Public.

### AFFIDAVIT OF ATTENDING PHYSICIAN OR MID-WIFE.

UNITED STATES OF AMERICA, Indian Territory, }
Central   DISTRICT. }

I,   N.L. Linker   , a   midwife   , on oath state that I attended on Mrs.   Nettie W Payte   , wife of   AJ. Payte   on the   17   day of   May   , 1905[sic]; that there was born to her on said date a   male   child; that said child was living March 4, 1905, and is said to have been named Roy K Payte

her
N. L. x Linker
mark

Witnesses To Mark:
{ T.W. Jones
{ J.M. Grist

111

## Applications for Enrollment of Choctaw Newborn
## Act of 1905   Volume IX

Subscribed and sworn to before me this   21   day of       March        , 1905

                                            John H Cross
                                                Notary Public.

---

**BIRTH AFFIDAVIT.**

### DEPARTMENT OF THE INTERIOR.
### COMMISSION TO THE FIVE CIVILIZED TRIBES.

---

IN RE APPLICATION FOR ENROLLMENT, as a citizen of the    Choctaw    Nation, of   Roy K. Payte   , born on the   17   day of   May   , 1903

Name of Father:  A. J. Payte            a citizen of the   U. S.    Nation.
Name of Mother:  Nettie W. Payte        a citizen of the   Choctaw  Nation.

                      Postoffice    Nixon I.T.

---

**AFFIDAVIT OF MOTHER.**

UNITED STATES OF AMERICA, Indian Territory, }
   Central              DISTRICT. }

I,   Nettie W. Payte   , on oath state that I am   19   years of age and a citizen by   blood  , of the   Choctaw   Nation; that I am the lawful wife of   A.J. Payte   , who is a citizen, by —— of the   United States   Nation; that a   male   child was born to me on   17   day of   May   , 1903; that said child has been named   Roy K Payte   , and was living March 4, 1905.

                                      Nettie W Payte

Witnesses To Mark:
{

Subscribed and sworn to before me this   8   day of    June    , 1905

                                      John H Cross
                                      Notary Public.

---

**AFFIDAVIT OF ATTENDING PHYSICIAN OR MID-WIFE.**

UNITED STATES OF AMERICA, Indian Territory, }
   Central              DISTRICT. }

I,   N.L. Linker   , a   midwife   , on oath state that I attended on Mrs.   Nettie W Payte   , wife of   AJ. Payte   on the   17   day of   May   ,1903;

## Applications for Enrollment of Choctaw Newborn
## Act of 1905   Volume IX

that there was born to her on said date a   male   child; that said child was living March 4, 1905, and is said to have been named Roy K Payte

her<br>N. L. x Linker<br>mark

Witnesses To Mark:
{ A C Randell[sic]
  M E Cross

Subscribed and sworn to before me this  8  day of   June   , 1905

John H Cross<br>Notary Public.

---

Choc New Born 544
    Nita Jacobs   b.  10-17-03

N. B. 544

Muskogee, Indian Territory, April 8, 1905.

Isaac A. Jacobs,
    Muldrow, Indian Territory.

Dear Sir:

You are hereby advised that before the application for the enrollment of Nita Jacobs can be finally disposed of, it will be necessary for you to furnish the Commission with either the original or a certified copy of the license and certificate of your marriage to Lizzie M. Jacobs.

Please give this matter your immediate attention.

Respectfully,

Commissioner in Charge.

# Applications for Enrollment of Choctaw Newborn
## Act of 1905   Volume IX

Choctaw 5820.

Muskogee, Indian Territory, April 4, 1905.

Isaac A. Jacobs,
  Muldrow, Indian Territory.

Dear Sir:

Receipt is hereby acknowledged of the affidavits of Lizzie M. Jacobs and Samuel R. Bates to the birth of Nita Jacobs, daughter of Isaac A. and Lizzie M. Jacobs, October 17, 1903, and the same have been filed with our records as an application for the enrollment of said child.

Respectfully,

Commissioner in Charge.

---

**BIRTH AFFIDAVIT.**

### DEPARTMENT OF THE INTERIOR.
### COMMISSION TO THE FIVE CIVILIZED TRIBES.

---

**IN RE APPLICATION FOR ENROLLMENT,** as a citizen of the Choctaw Nation, of Nita Jacobs, born on the 17" day of Oct, 1903

Name of Father: Isaac A. Jacobs           a citizen of the Choctaw Nation.
*6/33*
Name of Mother: Lizzie M Jacobs           a citizen of the Choctaw Nation.

Postoffice   Muldrow Ind Ter.

---

**AFFIDAVIT OF MOTHER.**

UNITED STATES OF AMERICA, Indian Territory, }
  Northern       DISTRICT.                  }

I, Lizzie M Jacobs, on oath state that I am 33 years of age and a citizen by blood, of the Choctaw Nation; that I am the lawful wife of Isaac A Jacobs, who is a citizen, by blood of the Choctaw Nation; that a Female child was born to me on 17" day of October, 1903; that said child has been named Nita Jacobs, and was living March 4, 1905.

Lizzie M Jacobs

Witnesses To Mark:

## Applications for Enrollment of Choctaw Newborn
## Act of 1905 Volume IX

Subscribed and sworn to before me this 29 day of March , 1905

J H Bowers
Notary Public.

---

#### AFFIDAVIT OF ATTENDING PHYSICIAN OR MID-WIFE.

UNITED STATES OF AMERICA, Indian Territory,
................................................. DISTRICT.

I, Samuel R Bates , a Physician , on oath state that I attended on Mrs. Lizzie M Jacobs , wife of Isaac A Jacobs on the $17^{th}$ day of October , 1903; that there was born to her on said date a female child; that said child was living March 4, 1905, and is said to have been named Nita Jacobs

Witnesses To Mark:
{

Samuel R Bates M.D.
mark

Subscribed and sworn to before me this $29^{th}$ day of March , 1905

J H Bowers
Notary Public.

---

Choc New Born 545
Atha E. Tucker  b. 11-29-04

---

BIRTH AFFIDAVIT.
#### DEPARTMENT OF THE INTERIOR.
#### COMMISSION TO THE FIVE CIVILIZED TRIBES.

---

IN RE APPLICATION FOR ENROLLMENT, as a citizen of the Choctaw Nation, of Atha E. Tucker , born on the 29 day of Nov , 1904

Name of Father: Joseph S Tucker           a citizen of the Choctaw Nation.
Name of Mother: Martha M Tucker        a citizen of the Choctaw Nation.

Postoffice    Cameron I.T.

# Applications for Enrollment of Choctaw Newborn
## Act of 1905   Volume IX

### AFFIDAVIT OF MOTHER.

UNITED STATES OF AMERICA, Indian Territory,}
Central                DISTRICT.

I, Martha M. Tucker, on oath state that I am 25 years of age and a citizen by blood, of the Choctaw Nation; that I am the lawful wife of Joseph S Tucker, who is a citizen, by Marriage of the Choctaw Nation; that a female child was born to me on 29th day of November, 1904, that said child has been named Atha E. Tucker, and is now living.

Martha M Tucker

Witnesses To Mark:

Subscribed and sworn to before me this 30th day of March, 1905.

Wirt Franklin
Notary Public.

### AFFIDAVIT OF ATTENDING PHYSICIAN OR MID-WIFE.

UNITED STATES OF AMERICA, Indian Territory,}
Central                DISTRICT.

I, M.W. Harrison, a Physician, on oath state that I attended on Mrs. Martha M Tucker, wife of Joseph S Tucker on the 29 day of Nov, 1904; that there was born to her on said date a female child; that said child is now living and is said to have been named Atha E. Tucker

q                                          M. W. Harrison M.D.
Witnesses To Mark:
  Oscar Tucker
  T.W. Dornell

Subscribed and sworn to before me this 29 day of March, 1905.

Hasrod Pilgreen
Notary Public.

My Com expires Oct 9-07

# Applications for Enrollment of Choctaw Newborn
## Act of 1905 Volume IX

**NEW-BORN AFFIDAVIT.**

Number............

...Choctaw Enrolling Commission...

IN THE MATTER OF THE APPLICATION FOR ENROLLMENT, as a citizen of the Choctaw Nation, of Atha E Tucker

born on the 29 day of Nov 190 4

Name of father Joseph S Tucker  a citizen of Choctaw
Nation final enrollment No. 41
Name of mother Martha M Tucker  a citizen of Choctaw
Nation final enrollment No. 6992

Postoffice Cameron I.T.

**AFFIDAVIT OF MOTHER.**

UNITED STATES OF AMERICA
INDIAN TERRITORY
Central DISTRICT

I Martha M Tucker , on oath state that I am 25 years of age and a citizen by Blood of the Choctaw Nation, and as such have been placed upon the final roll of the Choctaw Nation, by the Honorable Secretary of the Interior my final enrollment number being 6992 ; that I am the lawful wife of Joseph S Tucker , who is a citizen of the Choctaw Nation, and as such has been placed upon the final roll of said Nation by the Honorable Secretary of the Interior, his final enrollment number being 41 and that a female child was born to me on the 29 day of Nov 190 4; that said child has been named Atha E Tucker , and is now living.

Martha M Tucker

Witnesseth.
Must be two Witnesses who are Citizens.
J T Reynolds
Clyde M<sup>c</sup>Murtrey

Subscribed and sworn to before me this 27 day of Feb 190 5

Hasrod Pilgreen
Notary Public.

My commission expires: Dec 9-07

# Applications for Enrollment of Choctaw Newborn
## Act of 1905 Volume IX

## AFFIDAVIT OF ATTENDING PHYSICIAN OR MIDWIFE

UNITED STATES OF AMERICA
INDIAN TERRITORY
Central   DISTRICT

I, M.W. Harrison a Physician on oath state that I attended on Mrs. Martha M Tucker wife of Joseph S Tucker on the 29 day of Nov , 190 4, that there was born to her on said date a female child, that said child is now living, and is said to have been named Atha E Tucker

M.W. Harrison   M.D.

WITNESSETH:
Must be two witnesses who are citizens and know the child.
{ J.T. Reynolds
  Clyde M$^c$Murtrey

Subscribed and sworn to before me this, the 27 day of Feb 190 5

Hasrod Pilgreen   Notary Public.

We hereby certify that we are well acquainted with M.W. Harrison a Physician and know him to be reputable and of good standing in the community.

{ J T Reynolds
  Clyde McMurtrey

---

Choc New Born 546
  Clarence J. Tucker  b. 8-25-04

**COPY**   N. B. 546

Muskogee, Indian Territory, April 8, 1905.

Oscar Tucker,
  Cameron, Indian Territory.

Dear Sir:

There is inclosed you herewith for execution application for the enrollment of your infant child, Clarence J. Tucker, born August 25, 1904.

## Applications for Enrollment of Choctaw Newborn
## Act of 1905  Volume IX

It appears from the affidavits heretofore filed with the Commission that the physician has given the name of the father as "Joseph B. Tucker". It will, therefore, be necessary that the application be re-executed.

In having these affidavits executed care should be exercised to see that all names are written in full, as they appear in the body of the affidavit, and in the event that either of the persons signing the affidavit are unable to write, signatures by mark must be attested by two witnesses. Each affidavit must be executed before a Notary Public and the notarial seal and signature of the officer must be attached to each separate affidavit.

Respectfully,

SIGNED

*T. B. Needles.*

LM 8-36                    Commissioner in Charge.

---

Choctaw N.B. 546.

**COPY**

Muskogee, Indian Territory, April 21, 1905.

Oscar Tucker,
    Cameron, Indian Territory.

Dear Sir:

Receipt is hereby acknowledged of the affidavits of Martha Belle Tucker and M. W. Harrison to the birth of Clarence J. Tucker, son of Oscar and Martha Belle Tucker, August 25, 1904 and the same have been filed with our records in the matter of the enrollment of said child.

Respectfully,

SIGNED

*Tams Bixby*
Chairman.

Applications for Enrollment of Choctaw Newborn
Act of 1905   Volume IX

**NEW-BORN AFFIDAVIT.**

Number..........

...Choctaw Enrolling Commission...

IN THE MATTER OF THE APPLICATION FOR ENROLLMENT, as a citizen of the Choctaw Nation, of Clarence J. Tucker

born on the 25 day of Aug 190 4

Name of father    Oscar Tucker                a citizen of ~~non~~
Nation final enrollment No. ..........
Name of mother    Martha B Tucker            a citizen of    Choctaw
Nation final enrollment No. 14732

Postoffice    Cameron I.T.

**AFFIDAVIT OF MOTHER.**

UNITED STATES OF AMERICA
INDIAN TERRITORY
   Central    DISTRICT

I    Martha B Tucker    , on oath state that I am 23 years of age and a citizen by Blood of the Choctaw Nation, and as such have been placed upon the final roll of the Choctaw Nation, by the Honorable Secretary of the Interior my final enrollment number being 14732 ; that I am the lawful wife of Oscar Tucker , who is a ~~non~~ citizen of the ——— Nation, and as such has been placed upon the final roll of said Nation by the Honorable Secretary of the Interior, his final enrollment number being —— and that a Male child was born to me on the 25 day of Aug 190 4; that said child has been named Clarence J Tucker , and is now living.

Martha B Tucker

Witnesseth.
   Must be two   } Alfred Wade M^cClure
   Witnesses who
   are Citizens.     Laura Walker

Subscribed and sworn to before me this    11 day of Feb 190 5

Hasrod Pilgreen
Notary Public.

My commission expires:  Dec 9-07

# Applications for Enrollment of Choctaw Newborn
## Act of 1905 Volume IX

## AFFIDAVIT OF ATTENDING PHYSICIAN OR MIDWIFE

UNITED STATES OF AMERICA
INDIAN TERRITORY
Central DISTRICT

I, M.W. Harrison a Physician on oath state that I attended on Mrs. Martha B Tucker wife of Oscar Tucker on the 25 day of Aug , 190 4, that there was born to her on said date a male child, that said child is now living, and is said to have been named Clarence J Tucker

M.W. Harrison M.D.

WITNESSETH:
Must be two witnesses who are citizens and know the child. { Alfred Wade M<sup>c</sup>Clure
Laura Walker

Subscribed and sworn to before me this, the 11 day of Feb 190 5

Hasrod Pilgreen Notary Public.

We hereby certify that we are well acquainted with M.W. Harrison a Physician and know him to be reputable and of good standing in the community.

{ Alfred Wade M<sup>c</sup>Clure
Laura Walker

BIRTH AFFIDAVIT.

## DEPARTMENT OF THE INTERIOR.
## COMMISSION TO THE FIVE CIVILIZED TRIBES.

IN RE APPLICATION FOR ENROLLMENT, as a citizen of the Choctaw Nation, of Clarence J. Tucker , born on the 25 day of Aug , 1904

Name of Father: Oscar Tucker  non  a citizen of the Choctaw Nation.
Name of Mother: Martha B. Tucker a citizen of the Choctaw Nation.

Postoffice Cameron I.T.

# Applications for Enrollment of Choctaw Newborn
## Act of 1905 Volume IX

### AFFIDAVIT OF MOTHER.

UNITED STATES OF AMERICA, Indian Territory,
Central DISTRICT.

I, Martha B Tucker, on oath state that I am 23 years of age and a citizen by blood, of the Choctaw Nation; that I am the lawful wife of Oscar Tucker, who is a citizen, ~~by~~ .................. of the United States Nation; that a male child was born to me on 25th day of August, 1904, that said child has been named Clarence J Tucker, and is now living.

Martha B Tucker

Witnesses To Mark:

Subscribed and sworn to before me this 30th day of March, 1905.

Wirt Franklin
Notary Public.

### AFFIDAVIT OF ATTENDING PHYSICIAN OR MID-WIFE.

UNITED STATES OF AMERICA, Indian Territory,
Central DISTRICT.

I, M.W. Harrison, a Physician, on oath state that I attended on Mrs. Martha B Tucker, wife of Joseph B[sic] Tucker on the 25 day of Aug, 1904; that there was born to her on said date a male child; that said child is now living and is said to have been named Clarence J Tucker

M.W. Harrison M.D.

Witnesses To Mark:
JB Pilgreen
*(Name Illegible)*

Subscribed and sworn to before me this 29 day of March, 1905.

Hasrod Pilgreen
Notary Public.

My Com expires Dec 9-07

## Applications for Enrollment of Choctaw Newborn
## Act of 1905   Volume IX

BIRTH AFFIDAVIT.

### DEPARTMENT OF THE INTERIOR.
### COMMISSION TO THE FIVE CIVILIZED TRIBES.

IN RE APPLICATION FOR ENROLLMENT, as a citizen of the   Choctaw   Nation, of Clarence J Tucker   , born on the   25   day of August   , 1904

Name of Father: Oscar Tucker         a citizen of the   U. S.   Nation.
Name of Mother: Martha Belle Tucker   a citizen of the   Choctaw   Nation.

Postoffice   Cameron I.T.

### AFFIDAVIT OF MOTHER.

UNITED STATES OF AMERICA, Indian Territory, }
.................................... DISTRICT.

I,   Martha Belle Tucker   , on oath state that I am   23   years of age and a citizen by   blood   , of the   Choctaw   Nation; that I am the lawful wife of Oscar Tucker   , who is a citizen, ~~by~~ ................ of the   United States ~~Nation~~; that a   Male   child was born to me on 25"   day of   August   , 1904; that said child has been named   Clarence J Tucker   , and was living March 4, 1905.

Martha Belle Tucker

Witnesses To Mark:
{

Subscribed and sworn to before me this   17   day of   April   , 1905

Hasrod Pilgreen
Notary Public.

### AFFIDAVIT OF ATTENDING PHYSICIAN OR MID-WIFE.

UNITED STATES OF AMERICA, Indian Territory, }
   Central   DISTRICT.

I,   M.W. Harrison   , a Physician   , on oath state that I attended on Mrs.   Martha Belle Tucker   , wife of   Oscar Tucker   on the   25" day of August   , 1904; that there was born to her on said date a   male   child; that said child was living March 4, 1905, and is said to have been named Clarence J Tucker

M.W. Harrison M.D.

Witnesses To Mark:
{

## Applications for Enrollment of Choctaw Newborn
## Act of 1905  Volume IX

Subscribed and sworn to before me this 17 day of April , 1905

Hasrod Pilgreen
Notary Public.

---

Choc New Born 547
Thomas Hunter  b. 3-30-04

DEPARTMENT OF THE INTERIOR,
COMMISSIONER TO THE FIVE CIVILIZED TRIBES.

Record in the matter of the application for enrollment as a citizen by blood of the Choctaw Nation of:

THOMAS HUNTER         7-NB-547.

**BIRTH AFFIDAVIT.**
**DEPARTMENT OF THE INTERIOR.**
**COMMISSION TO THE FIVE CIVILIZED TRIBES.**

**IN RE APPLICATION FOR ENROLLMENT**, as a citizen of the Choctaw Nation, of Thomas Hunter , born on the 30th day of March , 1904

Name of Father: George Hunter        a citizen of the Choctaw Nation.
Name of Mother: Minnie Hunter (nee Jones)   a citizen of the Choctaw Nation.

Postoffice  Boswell, I.T.

**AFFIDAVIT OF MOTHER.**

UNITED STATES OF AMERICA, Indian Territory,
Central        DISTRICT.

I, Minnie Hunter , on oath state that I am 19 yrs years of age and a citizen by blood , of the Choctaw Nation; that I am the lawful wife of George Hunter , who is a citizen, by Blood of the Choctaw Nation; that a male child was born to me on 30th day of Mar , 1904; that said

# Applications for Enrollment of Choctaw Newborn
## Act of 1905   Volume IX

child has been named   Thomas Hunter   , and was ~~living~~ *dead* March 4, 1905. *having died Aug 8, 1904*

                                      Minnie Hunter

Witnesses To Mark:
{

    Subscribed and sworn to before me this 25th   day of   Mar   , 1905

(Seal)
                                    J R Armstrong
                                        Notary Public.

---

**AFFIDAVIT OF ATTENDING PHYSICIAN OR MID-WIFE.**

UNITED STATES OF AMERICA, Indian Territory, }
   Central                DISTRICT. }

    I,   Belle Vinson   , a   midwife   , on oath state that I attended on Mrs.   Minnie Hunter   , wife of   George Hunter   on the 30th day of   March , 1904; that there was born to her on said date a   male   child; that said child was ~~living~~ *dead* March 4, 1905, *having died Aug 8, 1904* and is said to have been named   Thomas Hunter

                                        her
                                  Belle  x  Vinson

Witnesses To Mark:                      mark
{ Edwin Dwight
{ Emma Dwight

    Subscribed and sworn to before me this 25   day of   Mar   , 1905

(Seal)
                                    J R Armstrong
                                        Notary Public.

---

                                                            7-NB-547.

                        Muskogee, Indian Territory, May 26, 1905.

George Hunter,
        Boswell, Indian Territory.

Dear Sir:

    Referring to the application for the enrollment of your infant child, Thomas Hunter, born March 30, 1904, it is noted from the affidavits heretofore filed in this office that the applicant died on August 8, 1904.

Applications for Enrollment of Choctaw Newborn
Act of 1905   Volume IX

If this is correct you will please execute and return to this office the enclosed proof of death, in order that this fact may be made a matter of record.

Respectfully,

Chairman.

Enclose D-C.

## DEPARTMENT OF THE INTERIOR.
## COMMISSION TO THE FIVE CIVILIZED TRIBES.

In the matter of the death of   Thomas Hunter   a citizen of the   Choctaw Nation, who formerly resided at or near   Boswell   , Ind. Ter., and died on the   $8^{th}$   day of Agust[sic]   , 1904

### AFFIDAVIT OF RELATIVE.

UNITED STATES OF AMERICA, Indian Territory, }
   Central         DISTRICT.

I,   Thomas W. Hunter   , on oath state that I am   36   years of age and a citizen by   blood   , of the   Choctaw   Nation; that my postoffice address is   Boswell   , Ind. Ter.; that I am   Uncle   of   Thomas Hunter   who was a citizen, by   blood   , of the   Choctaw   Nation and that said   Thomas Hunter   died on the   $8^{th}$   day of Agust[sic]   , 1904

Thomas W Hunter

Witnesses To Mark:
{

Subscribed and sworn to before me this   15"   day of   June   , 1905.

SH Downing
Notary Public.

### AFFIDAVIT OF ACQUAINTANCE.

UNITED STATES OF AMERICA, Indian Territory, }
   Central         DISTRICT.

I,   E.T. Dwight   , on oath state that I am ............ years of age, and a citizen by blood   of the   Choctaw   Nation; that my postoffice address is   Boswell   , Ind. Ter.; that I was personally acquainted with   Thomas Hunter   who was a citizen, by   blood   , of the   Choctaw   Nation; and that said   Thomas Hunter   died on the   $8^{th}$   day of Agust[sic]   , 1904

# Applications for Enrollment of Choctaw Newborn
## Act of 1905   Volume IX

Witnesses To Mark:

E. T. Dwight

{

Subscribed and sworn to before me this  17  day of  June  , 1905.

Thos W. Hunter
Notary Public.

*W.J.*
7-NB-547.

## DEPARTMENT OF THE INTERIOR,
## COMMISSIONER TO THE FIVE CIVILIZED TRIBES.

In the matter of the application for the enrollment of Thomas Hunter as a citizen by blood of the Choctaw Nation.

----oOo----

It appears from the record herein that on April 5, 1905 there was filed with the Commission to the Five Civilized Tribes an application for the enrollment of Thomas Hunter as a citizen by blood of the Choctaw Nation.

It further appears from the record herein and the records of this office that the applicant was born March 30, 1904; that he is a son of George Hunter and Minnie Hunter (enrolled as Minnie Jones), recognized and enrolled citizens by blood of the Choctaw Nation whose names appear opposite numbers 9616 and 13997, respectively, upon the final roll of citizens by blood of the Choctaw Nation, approved by the Secretary of the Interior on February 4, 1903 and March 19, 1903, respectively; and that said applicant died August 8, 1904.

The Act of Congress approved March 3, 1905 (Public No. 212) among other things provides:

"That the Commission to the Five Civilized Tribes is authorized for sixty days after the date of the approval of this act to receive and consider applications for enrollment of children born subsequent to September twenty-fifth, nineteen hundred and two, and prior to March fourth, nineteen hundred and five, and who were living on said latter date, to citizens by blood of the Choctaw and Chickasaw tribes of Indians whose enrollment has been approved by the Secretary of the Interior prior to the date of the approval of this act; and to enroll and make allotments to such children."

It is, therefore, hereby ordered that the application for the enrollment of Thomas Hunter as a citizen by blood of the Choctaw Nation be dismissed.

Tams Bixby  Commissioner.

Muskogee, Indian Territory.
OCT 6 1905

## Applications for Enrollment of Choctaw Newborn
## Act of 1905   Volume IX

7-NB-547.

Muskogee, Indian Territory, October 6, 1905.

**COPY**

George Hunter,
   Boswell, Indian Territory.

Dear Sir:

Inclosed herewith you will find a copy of the order of the Commissioner to the Five Civilized Tribes, dated October 6, 1905, dismissing the application for the enrollment of your minor son Thomas Hunter as a citizen by blood of the Choctaw Nation.

Respectfully,
SIGNED
*Tams Bixby*
Commissioner.

Register.
7-NB-547.

---

7-NB-547.

Muskogee, Indian Territory, October 6, 1905.
**COPY**

Mansfield, McMurray & Cornish,
   Attorneys for Choctaw and Chickasaw Nations,
      South McAlester, Indian Territory.

Gentlemen:

Inclosed herewith you will find a copy of the order of the Commissioner to the Five Civilized Tribes, dated October 6, 1905, dismissing the application for the enrollment of Thomas Hunter as a citizen by blood of the Choctaw Nation.

Respectfully,
SIGNED
*Tams Bixby*
Commissioner.

7-NB-547.

## Applications for Enrollment of Choctaw Newborn
## Act of 1905   Volume IX

7-5531

Muskogee, Indian Territory, April 4, 1905.

Thomas Hunter,
    Boswell, Indian Territory.

Dear Sir:

    Receipt is hereby acknowledged of the affidavits of Minnie Hunter and Belle Vinson to the birth of Thomas Hunter, son of George Hunter and Minnie Hunter, March 30, 1904.

    It appears from the affidavits that Thomas Hunter died August 8, 1904, and under the provisions of the act of Congress approved March 3, 1905, the Commission is authorized to receive only applications for the enrollment of those children born to enrolled citizens by blood of the Choctaw and Chickasaw Nations between September 25, 1902, and March 4, 1905 and living on said latter date.

    You will therefore see that the Commission is without authority to enroll children born subsequent to September 25, 1902, who were not living on March 4, 1905.

Respectfully,

Chairman.

---

7 NB 547

Muskogee, Indian Territory, June 21, 1905.

Thomas W. Hunter,
    Boswell, Indian Territory.

Dear Sir:

    Receipt is hereby acknowledged of the affidavits of Thomas W. Hunter and E. T. Dwight to the death of Thomas Hunter which occurred August 8, 1904, and the same have been filed with our records as evidence of the death of the above named citizen. of the death of the above named child.

Respectfully,

Chairman.

## Applications for Enrollment of Choctaw Newborn
## Act of 1905  Volume IX

Choc New Born 548
   Waldo Lindsey  b. 6-6-03

**BIRTH AFFIDAVIT.**

### DEPARTMENT OF THE INTERIOR.
### COMMISSION TO THE FIVE CIVILIZED TRIBES.

**IN RE APPLICATION FOR ENROLLMENT,** as a citizen of the    Choctaw    Nation, of Waldo Lindsey    , born on the  6th   day of   June   , 1903

Name of Father: Selden T. Lindsey         a citizen of the   Choctaw   Nation.
Name of Mother: Nina Lindsey              a citizen of the   Choctaw   Nation.

            Postoffice    Durwood, I.T.

#### AFFIDAVIT OF MOTHER.

UNITED STATES OF AMERICA, Indian Territory, }
   Southern           DISTRICT.            }

   I,  Nina Lindsey   , on oath state that I am  38   years of age and a citizen by blood  , of the  Choctaw  Nation; that I am the lawful wife of  Selden T. Lindsey  , who is a citizen, by  marriage   of the   Choctaw   Nation; that a   male  child was born to me on  6th  day of  June   , 1903; that said child has been named Waldo Lindsey   , and was living March 4, 1905.

                        Nina Lindsey
Witnesses To Mark:
   {
   {
   Subscribed and sworn to before me this  21st  day of   Mar   , 1905

                        Orrin M Redfield
                           Notary Public.

#### AFFIDAVIT OF ATTENDING PHYSICIAN OR MID-WIFE.

UNITED STATES OF AMERICA, Indian Territory, }
   Southern           DISTRICT.            }

   I,        Bettie Cunningham        , on oath state that I attended on Mrs.  Nina Lindsey  , wife of  Selden T Lindsey   on the  6th  day of  June  , 1903; that there was born to her on said date a   male   child; that said child was living March 4, 1905, and is said to have been named Waldo Lindsey

# Applications for Enrollment of Choctaw Newborn
## Act of 1905 Volume IX

Bettie Cunningham

Witnesses To Mark:
{

Subscribed and sworn to before me this 23 day of March , 1905

Jas. H Mulkey
Notary Public.

**COPY**

Choctaw N.B. 548

Muskogee, Indian Territory, April 28, 1905.

Nina Lindsey,
    Durwood, Indian Territory.

Dear Madam:

    Receipt is hereby acknowledged of your letter of April 24, asking if the application for the enrollment of your child, Waldo Lindsey, has been received.

    In reply to your letter you are advised that the affidavits heretofore forwarded to the birth of your child, Waldo Lindsey, have been filed with our records as an application for the enrollment of said child.

Respectfully,
SIGNED

*Tams Bixby*
Chairman.

---

Choc New Born 549
    Josephine Hancock  b. 7-12-03

## Applications for Enrollment of Choctaw Newborn
## Act of 1905   Volume IX

7-5557

Muskogee, Indian Territory, April 6, 1905.

Willis Hancock,
    Redoak, Indian Territory.

Dear Sir:

    Receipt is hereby acknowledged of the affidavit of Watson Hampton to the birth of Josephine Hancock, daughter of Willie[sic] and Jincey Hancock, July 12, 1903, and the same has been filed with our records as an application for the enrollment of said child.

    Respectfully,

    Commissioner in Charge.

---

7-NB-548.

Muskogee, Indian Territory, May 26, 1905.

Willis Hancock,
    Redoak, Indian Territory.

Dear Sir:

    Referring to the application for the enrollment of your infant child, Josephine Hancock, born July 12, 1903, it is noted in the mother's affidavit, heretofore filed in this office, that the midwife who attended upon your wife at the time of birth of the applicant is dead. In place of her affidavit there has been filed in this office the affidavits of yourself and Watson Hampton.

    Before this matter can be finally determined it will be necessary for you to file in this office the affidavits of two persons, who are disinterested and not related to the applicant, who have actual knowledge of the facts that the child was born, the date of her birth; that she was living on March 4, 1905, and that Jincey Hancock is her mother. The affidavit of Watson Hampton, above referred to, does not show that the applicant was living on March 4, 1905.

    In having these affidavits executed care should be exercised to see that all names are written in full, as they appear in the body of the affidavit, and in the event that either of the persons signing the affidavit are unable to write, signatures by mark must be attested by two witnesses. Each affidavit must be executed before a Notary Public and the notarial seal and signature of the officer must be attached to each separate affidavit.

# Applications for Enrollment of Choctaw Newborn
## Act of 1905   Volume IX

Respectfully,

Chairman.

VR 26-8.

7 NB 549

Muskogee, Indian Territory, June 22, 1905.

W. W. Ish,
   Redoak, Indian Territory.

Dear Sir:

   Receipt is hereby acknowledged of the affidavits of M. D. Carney and Ben Sockey to the birth of Josephine Hancock, daughter of Willis and Jincey Hancock, July 12, 1903, and the same have been filed with our records in the matter of the enrollment of said child.

Respectfully,

Chairman.

Red Oak I.T.  April 1$^{st}$ 1905

   This is to certify that I Watt Hampton do know that on the 12$^{th}$ day of July 1903 there was born to Willis and Jincy[sic] Hancock one daughter.

Signed,
                              Watson Hampton

Subscribed and sworn to before me this 1$^{st}$ of April 1905

C.L. Stone N.P.

Witness my hand and seal this 1$^{st}$ of April 1905

C.L. Stone Notary Public

# Applications for Enrollment of Choctaw Newborn
# Act of 1905   Volume IX

*(The affidavit below typed as given.)*

United States of America
Central Judicial Division of Ind Ter
   Red Oak, Choctaw Nation
       June 17-1905

On this day personly appeared before me a Notary Public for the a bove named Dist and Divis M.D. Carney who is well known to me and after beaing duly qualified says I am about 47 years old I live at Red Oak Choctaw Nation and says I know Willis Hancock and his wife for 8 or 10 years  we live in the same neighborhood I see his family often  I know his little girl Josephine  seen her shortley after she was born and often since I do not know the exact month that she was born but believe it was in July 1903. I know that they call her Josephine and that she is a live today give under my hand and *(illegible...)* I am a Choctaw by blood

                                  M.D. Carney

Subscribed and sworn to before me this sworn to before me this the 17 June 1905
                                                    W.W. Ish
Red Ok Choctaw Nation                            Notary Public

---

*(The affidavit below typed as given.)*

       United States of America
       Central Judicial Div of I T
          Red Oak Choctaw Nation
          June the 17-1905

on this day personly appear before ma a Notary Public for the bove district Ben Sockey who beaing duely qualified says my name is Ben Sockey near Red Oak Choctaw Nation I am 58 years old I know Willis Hancock and his wife  I seen Josephine Hancock when I think a bout a week old that was in July 1903 and have seen her often since.  some time every day and never but a fiew days a part and I know that she is a live today as Hancock is one of my neighbors I know that she is called Josephine Hancock I am a Choctaw by blood

                                  Ben Sockey

Subscribed and sworn before me to this 17 day of June 1905

                                W.W. Ish
                                Notary Public
                                Red Ok
                                Choctaw Nation

## Applications for Enrollment of Choctaw Newborn
## Act of 1905 Volume IX

BIRTH AFFIDAVIT.

### DEPARTMENT OF THE INTERIOR.
### COMMISSION TO THE FIVE CIVILIZED TRIBES.

---

IN RE APPLICATION FOR ENROLLMENT, as a citizen of the Choctaw Nation, of Josephine Hancock , born on the 12th day of July , 1903

Name of Father: Willis Hancock     a citizen of the Choctaw Nation.
Name of Mother: Jincey Hancock     a citizen of the Choctaw Nation.

Postoffice    Redoak, Ind Ter

---

### AFFIDAVIT OF MOTHER.

UNITED STATES OF AMERICA, Indian Territory,
Central      DISTRICT.

     I, Juicey[sic] Hancock , on oath state that I am 35 years of age and a citizen by blood , of the Choctaw Nation; that I am the lawful wife of Willis Hancock , who is a citizen, by blood of the Choctaw Nation; that a female child was born to me on 12th day of July , 1903; that said child has been named Josephine Hancock , and was living March 4, 1905. *and that the midwife who attended me at the birth of said child is dead*

                        her
                 Juicey x Hancock
                     mark

Witnesses To Mark:
   George N Wise
   Victor M Locke JR

Subscribed and sworn to before me this 27th day of March , 1905

                 Wirt Franklin
                     Notary Public.

---

### AFFIDAVIT OF ATTENDING PHYSICIAN OR MID-WIFE.

UNITED STATES OF AMERICA, Indian Territory,
Central      DISTRICT.

     I, Willis Hancock , a~~~~~~, *am husband of* , on oath state that I ~~attended on~~ Mrs. Juicey Hancock , ~~wife of~~ that on the 12th day of July , 1903; that there was born to her on said date a female child; that said child was living March 4, 1905, and ~~is said to have~~ *has* been named Josephine Hancock

# Applications for Enrollment of Choctaw Newborn
## Act of 1905  Volume IX

Witnesses To Mark:
{

Willis Hancock

Subscribed and sworn to before me this 27th day of March , 1905

Wirt Franklin
Notary Public.

---

Choc New Born 550
Carl Ocey Merryman  b. 8-26-04

**BIRTH AFFIDAVIT.**

### DEPARTMENT OF THE INTERIOR.
### COMMISSION TO THE FIVE CIVILIZED TRIBES.

IN RE APPLICATION FOR ENROLLMENT, as a citizen of the Choctaw Nation, of Carl Ocey Merryman , born on the 26th day of August , 1904

Name of Father: Leonidas Merryman     a citizen of the Choctaw Nation.
Name of Mother: Sarah Merryman        a citizen of the Choctaw Nation.

Postoffice  Spiro, Ind. Ter.

### AFFIDAVIT OF MOTHER.

UNITED STATES OF AMERICA, Indian Territory, }
Central        DISTRICT.

I, Sarah Merryman , on oath state that I am 29 years of age and a citizen by marriage , of the Choctaw Nation; that I am the lawful wife of Leonidas Merryman , who is a citizen, by blood of the Choctaw Nation; that a male child was born to me on 26th day of August , 1904; that said child has been named Carl Ocey Merryman , and was living March 4, 1905.

her
Sarah x Merryman
mark

Witnesses To Mark:
{ Louie LeFlore
  E A Moore

# Applications for Enrollment of Choctaw Newborn
## Act of 1905  Volume IX

Subscribed and sworn to before me this 30th day of March, 1905

Wirt Franklin
Notary Public.

---

### AFFIDAVIT OF ATTENDING PHYSICIAN OR MID-WIFE.

UNITED STATES OF AMERICA, Indian Territory,
Central                          DISTRICT.

I, W. O. Hartshorne, a physician, on oath state that I attended on Mrs. Sarah Merryman, wife of Leonidas Merryman on the 26th day of August, 1904; that there was born to her on said date a male child; that said child was living March 4, 1905, and is said to have been named Carl Ocey Merryman

W.O. Hartshorne

Witnesses To Mark:

Subscribed and sworn to before me this 30th day of March, 1905

Wirt Franklin
Notary Public.

---

## AFFIDAVIT OF ATTENDING PHYSICIAN OR MIDWIFE

UNITED STATES OF AMERICA
INDIAN TERRITORY
Central     DISTRICT

I, W.O. Hartshorne a Practicing Physician on oath state that I attended on Mrs. Sarah E Merryman wife of Leonidas E. Merryman on the 26 day of August, 190 4, that there was born to her on said date a male child, that said child is now living, and is said to have been named Carl O. Merryman

W.O. Hartshorne  *M.D.*

Subscribed and sworn to before me this, the 1 day of February 190 5

WITNESSETH:                      James Bower   Notary Public.
Must be two witnesses   E.A. Moore
who are citizens
                        E.L. Hickman

## Applications for Enrollment of Choctaw Newborn
## Act of 1905   Volume IX

We hereby certify that we are well acquainted with    W.O. Hartshorne   a  Practicing Physician    and know   him   to be reputable and of good standing in the community.

E.A. Moore

E. L. Hickman

**NEW-BORN AFFIDAVIT.**

Number..........

...Choctaw Enrolling Commission...

IN THE MATTER OF THE APPLICATION FOR ENROLLMENT, as a citizen of the Choctaw   Nation, of    Carl O. Merryman

born on the   26   day of ____August____ 190 4

Name of father    Leonidas E Merryman    a citizen of    Choctaw   Nation final enrollment No.  8181
Name of mother   Sarah E Merryman    a citizen of ..............................   Nation final enrollment No. ...............

Postoffice   Spiro I.T.

**AFFIDAVIT OF MOTHER.**

UNITED STATES OF AMERICA
INDIAN TERRITORY
  Central    DISTRICT

I   Sarah E Merryman   , on oath state that I am  28   years of age and a citizen by ............. of the ............. Nation, and as such have been placed upon the final roll of the ............. Nation, by the Honorable Secretary of the Interior my final enrollment number being ............; that I am the lawful wife of   Leonidas E Merryman   , who is a citizen of the   Choctaw   Nation, and as such has been placed upon the final roll of said Nation by the Honorable Secretary of the Interior, his final enrollment number being    8181   and that a   Male   child was born to me on the   26   day of   August    190 4; that said child has been named   Carl O Merryman   , and is now living.

Sarah E Merryman

Witnesseth.
  Must be two  ⎫   E A Moore
  Witnesses who ⎬
  are Citizens.  ⎭   E L Hickman

## Applications for Enrollment of Choctaw Newborn
## Act of 1905 Volume IX

Subscribed and sworn to before me this 1 day of Feb 190 5

James Bower
Notary Public.

My commission expires:
Sept 23 1907

---

Choc New Born 551
Stella Russell  b. 11-12-03

### *Affidavit of Attending Physician or Midwife*

UNITED STATES OF AMERICA,  
INDIAN TERRITORY,  
Central   DISTRICT

I, Mrs S. A. Harris a Midwife on oath state that I attended on Mrs. Dora Russell wife of Robert Russell on the 12 day of November , 190 3, that there was born to her on said date a female child, that said child is now living, and is said to have been named Stella Russell

S. A. Harris   M. D.

Subscribed and sworn to before me this the 22 day of February 1905

James Bower
Notary Public.

WITNESSETH:

Must be two witnesses who are citizens and know the child. { Frank R *(Illegible)*
Travis Williams

We hereby certify that we are well acquainted with Mrs S A Harris a midwife and know her to be reputable and of good standing in the community.

Must be two citizen witnesses. { Frank R *(Illegible)*
Travis Williams

## Applications for Enrollment of Choctaw Newborn
## Act of 1905 Volume IX

BIRTH AFFIDAVIT.

### DEPARTMENT OF THE INTERIOR.
### COMMISSION TO THE FIVE CIVILIZED TRIBES.

IN RE APPLICATION FOR ENROLLMENT, as a citizen of the Choctaw Nation, of Stella Russell, born on the 12th day of November, 1903

Name of Father: Robert Russell    a citizen of the Choctaw Nation.
Name of Mother: Dora Russell    a citizen of the Choctaw Nation.

Postoffice    Spiro, Ind. Ter.

### AFFIDAVIT OF MOTHER.

UNITED STATES OF AMERICA, Indian Territory, }
     Central      DISTRICT.

I, Dora Russell, on oath state that I am 22 years of age and a citizen by marriage, of the Choctaw Nation; that I am the lawful wife of Robert Russell, who is a citizen, by blood of the Choctaw Nation; that a female child was born to me on 12th day of November, 1903; that said child has been named Stella Russell, and was living March 4, 1905.

                         Dora Russell

Witnesses To Mark:
{

Subscribed and sworn to before me this 30th day of March, 1905

                         Wirt Franklin
                         Notary Public.

### AFFIDAVIT OF ATTENDING PHYSICIAN OR MID-WIFE.

UNITED STATES OF AMERICA, Indian Territory, }
     Central      DISTRICT.

I, A.P. Thompson, a physician, on oath state that I attended on Mrs. Dora Russell, wife of Robert Russell on the 12th day of November, 1903; that there was born to her on said date a female child; that said child was living March 4, 1905, and is said to have been named Stella Russell

                         A.P. Thompson

Witnesses To Mark:
{

Applications for Enrollment of Choctaw Newborn
Act of 1905   Volume IX

Subscribed and sworn to before me this  30th   day of   March   , 1905

Wirt Franklin
Notary Public.

# NEW BORN AFFIDAVIT

No _____

## CHOCTAW ENROLLING COMMISSION

IN THE MATTER OF THE APPLICATION FOR ENROLLMENT as a citizen of the Choctaw Nation, of   Stella Russell   born on the   12   day of   November   190 3

Name of father   Robert Russell   a citizen of   Choctaw   Nation, final enrollment No.   8018
Name of mother   Dora Russell   a citizen of   Choctaw   Nation, final enrollment No.   1111

Spiro I.T.   Postoffice.

**AFFIDAVIT OF MOTHER**

UNITED STATES OF AMERICA
INDIAN TERRITORY
DISTRICT   Central

I   Dora Russell   , on oath state that I am   22   years of age and a citizen by   Intermarriage   of the   Choctaw   Nation, and as such have been placed upon the final roll of the   Choctaw   Nation, by the Honorable Secretary of the Interior my final enrollment number being   1111   ; that I am the lawful wife of   Robert Russell   , who is a citizen of the   Choctaw   Nation, and as such has been placed upon the final roll of said Nation by the Honorable Secretary of the Interior, his final enrollment number being   8018   and that a   female   child was born to me on the   12   day of   November   190 3; that said child has been named   Stella Russell   , and is now living.

Dora Russell

WITNESSETH:
Must be two witnesses who are citizens   { Frank R. *(Illegible)*
                                            Travis Williams

141

## Applications for Enrollment of Choctaw Newborn
## Act of 1905  Volume IX

Subscribed and sworn to before me this, the 22 day of February, 1905

James Bower
Notary Public.

My Commission Expires:
Sept 23-1907

---

Choc New Born 552
   Louie Fudge LeFlore   b. 9-11-03

## AFFIDAVIT OF ATTENDING PHYSICIAN OR MIDWIFE

UNITED STATES OF AMERICA
INDIAN TERRITORY
   Central   DISTRICT

I, C.H. Mahar  a  Physician on oath state that I attended on Mrs. Mary B. LeFlore  wife of  Louis[sic] LeFlore on the 11 day of September, 1903, that there was born to her on said date a Male child, that said child is now living, and is said to have been named Louie Fudge LeFlore

Charles H Mahar    𝑚.𝒟.

Subscribed and sworn to before me this, the 22 day of February 1905

James Bower   Notary Public.

WITNESSETH:
Must be two witnesses   { E L Hickman
who are citizens           Robert Russell

We hereby certify that we are well acquainted with  C H Mahan a  Practicing Physician  and know him  to be reputable and of good standing in the community.

_____      E. L. Hickman

_____      Robert Russell

142

Applications for Enrollment of Choctaw Newborn
Act of 1905   Volume IX

**NEW-BORN AFFIDAVIT.**

Number..........

...Choctaw Enrolling Commission...

IN THE MATTER OF THE APPLICATION FOR ENROLLMENT, as a citizen of the Choctaw Nation, of    Louie Fudge LeFlore

born on the  11  day of __September__  190 3

Name of father   Louie LeFlore          a citizen of    Choctaw
Nation final enrollment No.  7749
Name of mother   Mary B LeFlore        a citizen of    Choctaw
Nation final enrollment No.  14741

Postoffice   Oak Lodge, I.T.

**AFFIDAVIT OF MOTHER.**

UNITED STATES OF AMERICA
INDIAN TERRITORY
  Central     DISTRICT

I    Mary B. LeFlore    , on oath state that I am  30  years of age and a citizen by  marriage  of the    Choctaw    Nation, and as such have been placed upon the final roll of the    Choctaw   Nation, by the Honorable Secretary of the Interior my final enrollment number being    14741  ; that I am the lawful wife of   Louie LeFlore   , who is a citizen of the    Choctaw    Nation, and as such has been placed upon the final roll of said Nation by the Honorable Secretary of the Interior, his final enrollment number being    2709   and that a    Male    child was born to me on the   11   day of   September    190 3; that said child has been named   Louie Fudge LeFlore   , and is now living.

Mary B LeFlore

Witnesseth.
  Must be two  ⎫   E. L. Hickman
  Witnesses who ⎬
  are Citizens.  ⎭   Robert Russell

Subscribed and sworn to before me this  2  day of   Feb   190 5

James Bower
Notary Public.

My commission expires:
  Sept 23 - 1907

# Applications for Enrollment of Choctaw Newborn
## Act of 1905   Volume IX

BIRTH AFFIDAVIT.

### DEPARTMENT OF THE INTERIOR.
### COMMISSION TO THE FIVE CIVILIZED TRIBES.

IN RE APPLICATION FOR ENROLLMENT, as a citizen of the Choctaw Nation, of Louie Fudge LeFlore, born on the 11th day of September, 1903

Name of Father: Louie LeFlore   a citizen of the Choctaw Nation.
Name of Mother: Mayme B. LeFlore   a citizen of the Choctaw Nation.

Postoffice   Oaklodge, Ind. Ter.

### AFFIDAVIT OF MOTHER.

UNITED STATES OF AMERICA, Indian Territory,
Central DISTRICT.

I, Mayme B LeFlore, on oath state that I am 31 years of age and a citizen by marriage, of the Choctaw Nation; that I am the lawful wife of Louie LeFlore, who is a citizen, by blood of the Choctaw Nation; that a male child was born to me on 11th day of September, 1903; that said child has been named Louie Fudge LeFlore, and was living March 4, 1905.

Mrs. Mayme B. LeFlore

Witnesses To Mark:

Subscribed and sworn to before me this 30th day of March, 1905

Wirt Franklin
Notary Public.

### AFFIDAVIT OF ATTENDING PHYSICIAN OR MID-WIFE.

UNITED STATES OF AMERICA, Indian Territory,
Central DISTRICT.

I, Charles H Mahar, a physician, on oath state that I attended on Mrs. Mayme B LeFlore, wife of Louie LeFlore on the 11th day of September, 1903; that there was born to her on said date a male child; that said child was living March 4, 1905, and is said to have been named Louie Fudge LeFlore

Charles H Mahar M.D.

Witnesses To Mark:

Applications for Enrollment of Choctaw Newborn
Act of 1905 Volume IX

Subscribed and sworn to before me this 30th day of March, 1905

Wirt Franklin
Notary Public.

Choc New Born 553
Ethan Allen Moore  b. 7-20-03

## AFFIDAVIT OF ATTENDING PHYSICIAN OR MIDWIFE

UNITED STATES OF AMERICA
INDIAN TERRITORY
Central  DISTRICT

I, C H Mahar  a  Practicing Physician on oath state that I attended on Mrs. Ida N Moore  wife of Lyman R Moore on the 20th day of July, 190 3, that there was born to her on said date a Male child, that said child is now living, and is said to have been named Ethan Allen Moore

C H Mahar  M.D.

Subscribed and sworn to before me this, the  26  day of January  190 5

WITNESSETH:                         James Bower  Notary Public.
  Must be two witnesses   { E A Moore
  who are citizens
                            (Name Illegible)

We hereby certify that we are well acquainted with  CH Mahar a Practicing Physician  and know him  to be reputable and of good standing in the community.

_____          E.A. Moore

_____          (Name Illegible)

## Applications for Enrollment of Choctaw Newborn
## Act of 1905   Volume IX

**NEW-BORN AFFIDAVIT.**

Number............

### ...Choctaw Enrolling Commission...

IN THE MATTER OF THE APPLICATION FOR ENROLLMENT, as a citizen of the Choctaw Nation, of Ethan Allen Moore

born on the 20 day of __July__ 190 3

Name of father   Lyman R Moore         a citizen of   Choctaw Nation
Nation final enrollment No.  7844
Name of mother   Ida N Moore nee M$^c$Curtain   a citizen of   Choctaw ~~Nation~~
Nation final enrollment No.  5407

Postoffice   Spiro I.T.

**AFFIDAVIT OF MOTHER.**

UNITED STATES OF AMERICA
INDIAN TERRITORY
   Central       DISTRICT

*(nee M$^c$Curtain)*

I   Ida N Moore          , on oath state that I am ............ years of age and a citizen by  Blood  of the   Choctaw   Nation, and as such have been placed upon the final roll of the   Choctaw   Nation, by the Honorable Secretary of the Interior my final enrollment number being ............ ; that I am the lawful wife of   Lyman R Moore   , who is a citizen of the   Choctaw   Nation, and as such has been placed upon the final roll of said Nation by the Honorable Secretary of the Interior, his final enrollment number being ............ and that a   Male   child was born to me on the 20$^{th}$ day of   July   190 3; that said child has been named   Ethan Allen Moore  , and is now living.

                                        Ida N Moore

Witnesseth.
   Must be two  ⎫   E A Moore
   Witnesses who ⎬
   are Citizens. ⎭   *(Name Illegible)*

Subscribed and sworn to before me this  22  day of  Feb   190 5

                           James Bower
                                 Notary Public.

My commission expires:
   Sept 23 - 1907

# Applications for Enrollment of Choctaw Newborn
## Act of 1905 Volume IX

BIRTH AFFIDAVIT.

### DEPARTMENT OF THE INTERIOR.
### COMMISSION TO THE FIVE CIVILIZED TRIBES.

IN RE APPLICATION FOR ENROLLMENT, as a citizen of the Choctaw Nation, of Ethan Allen Moore, born on the 20th day of July, 1903

Name of Father: Lyman R Moore      a citizen of the Choctaw Nation.
Name of Mother: Ida N Moore        a citizen of the Choctaw Nation.

Postoffice   Spiro, Ind. Ter.

#### AFFIDAVIT OF MOTHER.

UNITED STATES OF AMERICA, Indian Territory,
Central DISTRICT.

I, Ida N Moore, on oath state that I am 27 years of age and a citizen by blood, of the Choctaw Nation; that I am the lawful wife of Lyman R Moore, who is a citizen, by blood of the Choctaw Nation; that a male child was born to me on 20th day of July, 1903; that said child has been named Ethan Allen Moore, and was living March 4, 1905.

                                             Ida N Moore
Witnesses To Mark:
{

Subscribed and sworn to before me this 30th day of March, 1905

                                             Wirt Franklin
                                             Notary Public.

#### AFFIDAVIT OF ATTENDING PHYSICIAN OR MID-WIFE.

UNITED STATES OF AMERICA, Indian Territory,
Central DISTRICT.

I, Charles H Mahar, a physician, on oath state that I attended on Mrs. Ida N Moore, wife of Lyman R Moore on the 20th day of July, 1903; that there was born to her on said date a male child; that said child was living March 4, 1905, and is said to have been named Ethan Allen Moore

                                             Charles H Mahar M.D.
Witnesses To Mark:
{

## Applications for Enrollment of Choctaw Newborn
## Act of 1905   Volume IX

Subscribed and sworn to before me this 30th day of March, 1905

        Wirt Franklin
        Notary Public.

---

Choc New Born 554
 John R. Brown, Jr  b. 10-16-02

              N. B. 554
      **COPY**
    Muskogee, Indian Territory, April 10, 1905.

John R. Brown,
 Midway, Indian Territory.

Dear Sir:

 There is inclosed you herewith for execution application for the enrollment of your infant child, John R. Brown Jr., born October 16, 1902.

 The affidavits heretofore filed with the Commission show the child was living on January 12, 1905. It is necessary, for the child to be enrolled, that he was living on March 4, 1905.

 In having these affidavits executed care should be exercised to see that all names are written in full, as they appear in the body of the affidavit, and in the event that either of the persons signing the affidavit are unable to write, signatures by mark must be attested by two witnesses. Each affidavit must be executed before a Notary Public and the notarial seal and signature of the officer must be attached to each separate affidavit.

      Respectfully,
      SIGNED
      *T. B. Needles.*
LM- - 10-45     Commissioner in Charge.

## Applications for Enrollment of Choctaw Newborn
## Act of 1905  Volume IX

Choctaw N.B. 554.

**COPY**

Muskogee, Indian Territory, April 21, 1905.

John R. Brown,
    Midway, Indian Territory.

Dear Sir:

    Receipt is hereby acknowledged of your letter of April 17, transmitting the affidavits of Henrietta Hodges Brown and H. G. Goben to the birth of John R. Brown, Jr., son of John R. and Henrietta Brown (Hodges), October 16, 1902, and the same have been filed with our records in the matter of the enrollment of said child.

    Replying to that portion of your letter in which you ask if your child born March 21, 1905[sic], may be enrolled, you are advised that the Act of Congress approved March 3, 1905, authorizes the Commission for a period of sixty days from that date to receive applications for the enrollment of children born to enrolled citizens by blood of the Choctaw and Chickasaw Nations, subsequent to September 25, 1902 and prior to March 4, 1905 and living on the latter date.

    You will therefore see that the Commission is without authority to enroll children born subsequent to March 4, 1905.

Respectfully,
SIGNED

*Tams Bixby*
Chairman.

---

7-NB-554

Muskogee, Indian Territory, May 22, 1906.

John R. Brown,
    Midway, Indian Territory.

Dear Sir:

    Receipt is hereby acknowledged of your letter of May 15, 1906, in which you state that in accordance with instructions issued in circulars, you sent the name of John R. Brown, Jr., a Choctaw, whose enrollment number is 536.

    In reply to your letter you are advised that John R. Brown, Jr., has already been enrolled as a new born citizen of the Choctaw Nation under the act of Congress approved March 3, 1905, and his enrollment as such was approved by the Secretary of the Interior,

# Applications for Enrollment of Choctaw Newborn
## Act of 1905   Volume IX

July 22, 1905 and it will not therefore be necessary to make further application for the enrollment of this child.

Respectfully,

Acting Commissioner.

---

## AFFIDAVIT OF ATTENDING PHYSICIAN OR MIDWIFE

UNITED STATES OF AMERICA }
INDIAN TERRITORY
Central   DISTRICT

I, H.G. Goben   a   Practicing Physician on oath state that I attended on Mrs. Henrietta Brown   wife of   John R. Brown on the   16   day of   October   , 190 2 , that there was born to her on said date a   Male child, that said child is now living, and is said to have been named   John R. Brown Jr.

H.G. Goben   M.D.

Subscribed and sworn to before me this, the   14   day of   January   190 5

CH Ewing

Notary Public.

WITNESSETH:
Must be two witnesses who are citizens and know the child.

(Name Illegible)

W.C. James

We hereby certify that we are well acquainted with   H.G. Goben   a   Physician   and know   him   to be reputable and of good standing in the community.

(Name Illegible)

W.C. James

Applications for Enrollment of Choctaw Newborn
Act of 1905   Volume IX

**NEW-BORN AFFIDAVIT.**

Number..............

## Choctaw Enrolling Commission.

IN THE MATTER OF THE APPLICATION FOR ENROLLMENT, as a citizen of the Choctaw Nation, of John R. Brown, Jr

born on the  16  day of  October  1902

Name of father  John R Brown  a citizen of  Choctaw
Nation final enrollment No ———  *nee Hodges*
Name of mother  Henrietta Brown  a citizen of  Choctaw
Nation final enrollment No  11998

Postoffice  Midway I.T.

**AFFIDAVIT OF MOTHER.**

UNITED STATES OF AMERICA,
  INDIAN TERRITORY,
  Central  DISTRICT

I  Henrietta Brown  on oath state that I am  25  years of age and a citizen by  blood  of the  Choctaw  Nation, and as such have been placed upon the final roll of the  Choctaw  Nation, by the Honorable Secretary of the Interior my final enrollment number being  11998  ; that I am the lawful wife of  John R. Brown  , who is a citizen of the  white  Nation, and as such has been placed upon the final roll of said Nation by the Honorable Secretary of the Interior, his final enrollment number being —— and that a  male  child was born to me on the 16 day of  October  1902 ; that said child has been named  John R Brown, Jr.  , and is now living.

Henrietta Brown

WITNESSETH:
  Must be two
  Witnesses who
  are Citizens.
  A.N. Mathews
  Wallis G Plummer

Subscribed and sworn to before me this  12<sup>th</sup>  day of  January  1905

W.A. Shoney
Notary Public.

My commission expires  Jan 11<sup>th</sup> 1909

# Applications for Enrollment of Choctaw Newborn
## Act of 1905   Volume IX

BIRTH AFFIDAVIT.

## DEPARTMENT OF THE INTERIOR.
## COMMISSION TO THE FIVE CIVILIZED TRIBES.

IN RE APPLICATION FOR ENROLLMENT, as a citizen of the   Choctaw   Nation, of John R Brown Jr, born on the 16 day of October, 1902

Name of Father: John R Brown    a citizen of the United States Nation.

Name of Mother: Henrietta Brown *formerly Henrietta Hodges*    a citizen of the Choctaw Nation.

Postoffice    Midway I.T.

### AFFIDAVIT OF MOTHER.

UNITED STATES OF AMERICA, Indian Territory,  
Central   DISTRICT.

I, Henrietta Brown *formerly Henrietta Hodges*, on oath state that I am 21 years of age and a citizen by blood, of the Choctaw Nation; that I am the lawful wife of John R Brown, who is a citizen, ~~by~~ .......... of the United States ~~Nation~~; that a male child was born to me on 16 day of October, 1902, that said child has been named John R Brown Jr, and is now living.

Henrietta Brown

Witnesses To Mark:

Subscribed and sworn to before me this 12 day of January, 1905.

CH Ewing  
Notary Public.

### AFFIDAVIT OF ATTENDING PHYSICIAN OR MID-WIFE.

UNITED STATES OF AMERICA, Indian Territory,  
Central   DISTRICT.

I, H G Goben, a physician, on oath state that I attended on Mrs. Henrietta Brown, wife of John R Brown on the 16 day of October, 1902; that there was born to her on said date a male child; that said child is now living and is said to have been named John R Brown Jr

H.G. Goben M.D.

# Applications for Enrollment of Choctaw Newborn
## Act of 1905   Volume IX

Witnesses To Mark:

{

Subscribed and sworn to before me this 12 day of January, 1905.

CH Ewing
Notary Public.

**BIRTH AFFIDAVIT.**

### DEPARTMENT OF THE INTERIOR.
### COMMISSION TO THE FIVE CIVILIZED TRIBES.

IN RE APPLICATION FOR ENROLLMENT, as a citizen of the Choctaw Nation, of John R Brown, born on the 16$^{th}$ day of Oct, 1902

Name of Father: John R Brown        a citizen of the _____ Nation.
Name of Mother: Henrietta Hodges Brown    a citizen of the Choctaw Nation.

Postoffice   Midway I.T.

**AFFIDAVIT OF MOTHER.**

UNITED STATES OF AMERICA, Indian Territory,
Central                         DISTRICT.

I, Henrietta Hodges Brown, on oath state that I am 21 years of age and a citizen by blood, of the Choctaw Nation; that I am the lawful wife of John R Brown, who is a citizen, by _____ of the _____ Nation; that a male child was born to me on 16th day of Oct, 1902; that said child has been named John R Brown, and was living March 4, 1905.

Henrietta Hodges Brown

Witnesses To Mark:

{

Subscribed and sworn to before me this 8th day of April, 1905

A T West
Notary Public.

## Applications for Enrollment of Choctaw Newborn
## Act of 1905   Volume IX

### AFFIDAVIT OF ATTENDING PHYSICIAN OR MID-WIFE.

UNITED STATES OF AMERICA, Indian Territory,  
Central         DISTRICT.

I,   H G Goben   , a  Physician   , on oath state that I attended on Mrs.   Henrietta Hodges Brown  , wife of   J R Brown      on the  16th day of   Oct  , 1902; that there was born to her on said date a      male     child; that said child was living March 4, 1905, and is said to have been named John R Brown

                                          H G Goben M.D.

Witnesses To Mark:
{

    Subscribed and sworn to before me this  8th   day of      April     , 1905

                                A T West
                                      Notary Public.

---

**BIRTH AFFIDAVIT.**

### DEPARTMENT OF THE INTERIOR.
### COMMISSION TO THE FIVE CIVILIZED TRIBES.

**IN RE APPLICATION FOR ENROLLMENT,** as a citizen of the     Choctaw     Nation, of John R Brown Jr   , born on the  16$^{th}$   day of   October   , 1902

Name of Father:  John R Brown          a citizen of the United States ~~Nation~~.  
Name of Mother:  Henrietta Brown (Hodges)    a citizen of the   Choctaw    Nation.

                          Postoffice     Midway I.T.

---

### AFFIDAVIT OF MOTHER.

UNITED STATES OF AMERICA, Indian Territory,  
Central         DISTRICT.

I,   Henrietta Brown (Hodges)   , on oath state that I am  21    years of age and a citizen by     blood   , of the    Choctaw    Nation; that I am the lawful wife of John R Brown   , who is a citizen, by _____ of the United States ~~Nation~~; that a male    child was born to me on  16$^{th}$    day of   October   , 1902; that said child has been named   John R Brown Jr   , and was living March 4, 1905.

                              Henrietta Hodges Brown

Witnesses To Mark:
{

# Applications for Enrollment of Choctaw Newborn
## Act of 1905  Volume IX

Subscribed and sworn to before me this 17th day of April, 1905

A T West
Notary Public.

---

**AFFIDAVIT OF ATTENDING PHYSICIAN OR MID-WIFE.**

UNITED STATES OF AMERICA, Indian Territory,
Central  DISTRICT.

I, H G Goben, a Physician, on oath state that I attended on Mrs. Henrietta Brown (Hodges), wife of J R Brown on the 16$^{th}$ day of October, 1902; that there was born to her on said date a male child; that said child was living March 4, 1905, and is said to have been named John R Brown Jr.

H G Goben M.D.

Witnesses To Mark:

Subscribed and sworn to before me this 17th day of April, 1905

A T West
Notary Public.

---

Choc New Born 555
 Hellena Lansyann Gardner  b. 9-5-04

BIRTH AFFIDAVIT.

### DEPARTMENT OF THE INTERIOR.
### COMMISSION TO THE FIVE CIVILIZED TRIBES.

IN RE APPLICATION FOR ENROLLMENT, as a citizen of the Choctaw Nation, of Hellena Lansyann Gardner, born on the 5$^{th}$ day of September, 1904

Name of Father: James Dolphin Gardner  a citizen of the Choctaw Nation.
Name of Mother: Flora Ellen Gardner  a citizen of the non-citizen Nation.

Postoffice  Wynnwood

# Applications for Enrollment of Choctaw Newborn
## Act of 1905  Volume IX

### AFFIDAVIT OF MOTHER.

UNITED STATES OF AMERICA, Indian Territory,　}
　　Southern　　　　　　DISTRICT.

　　I,　Flora Ellen Gardner　, on oath state that I am　20　years of age and a citizen *of*　United States　, *but of no tribe or nation* ~~Nation~~; that I am the lawful wife of　James Dolphin Gardner　, who is a citizen, by Blood　of the Choctaw　Nation; that a　female　child was born to me on　5th　day of September　, 1904; that said child has been named　Hellena Lansyann Gardner　, and was living March 4, 1905.

　　　　　　　　　　　　　　　　　Flora Ellen Gardner

Witnesses To Mark:
{ James Dolphin Gardner
{ S.E. Hays

　　Subscribed and sworn to before me this　28th　day of　March　, 1905

　　　　　　　　　　　　　　　JT Wheeler
　　　　　　　　　　　　　　　　Notary Public.

---

### AFFIDAVIT OF ATTENDING PHYSICIAN OR MID-WIFE.

UNITED STATES OF AMERICA, Indian Territory,　}
　　Southern　　　　　　DISTRICT.

　　I,　A J Hoover　, a practicing physician　, on oath state that I attended on Mrs.　Flora Ellen Gardner　, wife of　James Dolphin Gardner　on the　5th　day of　September　, 1904; that there was born to her on said date a　female　child; that said child was living March 4, 1905, and is said to have been named　Hellena Lansyann Gardner

　　　　　　　　　　　　　　　Andrew J Hoover M.D.

Witnesses To Mark:
{

　　Subscribed and sworn to before me this　27th　day of　March　, 1905

　　　　　　　　　　　　　　　JT Wheeler
　　　　　　　　　　　　　　　　Notary Public.

# Applications for Enrollment of Choctaw Newborn
## Act of 1905 Volume IX

*(The affidavit below typed as given.)*

Southern District §
Indian Territory §

James W. Gardner, first being duly sworn deposes and says:

My name is James W. Gardner, my age 56 years my occupation farmer, and stock raiser and my postoffice, Wynnewood, I.T.

I am the father of James Adolphus Gardner, a Choctaw Indian by blood, who is enrolled as James Dolphin Gardner, his middle name having been by mistake spelled Dolphin instead of Adolphus as it should have been.

His Marriage License were issued to him with his proper enitials J.A., and not with the enitials that would appear on the rolls of the tribe or of the Commission.

However, the J.A. Gardner in the licenae to marry Flora Ellen Francis issued on Nov. 12th.1903, and under which authority they were married on the 15th. day of November, 1903, by J.W. Seeton, is the identical person who is known on the rolls of the Commission to the Five Civilized Tribes and the Rolls of the Nation as James Dolphin Gardner.

James W Gardner

Subscribed and sworn to before me this the 13th. day of April, 1905.

J.T. Wheeler
Notary Public.

---

*(The affidavit below typed as given.)*

Southern District §
§
Indian Territory §

James Adolphus Gardner, being first duly sworn deposes and says:

My name is James Adolphus Gardner, my age 21 years and my place of residence Wynnwood, I.T.; I am a Choctaw Indian By blood and enrolled under the Act of Congress approved March 3, 1905, as number name of James Dolphin Gardner, my name having been by mistake placed on the rolls of the tribe as Dolphin instead of Adolphus.

My marriage certificate or licens was issued to me in the name of J.A.Gardner, my proper enitials being J.A., and not J.D., as would appear on the rolls of the Commission or the tribe.

# Applications for Enrollment of Choctaw Newborn
## Act of 1905 Volume IX

I, James Adolphus Gardner, am the identical person enrolled as James Dolphin Gardner, that is James Dolphin Gardner and J.A.Gardner are one and the same person.

James Adolphus Gardner

Subscribed and sworn to before me this the 18th. day of April, 1905.

JT Wheeler<br>Notary Public.

---

## CERTIFICATE OF RECORD OF MARRIAGE

United States of America :
    Indian Territory     :   sct.
Southern   District     :

I, C. M. Campbell, Clerk of the United States Court, in the Territory and District aforesaid DO HEREBY CERTIFY, that the License for and Certificate of Marriage of Mr. J. A. Gardner and M Flora E. Francis were filed in my office in said Territory and District the 30th. day of November, A.D. 1903, and duly recorded in Book G. of Marriage Record, Page 506

    Witness my hand and seal of said Court, at Ardmore, this 30 day of Nov. A.D. 1903.
        C. M. Campbell
            CLERK.

---

Return this License to the United States Clerk at Ardmore, that it may be recorded, when it will be mailed to the proper address.

F I L E D
AT ARDMORE
Nov. 30 1903 8AM
C.M.Campbell, Clerk
and Exofficio Reocrder[sic]
District No 21 Ind.Ter.

# Applications for Enrollment of Choctaw Newborn
# Act of 1905   Volume IX

*(The license and certificate below typed as given.)*

Literal Copy of Marriage License and Certificate of
Marriag of J.A. Gardner and Flora Allen Francis.
*****************************************************************

No person is authorized to perform the Marriage Ceremony in the Indian Territory unless the proper credentials have first been in the Clerks office.

-----

## MARRIFE LICENSE

No. 2379

United States of America :  TO ANY PERSON AUTHORIZED BY LAW
 Indian Territory, : SS SOLEMNIZE MARRIAGE, GREETING:
 Southern District. :

YOU ARE HEREBY COMMANDED to solemnize the Rite and publish the Banns of Matrimony between Mr. J. A. Gardner, of Wynnewood, in the Indian Territory, age 20 years, and Miss Flora Ellen Francis, of Wynnewood, in the Indian Territory, aged 19 years, according to law; and do you officially sign and return this license to the parties therein named.

         WITNESS my hand and official Seal, this 12th.
         day of November, A.D. 1903.

         C.M. Campbell
(   Seal of Court   )    Clerk of the United States
         Coury.
         By S.H. Wootton, Day.

-----

## CERTIFICATE OF MARRIAGE

United States of America:
 Indian Territory : SS
 Southern District. :

        I, J.W. Seeton, M.G. do hereby certify that on the fifteenth day of November, A.D. 1903, I did duly and according to law, as commanded in the foregoing license, solemnize the Rite and publish the Banns of Matrimony between the parties therein named.

Witness my hand this 15th. day of Nov. A.D. 1903.

## Applications for Enrollment of Choctaw Newborn
## Act of 1905 Volume IX

      My credentials are recorded in the office of the Clerk of the United States Court in the Indian Territory, Southern District, at Ardmore, Book A page 123 & 124.

                                      J.W. Seeton
                                        M.C.

---

      NOTE.(a) This License and Certificate of Marriage must be retirned to the office of the Clerk of the United States Court in the Indian Territory at Ardmore, Indian Territory within sixty days from the date thereof, or the party to whom the license was issued will be liable in the sum of ONE HUNDERD DOALARS ($100).

************************************************************************
**********************************************************************

United States of America,
   INDIAN TERRITORY
Southern District.

                      I, J. T. Wheeler, a notary public in and for the Southern District of the Indian Territory do hereby certify that the above and foregoing is a true and literal copy of the License, Marriage Certificate and Certificate of Record of same, as exhibited to me by J.A. Gardner and now in his possession.
      In testimony whereof I have hereunto set my hand and seal of office as such notary public at Wynnewood, Indian Territory in said District and Territory this the 13th. day of April, 1905.

                                        J T Wheeler
                                        Notary Public.

---

$W^m O.B.$

COMMISSIONERS:
TAMS BIXBY,
THOMAS B. NEEDLES,
C.R. BRECKINBRIDGE.

**DEPARTMENT OF THE INTERIOR,**
**COMMISSIONER TO THE FIVE CIVILIZED TRIBES.**

REFER IN REPLY TO THE FOLLOWING:

N. B. 555

WM. O. BEALL
Secretary

          ADDRESS ONLY THE
  COMMISSION TO THE FIVE CIVILIZED TRIBES.

                                  Muskogee, Indian Territory, April 8, 1905.

James Dolphin Gardner,
      Wynnewood, Indian Territory.

Dear Sir:

      You are hereby advised that before the application for the enrollment[sic] of your child, Hellena Lausyann[sic] Gardner, can be finally disposed of, it will [sic]

## Applications for Enrollment of Choctaw Newborn
## Act of 1905   Volume IX

necessary that you furnish the Commission with either the original or a certified copy of the license and certificate of your marriage to Flora Ellen Gardner.

Please attend to this matter at once.

Respectfully,

T.B. Needles<br>Commissioner in Charge.

---

**COPY**

7 NB 555

Muskogee, Indian Territory, April 19, 1905.

James Dolphin Gardner,
  Wynnewood, Indian Territory.

Dear Sir:

Receipt is hereby acknowledged of the affidavits of James M. Gardner and James Adolphus Gardner and a certified copy of a marriage license and certificate between James Adolphus Gardner and Flora Ellen Francis which you offer in support of the application for the enrollment of your child Helena[sic] Lawsyann[sic] Gardner and the same have been filed with our records in this case.

Respectfully,<br>SIGNED

*Tams Bixby*<br>Chairman.

---

Choc New Born 556
  Wallace Mitchell Betts  b. 5-4-04
  Ida Florence Betts  b. 4-13-03
  No. 2 Dismissed 1-22-06

# Applications for Enrollment of Choctaw Newborn
## Act of 1905  Volume IX

7-4398

Muskogee, Indian Territory, March 20, 1905.

David C. Betts,
    Atoka, Indian Territory.

Dear Sir:

    Receipt is hereby acknowledged of the affidavits of Emma Betts and I. A. Briggs M. D., to the birth of Wallace Mitchell Betts, son of David C. and Emma Betts, May 4, 1904, and the same have been filed with our records as an application for the enrollment of said child.

                  Respectfully,

                                  Chairman.

---

7-4398

Muskogee, Indian Territory, March 22, 1905.

David C. Betts,
    Atoka, Indian Territory.

Dear Sir:

    Receipt is hereby acknowledged of the affidavit of Emma Betts to the birth of Ida Florence Betts, infant daughter of David C. and Emma Betts, April 13, 1903.

    It appears from the affidavit of the mother that said child died July 27, 1903, and under the provisions of the act of Congress approved March 3, 1905, the Commission was authorized for a period of sixty days from that date to receive applications for the enrollment of children born to enrolled citizens by blood of the Choctaw and Chickasaw Nations between September 25, 1902, and March 4, 1905 and living on the latter date. You will therefore see that the Commission is without authority to enroll children born to citizens of the Choctaw and Chickasaw Nations subsequent to September 25, 1902, who were not living on March 4, 1905.

                  Respectfully,

                                  Chairman.

## Applications for Enrollment of Choctaw Newborn
## Act of 1905   Volume IX

7-NB-556.

**COPY**

Muskogee, Indian Territory, January 22, 1906.

David C. Betts,
    Atoka, Indian Territory.

Dear Sir:

    You are hereby advised that on January 22, 1906, the Commissioner to the Five Civilized Tribes dismissed the application for the enrollment of your child, Ida Florence Betts, as a citizen by blood of the Choctaw Nation, for the reason that she died prior to March 4, 1905.

Respectfully,
SIGNED

*Tams Bixby*
Chairman.

---

**BIRTH AFFIDAVIT.**

**DEPARTMENT OF THE INTERIOR.**
**COMMISSION TO THE FIVE CIVILIZED TRIBES.**

---

**IN RE APPLICATION FOR ENROLLMENT**, as a citizen of the Choctaw Nation, of Ida Florence Betts, born on the 13th day of April, 1903

Name of Father: David C Betts     a citizen of the Choctaw Nation.
Name of Mother: Emma Betts     a citizen of the Choctaw Nation.

Postoffice    Atoka I.T.

---

**AFFIDAVIT OF MOTHER.**

UNITED STATES OF AMERICA, Indian Territory,
    Central      DISTRICT.

    I, Emma Betts, on oath state that I am 29 years of age and a citizen by Intermarriage, of the Choctaw Nation; that I am the lawful wife of David C. Betts, who is a citizen, by blood of the Choctaw Nation; that a female child was born to me on 13th day of April, 1903; that said child has been named Ida Florence Betts, and ~~was living March 4, 1905~~. *died July 27, 1903*

Emma Betts

Witnesses To Mark:

## Applications for Enrollment of Choctaw Newborn
## Act of 1905  Volume IX

Subscribed and sworn to before me this 15<sup>th</sup> day of March, 1905

W.H. Angell
Notary Public.

**NEW-BORN AFFIDAVIT.**

Number..............

...Choctaw Enrolling Commission...

IN THE MATTER OF THE APPLICATION FOR ENROLLMENT, as a citizen of the Choctaw Nation, of Wallace M Betts

born on the 4<sup>th</sup> day of May 190 4

Name of father David C. Betts  a citizen of Choctaw
Nation final enrollment No. 12264
Name of mother Emma Betts  a citizen of Choctaw
Nation final enrollment No. 426

Postoffice Atoka IT

**AFFIDAVIT OF MOTHER.**

UNITED STATES OF AMERICA
INDIAN TERRITORY
   Central      DISTRICT

I Emma Betts, on oath state that I am 29 years of age and a citizen by marriage of the Choctaw Nation, and as such have been placed upon the final roll of the Choctaw Nation, by the Honorable Secretary of the Interior my final enrollment number being 426 ; that I am the lawful wife of David C. Betts, who is a citizen of the Choctaw Nation, and as such has been placed upon the final roll of said Nation by the Honorable Secretary of the Interior, his final enrollment number being 12264 and that a Male child was born to me on the 4<sup>th</sup> day of May 190 4; that said child has been named Wallace M Betts, and is now living.

Emma Betts

Witnesseth.
  Must be two  } Bettie Betts
  Witnesses who
  are Citizens.   R.O. Sumter

## Applications for Enrollment of Choctaw Newborn
## Act of 1905 Volume IX

Subscribed and sworn to before me this 23$^d$ day of February 190 5

A.E. Folsom
Notary Public.

My commission expires:
Jan 9 - 1909

*Affidavit of Attending Physician or Midwife*

UNITED STATES OF AMERICA,  
   INDIAN TERRITORY,  
Central     DISTRICT

I, Mrs. M.E. Baxter a Mid wife on oath state that I attended on Mrs. Emma Betts wife of David C. Betts on the 4$^{th}$ day of May, 190 4, that there was born to her on said date a male child, that said child is now living, and is said to have been named Wallace M. Baxter[sic]

M.E. Baxter     M. D.

Subscribed and sworn to before me this the 23 day of February 1905

A.E. Folsom
Notary Public.

WITNESSETH:

Must be two witnesses who are citizens and know the child.
- Bettie Betts
- R.O. Sumter

We hereby certify that we are well acquainted with Mrs. M.E. Baxter a mid wife and know her to be reputable and of good standing in the community.

Must be two citizen witnesses.
- Bettie Betts
- Robt O. Sumter

## Applications for Enrollment of Choctaw Newborn
## Act of 1905   Volume IX

BIRTH AFFIDAVIT.

### DEPARTMENT OF THE INTERIOR.
### COMMISSION TO THE FIVE CIVILIZED TRIBES.

IN RE APPLICATION FOR ENROLLMENT, as a citizen of the  Choctaw  Nation, of Wallace Mitchell Betts  , born on the  $4^{th}$  day of  May  , 1904

Name of Father: David C Betts       a citizen of the  Choctaw  Nation.
Name of Mother: Emma Betts       a citizen of the  Choctaw  Nation.

Postoffice   Atoka Ind Ter

### AFFIDAVIT OF MOTHER.

UNITED STATES OF AMERICA, Indian Territory, }
Central        DISTRICT. }

I,  Emma Betts  , on oath state that I am  29  years of age and a citizen by intermarriage  , of the  Choctaw  Nation; that I am the lawful wife of  David C Betts  , who is a citizen, by  blood  of the  Choctaw  Nation; that a male  child was born to me on  $4^{th}$  day of  May  , 1904; that said child has been named  Wallace Mitchell Betts  , and was living March 4, 1905.

Emma Betts

Witnesses To Mark:
{

Subscribed and sworn to before me this  $15^{th}$  day of  March  , 1905

W.H. Angell
Notary Public.

### AFFIDAVIT OF ATTENDING PHYSICIAN OR MID-WIFE.

UNITED STATES OF AMERICA, Indian Territory, }
Central        DISTRICT. }

I,  I. A. Briggs M.D.  , a physician  , on oath state that I attended on Mrs.  Emma Betts  , wife of  David C Betts  on the  $4^{th}$  day of  May  , 1904; that there was born to her on said date a  male  child; that said child was living March 4, 1905, and is said to have been named  Wallace Mitchell Betts

I.A. Briggs M.D.

Witnesses To Mark:
{

# Applications for Enrollment of Choctaw Newborn
## Act of 1905   Volume IX

Subscribed and sworn to before me this 15$^{th}$ day of     March    , 1905

W.S. Fanner
Notary Public.

---

Choc New Born 557
Amy McDaniel  b. 11-25-02

BIRTH AFFIDAVIT.

### DEPARTMENT OF THE INTERIOR.
### COMMISSION TO THE FIVE CIVILIZED TRIBES.

**IN RE APPLICATION FOR ENROLLMENT,** as a citizen of the    Choctaw    Nation, of Amy M$^c$Daniel    , born on the 25th day of November , 1902

Name of Father: W$^m$ McDaniel         a citizen of the  Choctaw  Nation.
Name of Mother: Lucetta McDaniel       a citizen of the  Choctaw  Nation.

Postoffice    Ada, I.T.

---

**AFFIDAVIT OF MOTHER.**

UNITED STATES OF AMERICA, Indian Territory,
Southern              DISTRICT.

I,  W$^m$ M$^c$Daniel    , on oath state that I am   50   years of age and a citizen by marriage   , of the   Choctaw   Nation; that I am the lawful ~~wife of~~ *Husband of Lucetta McDaniel, deceased*   , who ~~is~~ *was* a citizen, by blood   of the   Choctaw Nation; that a    female    child was born to ~~me~~ *her* on   25th day of November  , 1902; that said child has been named    Amy M$^c$Daniel    , and was living March 4, 1905.

William M$^c$Daniel

Witnesses To Mark:
{

Subscribed and sworn to before me this  29th day of   March    , 1905

H.C. Miller
Notary Public.

## Applications for Enrollment of Choctaw Newborn
## Act of 1905 Volume IX

BIRTH AFFIDAVIT.                  *No. 37*

**DEPARTMENT OF THE INTERIOR.**
**COMMISSION TO THE FIVE CIVILIZED TRIBES.**

*Choctaw Delinquent (Illegible)*

                                                                                                                Choctaw

      IN RE APPLICATION FOR ENROLLMENT, as a citizen of the ~~Amy M°Daniel~~ Nation, of   Amy M°Daniel  , born on the   25  day of   November  , 1902

Name of Father: William M°Daniel       a citizen of the   Choctaw  Nation.
Name of Mother: Lucetta M°Daniel      a citizen of the   Choctaw  Nation.

                                  Postoffice    Ada, I.T.

---

### AFFIDAVIT OF MOTHER.

UNITED STATES OF AMERICA, Indian Territory, ⎫
   Sou               DISTRICT. ⎭

      I,   William M°Daniel  , on oath state that I am   fifty  years of age and a citizen by   Inter-marriage  , of the   Choctaw  Nation; that I am the lawful ~~wife~~ *husband* of   Lucetta McDaniel, decased[sic] *since 13 Dec 1904*  , who is a citizen, by blood   of the  Choctaw  Nation; that a   Female  child was born to me on 25$^{th}$   day of   Nov  , 1902, that said child has been named   Amy M°Daniel  , and is now living.

                                                                       W$^m$ M°Daniel

Witnesses To Mark:
{

      Subscribed and sworn to before me this   6  day of   Jan  , 1905.

                                                    W H Bealey
                                                         Notary Public.
                            My commission expires June 8$^{th}$ 1908

---

### AFFIDAVIT OF ATTENDING PHYSICIAN OR MID-WIFE.

UNITED STATES OF AMERICA, Indian Territory, ⎫
   Southern          DISTRICT. ⎭

      I,   Dr. J.L. Clark  , a   phisicion[sic]  , on oath state that I attended on Mrs.   Lucetta M°Daniel  , wife of   William M°Daniel  on the   25$^{th}$  day of   November  , 1902; that there was born to her on said date a   Female  child; that said child is now living and is said to have been named Amy M°Daniel

                                                   Dr. J. L. Clark

# Applications for Enrollment of Choctaw Newborn
## Act of 1905 Volume IX

Witnesses To Mark:
{

Subscribed and sworn to before me this 6$^{th}$ day of Jan, 1905.

W H Bealey
Notary Public.
My commission expires June 8$^{th}$ 1908

**BIRTH AFFIDAVIT.**

### DEPARTMENT OF THE INTERIOR.
### COMMISSION TO THE FIVE CIVILIZED TRIBES.

IN RE APPLICATION FOR ENROLLMENT, as a citizen of the Choctaw Nation, of Amy M$^c$Daniel, born on the 12$^{th}$ day of November, 1902

Name of Father: William McDaniel — a citizen of the Choctaw Nation.
Name of Mother: Lucetta McDaniel — a citizen of the Choctaw Nation.

Postoffice Ada, Indian Territory

**AFFIDAVIT OF MOTHER.**

UNITED STATES OF AMERICA, Indian Territory,
Southern DISTRICT.

I, W$^m$ M$^c$Daniel, on oath state that I am (50) fifty years of age and a citizen by marriage of the Choctaw Nation; that I am the lawful ~~wife of~~ Husband of Lucetta McDaniel, deceased, who ~~is was a~~ citizen, by blood of the Choctaw Nation; that a female child was born to ~~me~~ her on 12$^{th}$ day of November, 1902; that said child has been named Amy M$^c$Daniel, and was living March 4, 1905. That Lucetta M$^c$Daniel my wife died on the 13$^{th}$ day of December 1904

William M$^c$Daniel

Witnesses To Mark:
{

Subscribed and sworn to before me this 28th day of March, 1905

My Commission expires
Sept 28 - 1907

Robt. Wimlush
Notary Public.

# Applications for Enrollment of Choctaw Newborn
## Act of 1905  Volume IX

**AFFIDAVIT OF ATTENDING PHYSICIAN OR MID-WIFE.**

UNITED STATES OF AMERICA, ~~Indian Territory~~,
*Jackson County*
~~Southern~~          ~~DISTRICT~~.

I, J. L. Cark[sic], a Physician, on oath state that I attended on Mrs. Lucetta M$^c$Daniel, wife of William M$^c$Daniel on the 25$^{th}$ day of November, 1902; that there was born to her on said date a female child; that said child was living March 4, 1905, and is said to have been named Amy M$^c$Daniel

James L Clark

Witnesses To Mark:

Subscribed and sworn to before me this 25$^{th}$ day of March, 1905

My Commission expires December 7$^{th}$, 1907.      *(Illegible)* F. Rose
                                                     Notary Public.
                                    Notary Public Jackson County, Missouri.

---

7-50 - *557*
Muskogee, Indian Territory, April 17, 1905.

William McDaniel,
    Tyrola, Indian Territory.

Dear Sir:

Receipt is hereby acknowledged of the joint affidavit of Albert Perry and I. N. McClure to the birth of Amy McDaniel, daughter of William and Lucetta McDaniel November 25, 1902, and the same have been filed with our records as an application for the enrollment of said child.

Respectfully,

Chairman.

# Applications for Enrollment of Choctaw Newborn
## Act of 1905   Volume IX

**COPY**  N. B. 557

Muskogee, Indian Territory, April 8, 1905.

William McDaniel,
    Ada, Indian Territory.

Dear Sir:

    It appears from the papers heretofored[sic] filed with the Commission that your wife, Lucetta McDaniel, the mother of my McDaniel, is dead. It is therefore necessary that you secure the affidavits of two persons who have actual knowledge of the fact, that the child was born, was living on March 4, 1905, and that Lucetta McDaniel, was her mother.

    This matter should be given your immediate attention.

Respectfully,

SIGNED

*T. B. Needles.*
Commissioner in Charge.

---

THE UNITED STATES OF AMERICA @

Indian Territory      @    In the matter of the Application of

Southern District.      @   Amy McDaniel for enrollment as a citizen

                                   @   of the Choctaw Tribe of Indians.

    Albert Perry and I. N. McClure, each being by me duly sworn upon their oaths say that they were each and both acquainted with Mrs. Lucetta McDaniel in her lifetime; that she died on the 13th day of December, 1904 that she was the mother of Amy McDaniel, the applicant herein; that said Amy McDaniel was born unto the said Mrs. Lucetta McDaniel on the 25th day of November, 1902 and that the said Amy McDaniel was living on the 4th day of March, 1905, and is still living; affiants further say that the said Lucetta McDaniel was a member of the Choctaw Tribe of Indians and duly enrolled as such, and was the lawful wife of William McDaniel; that this affidavit is made from actual knowledge and not upon information and belief.

Albert Perry

I. N. M$^c$Clure

## Applications for Enrollment of Choctaw Newborn
## Act of 1905   Volume IX

Subscribed and sworn to before me this the 11th day of April A.D. 1905.

                                              Robt Wimlush
                                              Notary Public within and for the
                                              Southern District, Indian Territory.

My Commission expires
Sept. 28, 1907.

---

Choc New Born 558
        William Hamlin   b. 9-21-03

                                                            7-2261

                          Muskogee, Indian Territory, June 2, 1904.

Israel Hamlin,
        Wister, Indian Territory.

Dear Sir:

        Receipt is hereby acknowledged of the affidavits of Sallie and Israel Hamlin, relative to the birth of your infant son, William Hamlin, September 21, 1903, which it is presumed have been forwarded as an application for the enrollment of said child as a citizen by blood of the Choctaw Nation.

        You are informed that under the provisions of the Act of Congress approved July 1, 1902, the Commission is now without authority to receive or consider the original application for enrollment of any person whomsoever as a citizen of the Choctaw or Chickasaw Nation.

                                      Respectfully,

                                                      Chairman.

# Applications for Enrollment of Choctaw Newborn
## Act of 1905   Volume IX

**COPY**

N. B. 558

Muskogee, Indian Territory, April 8, 1905.

Israel Hamlin,
    Wister, Indian Territory.

Dear Sir:

    There is inclosed you herewith for execution application for the enrollment of your infant child, William Hamlin, born September 21, 1903.

    The affidavits heretofore filed with the Commission show the child was living on May 27, 1904. It is necessary, for the child to be enrolled, that he was living on March 4, 1905. Please insert the age of the mother in space provided for the purpose.

    In the above mentioned affidavits, the one of the attending physician or midwife was filled out by the father. If there was no one in attendance at the birth of said child, it will be necessary that you secure the affidavits of two persons who have actual knowledge of the fact, that the child was born, was living on March 4, 1905, and that Sallie Hamlin was his mother.

    In having these affidavits executed care should be exercised to see that all names are written in full, as they appear in the body of the affidavit, and in the event that either of the persons signing the affidavit are unable to write, signatures by mark must be attested by two witnesses. Each affidavit must be executed before a Notary Public and the notarial seal and signature of the officer must be attached to each separate affidavit.

                                      Respectfully,
                                        SIGNED

                                      *T. B. Needles.*

LM 8-30.                                Commissioner in Charge.

---

7 N.B. 558.

Muskogee, Indian Territory, May 4, 1905.

Israel Hamlin,
    Wister, Indian Territory.

Dear Sir:

    Receipt is hereby acknowledged of the affidavits of Sallie Hamlin and Jane Rose to the birth of William Hamlin, son of Israel and Sallie Hamlin, September 21, 1903, and the same have been filed with our records in the matter of the enrollment of said child.

## Applications for Enrollment of Choctaw Newborn
## Act of 1905 Volume IX

Respectfully,

Chairman.

**BIRTH AFFIDAVIT.**

DEPARTMENT OF THE INTERIOR.
**COMMISSION TO THE FIVE CIVILIZED TRIBES.**

IN RE APPLICATION FOR ENROLLMENT, as a citizen of the Choctaw Nation, of William Hamlin, born on the 21$^{st}$ day of September, 1903

Name of Father: Isreal Hamlin - dec'd.   a citizen of the Choctaw Nation.
Name of Mother: Sallie Hamlin   a citizen of the Choctaw Nation.

Postoffice   Wister, Ind. Ter.

**AFFIDAVIT OF MOTHER.**

UNITED STATES OF AMERICA, Indian Territory, } DISTRICT.

I, Sallie Hamlin, on oath state that I am about 25 years of age and a citizen by blood, of the Choctaw Nation; that I am the lawful wife of Isreal Hamlin, who is a citizen, by blood of the Choctaw Nation; that a male child was born to me on 21$^{st}$ day of September, 1903; that said child has been named William Hamlin, and was living March 4, 1905.

                                        her
                                Sallie x Hamlin
Witnesses To Mark:        mark
{ *(Name Illegible)*
  *(Name Illegible)*

Subscribed and sworn to before me this 1$^{st}$ day of April, 1905

                              Lacey P Bobo
                                Notary Public.

## Applications for Enrollment of Choctaw Newborn
## Act of 1905    Volume IX

**AFFIDAVIT OF ATTENDING PHYSICIAN OR MID-WIFE.**

UNITED STATES OF AMERICA, Indian Territory,
................................................ DISTRICT.

*visited*

I,   Henry Jackson   , a  Choctaw citizen   , on oath state that I ~~attended on~~ Mrs.   Sally Hamlin   , wife of  Isreal Hamlin   on the  21st  day of  September, 1903; that there was born to her on said date a   male    child; that said child was living March 4, 1905, and is said to have been named William Hamlin

Henry Jackson

Witnesses To Mark:

Subscribed and sworn to before me this  1st  day of   April    , 1905

Lacey P Bobo
Notary Public.

*Sallie Hamlin's roll # is 6554*

# NEW BORN AFFIDAVIT

No ..................

## CHOCTAW ENROLLING COMMISSION

IN THE MATTER OF THE APPLICATION FOR ENROLLMENT as a citizen of the  Choctaw Nation, of    William Hamlin        born on the  21   day of  September    190 3

Name of father   Isreael[sic] Hamlin       a citizen of    Choctaw    Nation, final enrollment No.  ~~Sallie Hamlin~~  6553
Name of mother   Sallie Hamlin       a citizen of    Choctaw    Nation, final enrollment No.   6554

Wister I.T.                    Postoffice.

# Applications for Enrollment of Choctaw Newborn
## Act of 1905   Volume IX

**AFFIDAVIT OF MOTHER**

UNITED STATES OF AMERICA }
INDIAN TERRITORY }
DISTRICT   Central

I   Sallie Hamlin   , on oath state that I am   25   years of age and a citizen by   blood   of the   Choctaw   Nation, and as such have been placed upon the final roll of the   Choctaw   Nation, by the Honorable Secretary of the Interior my final enrollment number being   6554 ; that I ~~am~~ *was* the lawful wife of   Isreael[sic] Hamlin , who is a citizen of the   Choctaw   Nation, and as such has been placed upon the final roll of said Nation by the Honorable Secretary of the Interior, his final enrollment number being   6553   and that a   male   child was born to me on the   21   day of   September   190 3; that said child has been named   William Hamlin   , and is now living.

WITNESSETH:
Must be two witnesses { Forbis Mackey
who are citizens        { Israel Folsom

her
Sallie x Hamlin
mark

Subscribed and sworn to before me this, the   18   day of   February   , 190 5

James Bower
Notary Public.

My Commission Expires:
Sept 23 - 1907

## *Affidavit of Attending Physician or Midwife*

UNITED STATES OF AMERICA, }
INDIAN TERRITORY, }
Central   DISTRICT

I,   Jane Rose   a   midwife   on oath state that I attended on Mrs. Sallie Hamlin   wife of   Israel Hamlin (deceased) on the   21   day of   September , 190 3, that there was born to her on said date a   male   child, that said child is now living, and is said to have been named   William Hamlin

Jane Rose midwife       M. D.

Subscribed and sworn to before me this the   25   day of   Feb   1905

J J Riggs
Notary Public.

WITNESSETH:
Must be two witnesses   { Aaron Harris
who are citizens and    {
know the child.         { George Freeman

## Applications for Enrollment of Choctaw Newborn
## Act of 1905   Volume IX

We hereby certify that we are well acquainted with    Jane Rose    a    midwife    and know    her    to be reputable and of good standing in the community.

Must be two citizen witnesses. { Aaron Harris / George Freeman }

**BIRTH AFFIDAVIT.**

### DEPARTMENT OF THE INTERIOR.
### COMMISSION TO THE FIVE CIVILIZED TRIBES.

IN RE APPLICATION FOR ENROLLMENT, as a citizen of the    Choctaw    Nation, of    William Hamlin    , born on the   21"   day of   September   , 1903

Name of Father: Israel Hamlin     a citizen of the   Choctaw   Nation.
Name of Mother: Sallie Hamlin     a citizen of the   Choctaw   Nation.

Postoffice    Wister Ind Ter

**AFFIDAVIT OF MOTHER.**

UNITED STATES OF AMERICA, Indian Territory,
Central    DISTRICT.

I,  Sallie Hamlin  , on oath state that I am   25   years of age and a citizen by Blood  , of the   Choctaw   Nation; that I am the lawful wife of   Israel Hamlin  , who is a citizen, by Blood   of the    Choctaw    Nation; that a   Male   child was born to me on   21"  day of   September   , 1903; that said child has been named   William Hamlin   , and was living March 4, 1905.

Sallie x Hamlin
her    mark

Witnesses To Mark:
{ Simpson Thompson
Israel Folsom

Subscribed and sworn to before me this   29  day of    Apr    , 1905

J J Riggs
Notary Public.

## Applications for Enrollment of Choctaw Newborn
## Act of 1905 Volume IX

### AFFIDAVIT OF ATTENDING PHYSICIAN OR MID-WIFE.

UNITED STATES OF AMERICA, Indian Territory,
Central DISTRICT.

I, Jane Rose , a midwife , on oath state that I attended on Mrs. Sallie Hamlin , wife of Israel Hamlin on the 21" day of September, 1903; that there was born to her on said date a Male child; that said child was living March 4, 1905, and is said to have been named William Hamlin

                                    her
                        Jane x Rose
Witnesses To Mark:          mark
    { Milton Monroe
      Israel Folsom

Subscribed and sworn to before me this 1 day of Mar , 1905

                         J.J. Riggs
                              Notary Public.

BIRTH AFFIDAVIT.

## DEPARTMENT OF THE INTERIOR,
### COMMISSION TO THE FIVE CIVILIZED TRIBES.

**In Re Application for Enrollment,** as a citizen of the Choctaw Nation, of William Hamlin , born on the 21 day of September , 1903

Name of Father: Isreal Hamlin      a citizen of the Choctaw Nation.
Name of Mother: Sallie Hamlin      a citizen of the Choctaw Nation.

                     Post-office    Wister I.T.

### AFFIDAVIT OF MOTHER.

UNITED STATES OF AMERICA,
     INDIAN TERRITORY,
    Central      District.

I, Sallie Hamlin , on oath state that I am 44 years of age and a citizen by Blood , of the Choctaw Nation; that I am the lawful wife of Isreal Hamlin , who is a citizen, by Blood of the Choctaw Nation; that a male child was born to me on 21 day of September , 1903 , that said child has been named William Hamlin , and is now living.

# Applications for Enrollment of Choctaw Newborn
## Act of 1905 Volume IX

                                                    her
                                        Sallie x Hamlin

**WITNESSES TO MARK:**                             mark
{ HG Jackson
Minnie Baldwin

Subscribed and sworn to before me this 27 day of May , 1904

                                    J J Riggs
                                    **NOTARY PUBLIC.**

---

**AFFIDAVIT OF ATTENDING PHYSICIAN OR MID-WIFE.**

UNITED STATES OF AMERICA,
    INDIAN TERRITORY,
    Central        District.

I, Isreal Hamlin , a ......................., on oath state that I attended on Mrs. Sallie Hamlin , wife of my wife on the 21 day of September , 1903 ; that there was born to her on said date a male child; that said child is now living and is said to have been named William Hamlin

                                    Israel Hamlin

**WITNESSES TO MARK:**

Subscribed and sworn to before me this 27 day of May , 1904

                                    J.J. Riggs
                                    **NOTARY PUBLIC.**

---

Choc New Born 559
        John Leo Mann b. 3-3-05

## Applications for Enrollment of Choctaw Newborn
## Act of 1905  Volume IX

7-4047

Muskogee, Indian Territory, April 5, 1905.

Jewel Mann,
Wapanucka, Indian Territory.

Dear Sir:

Receipt is hereby acknowledged of the affidavits of Stella Mann and S. A. Rice to the birth of John Leo Mann, son of Jewwll[sic] and Stella Mann, March 3, 1905, and the same have been filed with our records as an application for the enrollment of said child.

Respectfully,

Commissioner in Charge.

---

**BIRTH AFFIDAVIT.**

### DEPARTMENT OF THE INTERIOR.
### COMMISSION TO THE FIVE CIVILIZED TRIBES.

IN RE APPLICATION FOR ENROLLMENT, as a citizen of the Choctaw Nation, of John Leo Mann, born on the 3d day of March, 1905

Name of Father: Jewell Mann          a citizen of the United States Nation.
Name of Mother: Stella Mann          a citizen of the Choctaw Nation.

Postoffice  Wapanucka I.T.

---

**AFFIDAVIT OF MOTHER.**

UNITED STATES OF AMERICA, Indian Territory,
Central DISTRICT.

I, Stella Mann, on oath state that I am 22 years of age and a citizen by blood, of the Choctaw Nation; that I am the lawful wife of Jewell Mann, who is a citizen, by of the United States Nation; that a male child was born to me on third day of March, 1905; that said child has been named John Leo Mann, and was living March 4, 1905.

Stella Mann

Witnesses To Mark:

# Applications for Enrollment of Choctaw Newborn
## Act of 1905 Volume IX

Subscribed and sworn to before me this   20th  day of   March   , 1905

*(Name Illegible)*
Notary Public.

---

### AFFIDAVIT OF ATTENDING PHYSICIAN OR MID-WIFE.

UNITED STATES OF AMERICA, Indian Territory,  
Central    DISTRICT.

I,   S.A. Rice   , a   Physician   , on oath state that I attended on Mrs.   Stella Mann   , wife of   Jewell Mann   on the   third   day of   March   , 1905; that there was born to her on said date a   Male   child; that said child was living March 4, 1905, and is said to have been named   John Leo Mann

S.A. Rice M.D.

Witnesses To Mark:

Subscribed and sworn to before me this   24   day of   March   , 1905

W.A. Austin
Notary Public.

---

Choc New Born 560
Sena[sic] Jones  b. 8-24-04

### *Affidavit of Attending Physician or Midwife*

UNITED STATES OF AMERICA,  
INDIAN TERRITORY,  
Central     DISTRICT

I,   W. E. Jones   a    Practicing Physician on oath state that I attended on Mrs. Luena Jones (nee Noel)    wife of   Charley Jones   on the   24   day of   August   , 190 4, that there was born to her on said date a    female child, that said child is now living, and is said to have been named   Lela[sic] Jones

W. E. Jones     M. D.

## Applications for Enrollment of Choctaw Newborn
## Act of 1905 Volume IX

Subscribed and sworn to before me this the 18 day of February 1905

James Bower
Notary Public.

WITNESSETH:
Must be two witnesses who are citizens and know the child.

Barnabas Peter
his
Joseph Jones x
mark

We hereby certify that we are well acquainted with a Practicing Physician and know him W.E. Jones to be reputable and of good standing in the community.

Must be two citizen witnesses.

Barnabas Peter
his
Joseph Jones x
mark

---

BIRTH AFFIDAVIT.

### DEPARTMENT OF THE INTERIOR.
## COMMISSION TO THE FIVE CIVILIZED TRIBES.

---

IN RE APPLICATION FOR ENROLLMENT, as a citizen of the Choctaw Nation, of Lena Jones , born on the 24th day of August , 1904

Name of Father: Charles Jones     a citizen of the Choctaw Nation.
Name of Mother: Louina Jones     a citizen of the Choctaw Nation.

Postoffice    Wister, Ind. Ter

---

### AFFIDAVIT OF MOTHER.

UNITED STATES OF AMERICA, Indian Territory,
Central DISTRICT.

I, Louina Jones , on oath state that I am 16 years of age and a citizen by blood , of the Choctaw Nation; that I am the lawful wife of Charles Jones , who is a citizen, by blood of the Choctaw Nation; that a female child was born to me on 24th day of August , 1904; that said child has been named Lena Jones , and was living March 4, 1905.

Louina Jones

## Applications for Enrollment of Choctaw Newborn
## Act of 1905   Volume IX

Witnesses To Mark:
{ Victor M Locks Jr
{ James Mills

Subscribed and sworn to before me this 25th day of March, 1905

Wirt Franklin
Notary Public.

---

**AFFIDAVIT OF ATTENDING PHYSICIAN OR MID-WIFE.**

UNITED STATES OF AMERICA, Indian Territory, }
Central                        DISTRICT. }

I, Elsie Noel, a midwife, on oath state that I attended on Mrs. Louina Jones, wife of Charles Jones on the 24th day of August, 1904; that there was born to her on said date a female child; that said child was living March 4, 1905, and is said to have been named Lena Jones

her
Elsie x Noel
mark

Witnesses To Mark:
{ Victor M Locks Jr
{ James Mills

Subscribed and sworn to before me this 25th day of March, 1905

Wirt Franklin
Notary Public.

---

# NEW BORN AFFIDAVIT

No ................

## CHOCTAW ENROLLING COMMISSION

IN THE MATTER OF THE APPLICATION FOR ENROLLMENT as a citizen of the Choctaw Nation, of   Lena Jones   born on the 24 day of August  190 4

Name of father   Charley Jones   a citizen of   Choctaw   Nation, final enrollment No.   6520
Name of mother   Luena Jones (nee Noel)   a citizen of   Choctaw   Nation, final enrollment No.   14726

Wister I.T.                Postoffice.

# Applications for Enrollment of Choctaw Newborn
# Act of 1905  Volume IX

**AFFIDAVIT OF MOTHER**

UNITED STATES OF AMERICA  
INDIAN TERRITORY  
DISTRICT  Central

I Luena Jones (nee Noel), on oath state that I am 23 years of age and a citizen by blood of the Choctaw Nation, and as such have been placed upon the final roll of the Choctaw Nation, by the Honorable Secretary of the Interior my final enrollment number being 14726; that I am the lawful wife of Charley Jones, who is a citizen of the Choctaw Nation, and as such has been placed upon the final roll of said Nation by the Honorable Secretary of the Interior, his final enrollment number being 6520 and that a female child was born to me on the 24 day of August 190 4; that said child has been named Lela Jones, and is now living.

WITNESSETH:  
Must be two witnesses who are citizens { Barnabas Peter his mark  
Joseph Jones x mark

Luena x Jones  
her mark

Subscribed and sworn to before me this, the 18 day of February, 190 5

James Bower  
Notary Public.

My Commission Expires:  
Com expires  
Sept 23 - 1907

---

Choc New Born 561  
Clarence Owens  b. 4-26-03

# Applications for Enrollment of Choctaw Newborn
## Act of 1905   Volume IX

**COPY**

Muskogee, Indian Territory, March 28, 1905.

Ed Owens,
    McAlester, Indian Territory.

Dear Sir:

    There have been received at this office affidavits of Susie Owens and J. O. Grubbs to the birth of Clarence Owens, son of Ed and Susie Owens, April 26, 1903. It is stated in the affidavit of the mother that she is a citizen by blood of the Choctaw Nation, but the information contained therein is not sufficient to enable the Commission to identify her upon its records under this name. If you will state under what name your wife, Susie Owens, was enrolled, the names of her parents, and such other information as will enable us to identify her as an applicant for enrollment in the Choctaw Nation, the matter of the affidavits above referred to will receive further consideration.

    Respectfully,

SIGNED

*Tams Bixby*
Chairman.

---

7-4719

Muskogee, Indian Territory, April 6, 1905.

Susie Owens,
    McAlester, Indian Territory.

Dear Madam:

    Receipt is hereby acknowledged of your letter of March 30, 1905, in which you state that your maiden name was Susie Bevel; that you are a daughter of Alice Bevel and Joe T. Bevel.

    In reply to your letter you are advised that the information contained therein has enabled the Commission to identify you upon its records as an enrolled citizen of the Choctaw Nation, and your affidavit and the affidavit of J. O. Grubbs to the birth of Clarence Owens, son of Ed and Susie Owns, April 26, 1903, have been filed with our records as an application for the enrollment of said child.

    Respectfully,

Commissioner in Charge.

# Applications for Enrollment of Choctaw Newborn
## Act of 1905 Volume IX

## AFFIDAVIT OF ATTENDING PHYSICIAN OR MIDWIFE

UNITED STATES OF AMERICA
INDIAN TERRITORY
Central DISTRICT

I, John O Grubbs a Physician on oath state that I attended on Mrs. Susie Bevill Owens wife of Ed Owens on the 26 day of April, 1903, that there was born to her on said date a Male child, that said child is now living, and is said to have been named Clarence Owens

J.O. Grubbs M.D.

WITNESSETH:
Must be two witnesses who are citizens and know the child.
{ Alice E Bevill
  Roy Bevill

Subscribed and sworn to before me this, the 15 day of February 1905

RB Coleman Notary Public.

We hereby certify that we are well acquainted with John O Grubbs a Physician and know him to be reputable and of good standing in the community.

{ Alice E Bevill
  Roy Bevill

**NEW-BORN AFFIDAVIT.**

Number

## ...Choctaw Enrolling Commission...

IN THE MATTER OF THE APPLICATION FOR ENROLLMENT, as a citizen of the Choctaw Nation, of Clarence Owens

born on the 26 day of April 1903

Name of father  Ed Owens         a citizen of  United States
Nation final enrollment No. ............
Name of mother  Susie Bevill Owens   a citizen of  Choctaw
Nation final enrollment No. 13040

Postoffice  M$^c$Alester I.T.

# Applications for Enrollment of Choctaw Newborn
## Act of 1905   Volume IX

### AFFIDAVIT OF MOTHER.

UNITED STATES OF AMERICA
INDIAN TERRITORY
Central   DISTRICT

I   Susie Owens   , on oath state that I am   20   years of age and a citizen by   Blood   of the   Choctaw   Nation, and as such have been placed upon the final roll of the   Choctaw   Nation, by the Honorable Secretary of the Interior my final enrollment number being   13040   ; that I am the lawful wife of   Ed Owens   , who is a citizen of the   United States   Nation, and as such has been placed upon the final roll of said Nation by the Honorable Secretary of the Interior, his final enrollment number being .................... and that a   Male   child was born to me on the   26   day of   April   190 3; that said child has been named   Clarence Owens   , and is now living.

Susie Bevill Owens

Witnesseth.

Must be two Witnesses who are Citizens.   } Alice E Bevill
Roy Bevill

Subscribed and sworn to before me this   15   day of   Feby   190 5

R B Coleman
Notary Public.

My commission expires:   10 Oct 1905

---

BIRTH AFFIDAVIT.

### DEPARTMENT OF THE INTERIOR.
## COMMISSION TO THE FIVE CIVILIZED TRIBES.

IN RE APPLICATION FOR ENROLLMENT, as a citizen of the   Choctaw   Nation, of Clarence Owens   , born on the 26th   day of   April   , 1903

Name of Father: Ed Owens   a citizen of the United States ~~Nation~~.
Name of Mother: Susie Owens   a citizen of the   Choctaw   Nation.

Postoffice   McAlester, I.T.

---

### AFFIDAVIT OF MOTHER.

UNITED STATES OF AMERICA, Indian Territory, }
Central   DISTRICT.

I,   Susie Owens   , on oath state that I am   20   years of age and a citizen by blood   , of the   Choctaw   Nation; that I am the lawful wife of   Ed Owens   ,

## Applications for Enrollment of Choctaw Newborn
## Act of 1905   Volume IX

who is a citizen, ~~by~~ .................. of the   United States   ~~Nation~~; that a   male child was born to me on   26th   day of   April  , 1903, that said child has been named   Clarence Owens  , and is now living.

Susie Owens

Witnesses To Mark:
{

Subscribed and sworn to before me this   16th   day of   March  , 1905.

Wirt Franklin<br>Notary Public.

---

**AFFIDAVIT OF ATTENDING PHYSICIAN OR MID-WIFE.**

UNITED STATES OF AMERICA, Indian Territory, }
   Central         DISTRICT. }

I,   J.O. Grubbs  , a   physician  , on oath state that I attended on Mrs.   Susie Owens  , wife of   Ed Owens   on the   26th   day of April , 1903; that there was born to her on said date a   male   child; that said child is now living and is said to have been named   Clarence Owens

J.O. Grubbs MD

Witnesses To Mark:
{

Subscribed and sworn to before me this   17th   day of   March  , 1905.

Wirt Franklin<br>Notary Public.

---

Choc New Born 562
    Pearl Luetta Gertrude Hayes
      b. 9-16-04

# Applications for Enrollment of Choctaw Newborn
## Act of 1905   Volume IX

7 NB 562

Muskogee, Indian Territory, May 15, 1905.

Robert E. Lee,
    Attorney at Law,
        Ardmore, Indian Territory.

Dear Sir:

    Receipt is hereby acknowledged of your letter of May 10, 1905, enclosing marriage license and certificate between J. C. Hayes and Nancy L. Moore which you offer in support of the application for the enrollment of Pearlie Luella Gertrude Hayes, and the same have been filed with the record in this case.

                Respectfully,

                          Chairman.

---

COMMISSIONERS:
TAMS BIXBY,
THOMAS B. NEEDLES,
C.R. BRECKINBRIDGE.

**DEPARTMENT OF THE INTERIOR,**
**COMMISSIONER TO THE FIVE CIVILIZED TRIBES.**

WM. O. BEALL
Secretary

$W^m O. B.$

REFER IN REPLY TO THE FOLLOWING:

7-NB-562.

ADDRESS ONLY THE
COMMISSION TO THE FIVE CIVILIZED TRIBES.

Muskogee, Indian Territory, May 26, 1905.

Josephus Hayes,
    Hewitt, Indian Territory.

Dear Sir:

    There is enclosed you herewith for execution application for the enrollment of your infant child, Perlie[sic] Luella Gertrude Hayes, born September 16, 1904.

    The application filed in this office on the 6th instant, contains the affidavit of the mother, Nancy L. Hayes, to the birth of the applicant, and J. C. Hayes and W. A. McCall to the fact that the applicant was living on March 4, 1905. The affidavit of the attending physician was omitted.

    From the affidavits of January 28, 1905, it appears that Dr. John Tidmore was in attendance upon your wife at the time of birth of the applicant. If this is correct you will please file his affidavit, using the enclosed blank, in this office, but if you are unable to secure his affidavit it will be necessary that you secure the affidavits of <u>two</u> persons, who

## Applications for Enrollment of Choctaw Newborn
## Act of 1905   Volume IX

are disinterested and not related to the applicant, who have actual knowledge of the facts that the child was born, the date of her birth; that she was living on March 4, 1905, and that Nancy L. Hayes is her mother.

In having these affidavits executed care should be exercised to see that all names are written in full, as they appear in the body of the affidavit, and in the event that either of the persons signing the affidavit are unable to write, signatures by mark must be attested by two witnesses. Each affidavit must be executed before a Notary Public and the notarial seal and signature of the officer must be attached to each separate affidavit.

Respectfully,
Tams Bixby Chairman.

VR 26-2.

---

7 NB 562

Muskogee, Indian Territory, June 14, 1905.

Josephus Hayes,
    Hewitt, Indian Territory.

Dear Sir:

Receipt is hereby acknowledged of the affidavits of Nancy L. Hayes and Dr. John Tidmore to the birth of Perlie Luella Gertrude Hayes, daughter of Josephus and Nancy L. Hayes, September 16, 1904, and the same have been filed in the matter of the enrollment of said child.

Respectfully,

Chairman.

---

7-N.B. 562.

Muskogee, Indian Territory, May 6, 1905.

Robert E. Lee,
    Ardmore, Indian Territory.

Dear Sir:

Receipt is hereby acknowledged of your letter of May 1, enclosing the affidavits of Nancy L. Hayes, J. L. Hayes and W. A. McCall to the birth of Pearl Luetta[sic] Gertrude Hayes, daughter of Josephus and Nancy L. Hayes, September 16, 1904, and the same have been filed with our records in the matter of the enrollment of said child.

## Applications for Enrollment of Choctaw Newborn
## Act of 1905 Volume IX

Respectfully,

Commissioner in Charge.

N. B. 562

Muskogee, Indian Territory, April 10, 1905.

Josephus Hayes,
    Hewitt, Indian Territory.

Dear Sir:

    There is inclosed you herewith for execution application for the enrollment of your infant child, Perlie Luella Gertrude Hayes, born September 16, 1904.

    The affidavits heretofore filed with the Commission show the child was living on January 28, 1905. It is necessary, for the child to be enrolled, that she was living on March 4, 1905.

    The affidavits also show the applicant claims through you. It is, therefore, necessary that the license and the certificate of your marriage to the applicant's mother, Nancy L. Hayes, be forwarded with the return of the inclosed affidavits.

    In having these affidavits executed care should be exercised to see that all names are written in full, as they appear in the body of the affidavit, and in the event that either of the persons signing the affidavit are unable to write, signatures by mark must be attested by two witnesses. Each affidavit must be executed before a Notary Public and the notarial seal and signature of the officer must be attached to each separate affidavit.

Respectfully,

LM 10-47

Commissioner in Charge.

Applications for Enrollment of Choctaw Newborn
Act of 1905   Volume IX

## CERTIFICATE OF RECORD OF MARRIAGE

United States of America,  
   Indian Territory, } sct.  
      Southern District.

I, C. M. Campbell, Clerk of the United States Court, in the Territory and District aforesaid Do Hereby Certify, that the License for and Certificate of Marriage of

Mr     J.C. Hays     and  
M     Nancy L Moore

were filed in my office in said Territory and District the 15 day of December A.D., 190 3 and duly recorded in Book G of Marriage Record, Page 537

DEPARTMENT OF THE INTERIOR,  
Commission to the Five Civilized Tribes.

**FILED**

MAY 15 1905

*Tams Bixby* CHAIRMAN.

    Witness my hand and Seal of said Court, at Ardmore, this  15  day of December   A.D. 190 3

    C. M. Campbell
                  Clerk.

Return this License to the United States Clerk at Ardmore, that it may be recorded, when it will be mailed to the proper address.

Ardmoreite Steam Print.  
*Hewitt*

# MARRIAGE LICENSE

United States of America ,  
   Indian Territory, } ss:  
      Southern District.

To Any Person Authorized by Law to Solemnize Marriage, Greeting:

You are Hereby Commanded, to solemnize the Rite and publish the Banns of Matrimony between Mr.    J C Hayes    of    Hewitt    in the Indian Territory, aged  29  years, and M    Nancy L Moon[sic]    of    Hewitt

## Applications for Enrollment of Choctaw Newborn
## Act of 1905   Volume IX

*in the Indian Territory, aged* 17 *years, according to law; and do you officially sign and return this License to the parties therein named.*

Witness *my hand and official Seal, this* 7 *day of* Dec *A. D. 190* 3

CM Campbell
Clerk of the United States Court.

## Certificate of Marriage.

UNITED STATES OF AMERICA,  
INDIAN TERRITORY,   } ss:  
SOUTHERN DISTRICT.           I,   G.W. Thompson

Minister of the Gospel  *do hereby certify that on the* 13th *day of* Dec. *, A. D.* 190 3 *, I did duly according to law, as commanded in the foregoing License, solemnize the Rite and publish the Banns of Matrimony between the parties therein named.*

Witness *my hand this* 14th *day of* Dec *A. D. 190* 3

*My credentials are recorded in the office of the Clerk of the United States Court, Indian Territory, Southern District, at Ardmore, Book* A *, Page* 126

G.W. Thompson
Rick Ind. T.

---

Ardmore, Indian Territory,
Southern District.

I, William McCall, state on oath that I know the mother, Nannie[sic] L. Hayes, and the father, Josephus Hayes, of Pearl Luetta Gertrude Hayes, that applicant herein and that said child was living on the 4th, day of March, 1905.

W A McCall

Subscribed and sworn to before me, Ola Holloway, a Notary Public, within and for the Southern District of the Indian Territory, on this the 1st, day of May, 1905.

Ola Holloway
Notary Public.

My commission expires Jan. 17th, 1909.

# Applications for Enrollment of Choctaw Newborn
## Act of 1905   Volume IX

Ardmore, Indian Territory,
Southern District.

    I, Josephus Hayes, state on oath that I am the father of the said Pearl Luetta Gertrude Hayes, that I am a Choctaw Indian by blood, and that said child was living on the 4th, day of March, 1905.

                                       J. C. Hayes

    Subscribed and sworn to before me, Ola Holloway, a Notary Public, within and for the Southern District of the Indian Territory, on this the 1st, day of May, 1905.

                                    Ola Holloway
                                            Notary Public.

My commission expires, Jan. 17th, 1909.

---

**BIRTH AFFIDAVIT.**

### DEPARTMENT OF THE INTERIOR.
### COMMISSION TO THE FIVE CIVILIZED TRIBES.

    **IN RE APPLICATION FOR ENROLLMENT,** as a citizen of the Choctaw Nation, of Perlie Luella Gertrude Hayes, born on the 16th day of Sept, 1904

Name of Father: Josephus Hayes         a citizen of the Choctaw Nation.
Name of Mother: Nancy L Hayes         a citizen of the United States ~~Nation~~.

                        Postoffice    Hewitt I.T.

---

### AFFIDAVIT OF MOTHER.

**UNITED STATES OF AMERICA, Indian Territory,**
                                    **DISTRICT.**

    I, Nancy L Hayes, on oath state that I am 18 years of age and a citizen by blood, of the United States ~~Nation~~; that I am the lawful wife of Josephus Hayes, who is a citizen, by blood of the Choctaw Nation; that a Female child was born to me on 16th day of September, 1904; that said child has been named Perlie Luella Gertrude Hayes, and was living March 4, 1905.

                                                 her
                                    Nancy L  x  Hayes
Witnesses To Mark:                         mark
    { W.B. Fulton
      H L DeBilly

## Applications for Enrollment of Choctaw Newborn
## Act of 1905   Volume IX

Subscribed and sworn to before me this Eighth  day of   June   , 1905

W.A. Darling
Notary Public.

---

### AFFIDAVIT OF ATTENDING PHYSICIAN OR MID-WIFE.

UNITED STATES OF AMERICA, Indian Territory, }
............................................... DISTRICT. }

I, John Tidmore   , a Physician   , on oath state that I attended on Mrs. Nancy L Hayes   , wife of Josephus Hayes   on the   16$^{th}$   day of September   , 1904; that there was born to her on said date a   Female   child; that said child was living March 4, 1905, and is said to have been named   Perlie Luella Gertrude Hayes

Dr John Tidmore

Witnesses To Mark:
{

Subscribed and sworn to before me this Eighth day of   June   , 1905

W.A. Darling
Notary Public.

---

BIRTH AFFIDAVIT.
### DEPARTMENT OF THE INTERIOR.
## COMMISSION TO THE FIVE CIVILIZED TRIBES.

---

IN RE APPLICATION FOR ENROLLMENT, as a citizen of the   Choctaw   Nation, of Pearl Luetta Gertrude Hayes   , born on the 16   day of Sept   , 1904

Name of Father: Josephus Hayes        a citizen of the   Choctaw   Nation.
Name of Mother: Nancy L Hayes         a citizen of the   U.S.   ~~Nation~~.

Postoffice   Hewitt I.T.

---

### AFFIDAVIT OF MOTHER.

UNITED STATES OF AMERICA, Indian Territory, }
Southern           DISTRICT. }

I, Nancy L Hayes   , on oath state that I am   18   years of age and a citizen by — — —, of the   United States   ~~Nation~~; that I am the lawful wife of   Josephus Hayes   , who is a citizen, by   blood   of the   Choctaw   Nation; that a

## Applications for Enrollment of Choctaw Newborn
## Act of 1905    Volume IX

Female    child was born to me on    16    day of    September    , 1904; that said child has been named    Pearl Luetta Gertrude Hayes    , and was living March 4, 1905.

              her
          Nancy L  x  Hayes
Witnesses To Mark:        mark
 { *(Name Illegible)*
  Ola Halloway[sic]

  Subscribed and sworn to before me this  1$^{st}$   day of   May    , 1905

          Ola Halloway
          Notary Public.

---

**BIRTH AFFIDAVIT.**
       DEPARTMENT OF THE INTERIOR.
    **COMMISSION TO THE FIVE CIVILIZED TRIBES.**

---

  **IN RE APPLICATION FOR ENROLLMENT,** as a citizen of the    Choctaw    Nation, of   Perlie Luella Gertrude Hays    , born on the    16   day of   Sept   , 1904

Name of Father: Josephus C Hayes  a citizen of the   Choctaw    Nation.
Name of Mother:  Nancy L Hayes   a citizen of the      U S    Nation.

      Postoffice    Hewitt I.T.

---

     **AFFIDAVIT OF MOTHER.**

UNITED STATES OF AMERICA, Indian Territory, }
  So     DISTRICT.

  I,   Nancy L Hayes   , on oath state that I am 8[sic]   years of age and a citizen by   Birth   , of the    US    Nation; that I am the lawful wife of    Josephus C Hayes   , who is a citizen, by   Birth   of the   Choctaw    Nation; that a    Female    child was born to me on    16    day of    September    , 1904, that said child has been named  Perlie Luella Gertrude Hayes    , and is now living.

             her
         Nancy L  x  Hayes
Witnesses To Mark:       mark
 { G R Spence
  Dell Kimbrell

  Subscribed and sworn to before me this  28   day of    January   , 190....

         W A Darling
         Notary Public.

# Applications for Enrollment of Choctaw Newborn
# Act of 1905   Volume IX

### AFFIDAVIT OF ATTENDING PHYSICIAN OR MID-WIFE.

UNITED STATES OF AMERICA, Indian Territory,
So                    DISTRICT.

I,   John Tidmore  , a   Physician  , on oath state that I attended on Mrs.   Nancy L Hayes  , wife of   Josephus C Hayes   on the   16   day of   Sept , 1904; that there was born to her on said date a   Female   child; that said child is now living and is said to have been named   Perlie Luella Gertrude Hayes

                                        Dr. John Tidmore

Witnesses To Mark:

Subscribed and sworn to before me this   28   day of   Jan  , 1905.

                                        WA Darling
                                               Notary Public.

---

Choc New Born 563
      Gladys Jones   b.  4-25-03

                                                         7 NB 563

                      Muskogee, Indian Territory, June 16, 1905.

Bond & Melton,
       Attorneys at Law,
              Chickasha, Indian Territory.

Gentlemen:

    Receipt is hereby acknowledged of your letter of June 10, 1905, asking if an application for the enrollment of Gladys Jones, minor child of Frank and Maggie Jones has been filed with the Commission.

    In reply to your letter you are informed that an application has been made to this Commission for the enrollment of Gladys Jones, child of Frank H. and Maggie Jones, under the act of Congress approved March 3, 1905, and her name is being placed upon a

Applications for Enrollment of Choctaw Newborn
Act of 1905   Volume IX

schedule of citizens by blood of said Nation prepared for forwarding to the Secretary of the Interior. You will be notified when her enrollment is approved by the Department.

Respectfully,

Chairman.

---

**BIRTH AFFIDAVIT.**

*DEPARTMENT OF THE INTERIOR.*
## COMMISSION TO THE FIVE CIVILIZED TRIBES.

---

IN RE APPLICATION FOR ENROLLMENT, as a citizen of the Choctaw Nation of Gladys Jones, born on the 25$^{th}$ day of April, 1903

Name of Father: Frank H. Jones    a citizen of the ———— Nation.
Name of Mother: Maggie Jones    a citizen of the Choctaw Nation.

Postoffice  Tuttle, Ind. Terr.

---

*AFFIDAVIT OF MOTHER.*

UNITED STATES OF AMERICA, INDIAN TERRITORY,
    Southern      DISTRICT.

I, Maggie Jones, on oath state that I am 25 years of age and a citizen by Blood, of the Choctaw Nation; that I am the lawful wife of Frank H. Jones, who is a citizen, by ——— of the ————Nation; that a female child was born to me on 25$^{th}$ day of April, 1903, that said child has been named Gladys Jones, and is now living.

                      Maggie Jones

WITNESSES TO MARK:

Subscribed and sworn to before me this 27th day of March, 1905.

   Com expires 10/17-1908      *(Name Illegible)*
                                 Notary Public.

## Applications for Enrollment of Choctaw Newborn
## Act of 1905   Volume IX

AFFIDAVIT OF ATTENDING PHYSICIAN OR MID-WIFE.

UNITED STATES OF AMERICA, INDIAN TERRITORY,  
Southern                   DISTRICT.

I, We, Susan Frances Campbell, Annie Jones and Minnie Campbell , on oath state that I attended on Mrs.   Maggie Jones   , wife of   Frank H Jones   on the   25$^{th}$   day of April , 190 3; that there was born to her on said date a    female    child; that said child is now living and is said to have been named   Gladys Jones

                                                   her  
WITNESSES TO MARK:         Susan Frances x Campbell  
   Pearl Beardeley                       mark  
   J.H. Carlisle                  Annie Jones  
                                   Minnie Campbell

Subscribed and sworn to before me this   27th  day of   March   , 1905.

Com expires 10/17-1908        *(Name Illegible)*  
                                        Notary Public.

---

<u>Choc New Born 546</u>  
    Carl Logan Loving   b.  12-18-04

                                                      7-2282

                 Muskogee, Indian Territory, April 5, 1905.

M. A. Loving,  
    Calvin, Indian Territory.

Dear Sir:

    Receipt is hereby acknowledged of your letter of March 31, 1905, enclosing affidavits of Eva B. Loving and J. C. Bentley to the birth of Carl Logan Loving, son of M. A. and Eva B. Loving December 18, 1904, and the same have been filed with our records as an application for the enrollment of said child.

                                    Respectfully,

                                              Commissioner in Charge.

# Applications for Enrollment of Choctaw Newborn
## Act of 1905   Volume IX

### *Affidavit of Attending Physician or Midwife*

UNITED STATES OF AMERICA,  
INDIAN TERRITORY,  
Central   DISTRICT

I, J C Bentley a Physician on oath state that I attended on Mrs. Eva B Loving wife of M A Loving on the 18 day of Dec, 190 4, that there was born to her on said date a male child, that said child is now living, and is said to have been named Carl Logan Loving

J C Bentley   M. D.

Subscribed and sworn to before me this the 24 day of Feb 190  
My Commission Exp  
Jan 10/1906   H B Harrell  
Notary Public.

WITNESSETH:  
Must be two witnesses who are citizens and know the child. { Katie James  
Johnson Frazier

We hereby certify that we are well acquainted with J C Bentley a Physician and know him to be reputable and of good standing in the community.

Must be two citizen witnesses. { Katie James  
Johnson Frazier

**NEW-BORN AFFIDAVIT.**

Number

### ...Choctaw Enrolling Commission...

IN THE MATTER OF THE APPLICATION FOR ENROLLMENT, as a citizen of the Choctaw Nation, of Carl Logan Loving

born on the 18 day of December 190 4

Name of father   M A Loving    a citizen of  U. S.  
Nation final enrollment No.  
Name of mother   Eva B Loving    a citizen of  Choctaw  
Nation final enrollment No. 6615

Postoffice   Calvin

## Applications for Enrollment of Choctaw Newborn
## Act of 1905 Volume IX

### AFFIDAVIT OF MOTHER.

UNITED STATES OF AMERICA
INDIAN TERRITORY
Central    DISTRICT

I    Eva B Loving    , on oath state that I am 21 years of age and a citizen by Blood of the Choctaw Nation, and as such have been placed upon the final roll of the Choctaw Nation, by the Honorable Secretary of the Interior my final enrollment number being 6615 ; that I am the lawful wife of M A Loving , who is a citizen of the U. S. Nation, and as such has been placed upon the final roll of said Nation by the Honorable Secretary of the Interior, his final enrollment number being ............... and that a Male child was born to me on the 18 day of December 190 4; that said child has been named Carl Logan Loving , and is now living.

Eva B Loving

Witnesseth.

Must be two Witnesses who are Citizens.    Johnson Frazier
Katie James

Subscribed and sworn to before me this 7 day of Feb 190 5

H B Harrell
Notary Public.

My commission expires: Jan 10/1906

---

BIRTH AFFIDAVIT.

### DEPARTMENT OF THE INTERIOR.
### COMMISSION TO THE FIVE CIVILIZED TRIBES.

IN RE APPLICATION FOR ENROLLMENT, as a citizen of the Choctaw Nation, of Carl Logan Loving , born on the 18th day of December , 1904

Name of Father: M A Loving    a citizen of the United States ~~Nation~~.
Name of Mother: Eva B Loving    a citizen of the Choctaw Nation.

Postoffice    Calvin, I.T.

---

### AFFIDAVIT OF MOTHER.

UNITED STATES OF AMERICA, Indian Territory,
Central    DISTRICT.

I, Eva B Loving , on oath state that I am 21 years of age and a citizen by blood , of the Choctaw Nation; that I am the lawful wife of M.A. Loving ,

## Applications for Enrollment of Choctaw Newborn
## Act of 1905   Volume IX

who is a citizen, ~~by~~ ............ of the United States ~~Nation~~; that a male child was born to me on 18th day of December, 1904; that said child has been named Carl Logan Loving, and was living March 4, 1905.

                                          Eva B Loving

Witnesses To Mark:
{

    Subscribed and sworn to before me this 18th day of March, 1905

                                            Wirt Franklin
                                                Notary Public.

---

**AFFIDAVIT OF ATTENDING PHYSICIAN OR MID-WIFE.**

UNITED STATES OF AMERICA, Indian Territory, }
    Central           DISTRICT.

    I, J C Bentley, a Physician, on oath state that I attended on Mrs. Eva B Loving, wife of M A Loving on the 18 day of Dec, 1904; that there was born to her on said date a male child; that said child was living March 4, 1905, and is said to have been named Carl Logan Loving

                                          J c Bentley

Witnesses To Mark:
{ Hugh L Harrell
  J.W. Hendley

    Subscribed and sworn to before me this 31 day of March, 1905

My Commission exp                  H.B. Harrell
Jan 10/1906                              Notary Public.

---

Choc New Born 565
    Boyd Rabon   b. 10-31-03

# Applications for Enrollment of Choctaw Newborn
## Act of 1905  Volume IX

7-2848

Muskogee, Indian Territory, April 5, 1905.

Robert L. Rabon,
    Kingston, Indian Territory.

Dear Sir:

Receipt is hereby acknowledged of the affidavits of Cora E. Rabon and C. B. Martin to the birth of Boyd Rabon, son of Robert and Cora E. Rabon, October 31, 1903, and the same have been filed with our records as an application for the enrollment of said child.

Respectfully,

Commissioner in Charge.

**BIRTH AFFIDAVIT.**

## DEPARTMENT OF THE INTERIOR.
## COMMISSION TO THE FIVE CIVILIZED TRIBES.

**IN RE APPLICATION FOR ENROLLMENT,** as a citizen of the    Choctaw    Nation, of Boyd Rabon    , born on the  31  day of Oct  , 1903

Name of Father:  Robt L Rabon         a citizen of the   Choctaw    Nation.
Name of Mother:  Cora A Rabon         a citizen of the   Choctaw    Nation.

Postoffice    Kingston Ind Ter

**AFFIDAVIT OF MOTHER.**

UNITED STATES OF AMERICA, Indian Territory, }
            Southern        DISTRICT.

I,  Cora E Rabon  , on oath state that I am Twenty-Seven   years of age and a citizen by   blood  , of the   Choctaw   Nation; that I am the lawful wife of Robt L Rabon   , who is a citizen, by  intermarriage   of the   Choctaw Nation; that a   male   child was born to me on  31st  day of  Oct  , 1903; that said child has been named  Boyd Rabon  , and was living March 4, 1905.

Cora E Rabon

Witnesses To Mark:
{

# Applications for Enrollment of Choctaw Newborn
## Act of 1905   Volume IX

Subscribed and sworn to before me this 30 day of March , 1905

*(Name Illegible)*
Notary Public.

---

### AFFIDAVIT OF ATTENDING PHYSICIAN OR MID-WIFE.

UNITED STATES OF AMERICA, Indian Territory, }
Southern      DISTRICT.

I, C.B. Martin , a Physician , on oath state that I attended on Mrs. Cora E Rabon , wife of Robt L Rabon on the 31st day of Oct , 1903; that there was born to her on said date a male child; that said child was living March 4, 1905, and is said to have been named Boyd Rabon

C.B. Martin M.D.

Witnesses To Mark:
{

Subscribed and sworn to before me this 30 day of March , 1905

*(Name Illegible)*
Notary Public.

---

Choc New Born 566
Edgar Hendrix  b. 10-24-03

Choctaw 4616.

Muskogee, Indian Territory, April 4, 1905.

William Hendrix,
Bebee, Indian Territory.

Dear Sir:

Receipt is hereby acknowledged of the affidavits of Evelina Hendrix and S. C. Davis to the birth of Edgar Hendrix, son of William and Evelina Hendrix, October 24, 1903, and the same have been filed with our records as an application for the enrollment of said child.

## Applications for Enrollment of Choctaw Newborn
## Act of 1905 Volume IX

Respectfully,

Commissioner in Charge.

**BIRTH AFFIDAVIT.**

### DEPARTMENT OF THE INTERIOR.
### COMMISSION TO THE FIVE CIVILIZED TRIBES.

IN RE APPLICATION FOR ENROLLMENT, as a citizen of the Choctaw Nation, of Edgar Hendrix, born on the 24 day of October, 1904

Name of Father: William Hendrix   a citizen of the Choctaw Nation.
                                                              (by marriage)
Name of Mother: Evelina Hendrix   a citizen of the Choctaw Nation.

Postoffice   Bebee

**AFFIDAVIT OF MOTHER.**

UNITED STATES OF AMERICA, Indian Territory,
Southern DISTRICT.

I, Evelina Hendrix, on oath state that I am 25 years of age and a citizen by marriage, of the Choctaw Nation; that I am the lawful wife of William Hendrix, who is a citizen, by blood of the Choctaw Nation; that a male child was born to me on 24 day of October, 1903; that said child has been named Edgar Hendrix, and was living March 4, 1905.

                                          her
                                 Evelina x Hendrix
Witnesses To Mark:                       mark
  Jno. P. Crawford
  S.H. Wax

Subscribed and sworn to before me this 27 day of March, 1905

                              Jno. P. Crawford
                                  Notary Public.

## Applications for Enrollment of Choctaw Newborn
## Act of 1905   Volume IX

#### AFFIDAVIT OF ATTENDING PHYSICIAN OR MID-WIFE.

UNITED STATES OF AMERICA, Indian Territory,
  Southern               DISTRICT.

    I,   S C Davis   , a   Physician   , on oath state that I attended on Mrs.  Evelina Hendrix   , wife of   William Hendrix   on the  24  day of October   , 1903; that there was born to her on said date a   Male   child; that said child was living March 4, 1905, and is said to have been named   Edgar Hendrix

                                      S.C. Davis M.D.

Witnesses To Mark:
  { JM Thompson
    W A Lindsey

    Subscribed and sworn to before me this  23  day of   March   , 1905

                                    J.J. Hart
                                        Notary Public.

---

Choc New Born 567
    Abner James   b.  11-17-02
    Henry James   b.  12-26-04

**COPY**

                                                                                 7-297.

                        Muskogee, Indian Territory, March 28, 1905.

Mary James,
    Care Silas James,
        Coalgate, Indian Territory.

Dear Madam:

    There is enclosed herewith for execution application the enrollment of your infant children, Abner James, born November 17, 1902, and Arabel[sic] James, born June 23, 1903.

    The affidavits heretofore filed with the Commission show that Abner James was living April 20, 1904, and Arabel James on April 30, 1904. It is necessary, for these children to be enrolled, that they were living on March 4, 1905.

# Applications for Enrollment of Choctaw Newborn
## Act of 1905 Volume IX

In one of the above mentioned affidavits you state your age is "about twenty-two" while in the other you say it is twenty-five. You will please fill out the blank space left in the enclosed affidavits for that purpose, with your correct age.

It is also noted that one of these affidavits was signed by mark while it appears from the other that you are able to write. If you can do so you will please sign the enclosed affidavits in your own hand. In the event that either of the persons signing the affidavit are unable to write, signatures by mark must be attested by two witnesses.

In having these affidavits executed care should be exercised to see that all names are written in full, as they appear in the body of the affidavit. Each affidavit must be executed before a Notary Public and the notarial seal and signature of the officer must be attached to each separate affidavit.

Respectfully,

SIGNED
*Tams Bixby*
Chairman.

P.T. 10/28

---

7-297
7 N B 16

Muskogee, Indian Territory, April 15, 1905.

Silas James,
Talihina, Indian Territory.

Dear Sir:

Receipt is hereby acknowledged of the affidavits of Mary James and Parlee Robinson to the birth of Henry James, son of Silas and Mary James, December 26, 1904; also affidavits of Mary James and William J. Conley to the birth of Arabel James, daughter of Silas and Mary James, June 23, 1903, and the same have been filed with our records as an application for the enrollment of said children.

Respectfully,

Chairman.

Applications for Enrollment of Choctaw Newborn
Act of 1905 Volume IX

567

COPY 7 NB ~~15~~

Muskogee, Indian Territory, April 19, 1905.

Silas James,
    Talihina, Indian Territory.

Dear Sir:

    Receipt is hereby acknowledged of the affidavits of Mary James and Mary Jackson to the birth of Abner James, son of Silas and Mary James November 17, 1902, and the same have been filed with our records as an application for the enrollment of said child.

                  Respectfully,

SIGNED

*Tams Bixby*
Chairman.

---

BIRTH AFFIDAVIT.

## DEPARTMENT OF THE INTERIOR,
### COMMISSION TO THE FIVE CIVILIZED TRIBES.

---

    IN RE Application for Enrollment, as a citizen of the Choctaw Nation, of Abner James, born on the 17 day of November, 1902

Name of Father: Silas James      a citizen of the Choctaw Nation.
Name of Mother: Mary James     a citizen of the Choctaw Nation.

                Post-Office: Talihina Ind Ter

---

AFFIDAVIT OF MOTHER.

---

UNITED STATES OF AMERICA,
    INDIAN TERRITORY.
Central      District.

    I, Mary James, on oath state that I am about 22 years of age and a citizen by Blood, of the Choctaw Nation; that I am the lawful wife of Silas James, who is a citizen, by Blood of the Choctaw Nation; that a male child was born to me on 17 day of November, 1902, that said child has been named Abner James, and is now living.

# Applications for Enrollment of Choctaw Newborn
## Act of 1905   Volume IX

her<br>
Mary x James<br>
mark

**WITNESSES TO MARK:**
{ Alex M<sup>c</sup>Intosh
{ Silas James

*Subscribed and sworn to before me this* 20 *day of* April , 1904

Sam T. Roberts Jr
**NOTARY PUBLIC.**

---

**AFFIDAVIT OF ATTENDING PHYSICIAN OR MID-WIFE.**

UNITED STATES OF AMERICA,
   **INDIAN TERRITORY.**
Central      District.

I, Mary Jackson , a midwife , on oath state that I attended on Mrs. Mary James , wife of Silas James on the 17 day of November , 1904 ; that there was born to her on said date a male child; that said child is now living and is said to have been named Abner James

her<br>
Mary x Jackson<br>
mark

**WITNESSES TO MARK:**
{ Alex M<sup>c</sup>Intosh
{ Silas James

*Subscribed and sworn to before me this* 20 *day of* April , 1904

Sam T. Roberts Jr
**NOTARY PUBLIC.**

---

**BIRTH AFFIDAVIT.**

### DEPARTMENT OF THE INTERIOR.
### COMMISSION TO THE FIVE CIVILIZED TRIBES.

*Austin Billy Interpreter*

**IN RE APPLICATION FOR ENROLLMENT,** as a citizen of the Choctaw Nation, of Abner James , born on the 17 day of November , 1902

Name of Father: Silas James        a citizen of the Choctaw Nation.
Name of Mother: Mary James        a citizen of the Choctaw Nation.

Postoffice   Talihina I.T.

## Applications for Enrollment of Choctaw Newborn
## Act of 1905   Volume IX

**AFFIDAVIT OF MOTHER.**

UNITED STATES OF AMERICA, Indian Territory, }
Central       DISTRICT.

I,   Mary James   , on oath state that I am  about 20   years of age and a citizen by   Blood   , of the   Choctaw   Nation; that I am the lawful wife of   Silas James   , who is a citizen, by   Blood   of the   Choctaw   Nation; that a Male   child was born to me on   17   day of   November   , 1902; that said child has been named   Abner James   , and was living March 4, 1905.

                                                  her
                                       Mary  x  James

Witnesses To Mark:                   mark
{ Austin Billy
{ D Thomas

Subscribed and sworn to before me this  6   day of   April   , 1905

My commission expires Feb. 4, 1908
Commission from U.S. Court at So. McAlester I.T.
MY OFFICE TALIHINA, I. T.

                                  Sam T Roberts Jr
                                  Notary Public.

---

**AFFIDAVIT OF ATTENDING PHYSICIAN OR MID-WIFE.**

*G.W. Dukes Interpreter*

UNITED STATES OF AMERICA, Indian Territory, }
Central       DISTRICT.

I,   Mary Jackson   , a   midwife   , on oath state that I attended on Mrs.   Mary James   , wife of   Silas James   on the   17 day of   November   , 1902; that there was born to her on said date a _____ child; that said child was living March 4, 1905, and is said to have been named   Abner James

                                                  her
                                       Mary  x  Jackson

Witnesses To Mark:                   mark
{ G. W. Dukes
{ D. Thomas

Subscribed and sworn to before me this  14  day of   April   , 1905

                                  Sam T Roberts Jr
                                  Notary Public.

# Applications for Enrollment of Choctaw Newborn
## Act of 1905 Volume IX

BIRTH AFFIDAVIT.

### DEPARTMENT OF THE INTERIOR.
### COMMISSION TO THE FIVE CIVILIZED TRIBES.

IN RE APPLICATION FOR ENROLLMENT, as a citizen of the Choctaw Nation, of Henry James, born on the 26 day of December, 1904

Name of Father: Silas James    a citizen of the Choctaw Nation.
Name of Mother: Mary James    a citizen of the Choctaw Nation.

Postoffice    Talihina, I.T.

*Austin Billy Interpreter*

### AFFIDAVIT OF MOTHER.

UNITED STATES OF AMERICA, Indian Territory, }
Central    DISTRICT.

I, Mary James, on oath state that I am about 20 years of age and a citizen by Blood, of the Choctaw Nation; that I am the lawful wife of Silas James, who is a citizen, by Blood of the Choctaw Nation; that a Male child was born to me on 26 day of December, 1904; that said child has been named Henry James, and was living March 4, 1905.

                 her
         Mary x James
Witnesses To Mark:      mark
{ Austin Billy
   D. Thomas

Subscribed and sworn to before me this 6 day of April, 1905

My commission expires Feb. 4, 1908
Commission from U.S. Court at So. McAlester I.T.    Sam T Roberts Jr
MY OFFICE TALIHINA, I. T.      Notary Public.

### AFFIDAVIT OF ATTENDING PHYSICIAN OR MID-WIFE.

UNITED STATES OF AMERICA, Indian Territory, }
Central    DISTRICT.

I, Parlee Robinson, a midwife, on oath state that I attended on Mrs. Mary James, wife of Silas James on the 26 day of December, 1904; that there was born to her on said date a Male child; that said child was living March 4, 1905, and is said to have been named Henry James

               her
       Parlee x Robinson
              mark

# Applications for Enrollment of Choctaw Newborn
## Act of 1905  Volume IX

Witnesses To Mark:
{ Austin Billy
{ D. Thomas

Subscribed and sworn to before me this 6 day of April , 1905

Sam T Roberts Jr
Notary Public.

---

Choc New Born 568
Walter Monroe Daniel  b. 8-17-03

7-4452

Muskogee, Indian Territory, April 5, 1905.

J. F. Daniel,
Massey, Indian Territory.

Dear Sir:

Receipt is hereby acknowledged of the affidavits of Beatrice Daniel and Eliza Jane Daniel to the birth of Walter Monroe Daniel, son of J. F. and Beatrice Daniel, August 17, 1903, and the same have been filed with our records as an application for the enrollment of said child.

Respectfully,

Commissioner in Charge.

## AFFIDAVIT OF ATTENDING PHYSICIAN OR MIDWIFE

UNITED STATES OF AMERICA
INDIAN TERRITORY
Central  DISTRICT

I, Eliza Jane Daniel  a  Midwife on oath state that I attended on Mrs. Beatrice Daniel wife of J.F. Daniel on the 17 day of August , 190 3, that there was born to her on said date a Male child, that said child is now living, and is said to have been named Walter Monroe Daniel

Eliza Jane Daniel  M.D.

## Applications for Enrollment of Choctaw Newborn
## Act of 1905   Volume IX

Subscribed and sworn to before me this, the   1   day of   March   190 3[sic]

O.P. Swisher
Notary Public.

WITNESSETH:

Must be two witnesses who are citizens and know the child.
{ W W Massey
  Sarah A Harlan

We hereby certify that we are well acquainted with   Eliza Jane Daniel   a   midwife   and know   her   to be reputable and of good standing in the community.

{ W W Massey
  Sarah A Harlan

**NEW-BORN AFFIDAVIT.**

Number............

...Choctaw Enrolling Commission...

IN THE MATTER OF THE APPLICATION FOR ENROLLMENT, as a citizen of the Choctaw   Nation, of   Walter Monroe Daniel

born on the   17   day of   August   190 3

Name of father   J F Daniel                              a citizen of   The United States
Nation final enrollment No. ................
Name of mother   Beatrice Daniel                   a citizen of   Choctaw
Nation final enrollment No.   14421

Postoffice   Massey I.T.

**AFFIDAVIT OF MOTHER.**

UNITED STATES OF AMERICA
INDIAN TERRITORY
  Central   DISTRICT

I   Beatrice Daniel   , on oath state that I am   23   years of age and a citizen by   Blood   of the   Choctaw   Nation, and as such have been placed upon the final roll of the   Choctaw   Nation, by the Honorable Secretary of the Interior my final enrollment number being   14421  ; that I am the lawful wife of   J. F. Daniel   , who is a citizen of the   United States   Nation, and as such has been placed upon the final roll of said Nation by the Honorable Secretary of the Interior, his final enrollment number being ............ and that a   Male   child was born to me on the

213

## Applications for Enrollment of Choctaw Newborn
## Act of 1905   Volume IX

17 day of August    190 3; that said child has been named   Walter Monroe Daniel ,
and is now living.

                Beatrice Daniel

Witnesseth.
  Must be two   } W W Massey
  Witnesses who
  are Citizens.    Sarah A Harlan

    Subscribed and sworn to before me this  1  day of  March  190 5

              O P Swisher
                 Notary Public.
My commission expires:  Jan 14 1908

---

**BIRTH AFFIDAVIT.**
## DEPARTMENT OF THE INTERIOR.
## COMMISSION TO THE FIVE CIVILIZED TRIBES.

   **IN RE APPLICATION FOR ENROLLMENT,** as a citizen of the  Choctaw Nation   Nation,
of  Walter Monroe Daniel , born on the  17  day of  August , 1903

Name of Father: J F Daniel      a citizen of the United States Nation.
Name of Mother: Beatrice Daniel     a citizen of the  Choctaw   Nation.

         Postoffice   Massey, Indian Territory

---

### AFFIDAVIT OF MOTHER.

**UNITED STATES OF AMERICA, Indian Territory,** }
  Central      **DISTRICT.**

   I,  Beatrice Daniel , on oath state that I am  23  years of age and a citizen by  Blood , of the  Choctaw  Nation; that I am the lawful wife of  J F Daniel, who is a citizen, ~~by~~ ............. of the  United States   Nation; that a  Male child was born to me on  17  day of  August , 1903; that said child has been named  Walter Monroe Daniel , and was living March 4, 1905.

              Beatrice Daniel
Witnesses To Mark:
 {

   Subscribed and sworn to before me this  27  day of  March , 1905

My Commission expires Jan 14-1908   O P Swisher
                Notary Public.

# Applications for Enrollment of Choctaw Newborn
# Act of 1905   Volume IX

### AFFIDAVIT OF ATTENDING PHYSICIAN OR MID-WIFE.

UNITED STATES OF AMERICA, Indian Territory, }
Central                             DISTRICT. }

I, Eliza Jane Daniel , a mid-wife , on oath state that I attended on Mrs. Beatrice Daniel , wife of   J F Daniel   on the 17 day of   August  , 1903; that there was born to her on said date a   male   child; that said child was living March 4, 1905, and is said to have been named   Walter Monroe Daniel

Eliza Jane Daniel

Witnesses To Mark:
{

Subscribed and sworn to before me this  27 day of   March   , 1905

My Commission expires Jan 14-1908        O P Swisher
Notary Public.

---

Choc New Born 569
           Ruth McCartney  b. 3-27-04

7-2347

Muskogee, Indian Territory, April 5, 1905.

Elsie McCartney,
     Howe, Indian Territory.

Dear Madam:

Receipt is hereby acknowledged of your letter of March 31, 1905, enclosing affidavits of Elsie McCartney and Samuel C. Dean to the birth of Ruth McCartney, daughter of Charles and Elsie McCartney, March 27, 1904, and the same have been filed with our records as an application for the enrollment of said child.

Respectfully,

Commissioner in Charge.

## Applications for Enrollment of Choctaw Newborn
## Act of 1905   Volume IX

### Affidavit of Attending Physician or Midwife

UNITED STATES OF AMERICA,  
  INDIAN TERRITORY,  
  Central   DISTRICT

I, S.C. Dean a Physician on oath state that I attended on Mrs. Elsie M$^c$Cartney wife of Chas E M$^c$Cartney on the 27 day of March, 190 4, that there was born to her on said date a Female child, that said child is now living, and is said to have been named Rutha M$^c$Cartney

Samuel C Dean   M. D.

Subscribed and sworn to before me this the 17 day of February 1905

AL Bennett  
Notary Public.

WITNESSETH:  
Must be two witnesses who are citizens and know the child. { Earnest Powell  
A.W. Benton

We hereby certify that we are well acquainted with Dr. S.C. Dean a Physician and know him to be reputable and of good standing in the community.

Must be two citizen witnesses. { Earnest Powell  
E.W. Burton

# NEW BORN AFFIDAVIT

No _____

## CHOCTAW ENROLLING COMMISSION

IN THE MATTER OF THE APPLICATION FOR ENROLLMENT as a citizen of the Choctaw Nation, of Rutha McCartney born on the 27$^{th}$ day of March 190 4

Name of father Chas E. McCartney   a citizen of white Nation, final enrollment No. ——

Name of mother Elsie McCartney   a citizen of Choctaw Nation, final enrollment No. 6795

Howe I.T.   Postoffice.

## Applications for Enrollment of Choctaw Newborn
## Act of 1905 Volume IX

**AFFIDAVIT OF MOTHER**

UNITED STATES OF AMERICA  
INDIAN TERRITORY  
DISTRICT    Central

I    Elsie McCartney    , on oath state that I am    22    years of age and a citizen by    Blood    of the    Choctaw    Nation, and as such have been placed upon the final roll of the    Choctaw    Nation, by the Honorable Secretary of the Interior my final enrollment number being    6795    ; that I am the lawful wife of    Chas E McCartney    , who is a citizen of the    white    Nation, and as such has been placed upon the final roll of said Nation by the Honorable Secretary of the Interior, his final enrollment number being —    and that a    Female    child was born to me on the    27    day of    March    190 4; that said child has been named    Rutha McCartney    , and is now living.

WITNESSETH:                                                        Elsie McCartney  
Must be two witnesses ⎰ Earnest Powell  
who are citizens       ⎱ E W Benton

Subscribed and sworn to before me this, the    17    day of    February    , 190 5

A L Bennett  
Notary Public.

My Commission Expires:    Expires Nov 1st 1905

BIRTH AFFIDAVIT.

**DEPARTMENT OF THE INTERIOR.**
## COMMISSION TO THE FIVE CIVILIZED TRIBES.

IN RE APPLICATION FOR ENROLLMENT, as a citizen of the    Choctaw    Nation, of    Ruth McCartney    , born on the 27th    day of    March    , 1904

Name of Father: Charles McCartney              a citizen of the United States Nation.  
Name of Mother: Elsie McCartney               a citizen of the    Choctaw    Nation.

Postoffice    Howe, Ind. Ter.

# Applications for Enrollment of Choctaw Newborn
## Act of 1905  Volume IX

### AFFIDAVIT OF MOTHER.

UNITED STATES OF AMERICA, Indian Territory,  
Central  DISTRICT.

I, Elsie McCartney, on oath state that I am 22 years of age and a citizen by blood, of the Choctaw Nation; that I am the lawful wife of Charles McCartney, who is a citizen, by ............ of the United States ~~Nation~~; that a female child was born to me on 27th day of March, 1904; that said child has been named Ruth McCartney, and was living March 4, 1905.

Elsie McCartney

Witnesses To Mark:

Subscribed and sworn to before me this 28th day of March, 1905

Wirt Franklin  
Notary Public.

---

### AFFIDAVIT OF ATTENDING PHYSICIAN OR MID-WIFE.

UNITED STATES OF AMERICA, Indian Territory,  
Central  DISTRICT.

I, S.C. Dean, a Physician, on oath state that I attended on Mrs. Elsie McCartney, wife of Charles McCartney on the 27th day of March, 1904; that there was born to her on said date a Female child; that said child was living March 4, 1905, and is said to have been named Ruth McCartney

Sam'l C. Dean, M.D.

Witnesses To Mark:

Subscribed and sworn to before me this 31st day of March, 1905

W.N. Eston  
Notary Public.

Applications for Enrollment of Choctaw Newborn
Act of 1905   Volume IX

Choc New Born 570
Lewis Murray Lindsay   b. 8-6-03

BIRTH AFFIDAVIT.

## DEPARTMENT OF THE INTERIOR,
COMMISSION TO THE FIVE CIVILIZED TRIBES.

**In Re Application for Enrollment,** as a citizen of the Choctaw Nation, of James Murray Lindsay, born on the 6 day of August, 1903

Name of Father: Lewis E Murray          a citizen of the Choctaw Nation.
Name of Mother: Juanita Lindsay          a citizen of the Choctaw Nation.

Post-office   Lindsay

AFFIDAVIT OF MOTHER.

UNITED STATES OF AMERICA,
    INDIAN TERRITORY,
    Southern   District.

I, Juanita Lindsay, on oath state that I am 34 years of age and a citizen by blood, of the Choctaw Nation; that I am the lawful wife of Lewis E Lindsay, who is a citizen, by Intermarriage of the Choctaw Nation; that a male child was born to me on 6 day of August, 1903, that said child has been named James Murray Lindsay, and is now living.

Juanita Lindsay

WITNESSES TO MARK:

Subscribed and sworn to before me this 27$^{th}$ day of November, 1903

T.M. Bell
NOTARY PUBLIC.

# Applications for Enrollment of Choctaw Newborn
## Act of 1905 Volume IX

**AFFIDAVIT OF ATTENDING PHYSICIAN OR MID-WIFE.**

UNITED STATES OF AMERICA,
INDIAN TERRITORY,
Southern District.

I, Benj W Ralston , a Physician , on oath state that I attended on Mrs. Juanita Lindsay , wife of Lewis E Lindsay on the 6$^{th}$ day of August , 1903 ; that there was born to her on said date a male child; that said child is now living and is said to have been named James Murray Lindsay

Benj. W. Ralston M.D.

WITNESSES TO MARK:
*(Name Illegible)*
Emmett M$^c$Caughey

Subscribed and sworn to before me this 29$^{th}$ day of December , 1903

TM Bell
**NOTARY PUBLIC.**

( C O P Y )

Lain & Sheegog, Agents,
Lindsay, Ind. Ty.                                April 3, 1905.

Com. to the Five Civilized Tribes,

Dear Sirs:

The child spoken of, we changed its name to Lewis Murray Lindsay, which is the name to enroll him by.

Respectfully,

(Signed) Lewis Lindsay.

## Applications for Enrollment of Choctaw Newborn
## Act of 1905 Volume IX

7-177

**COPY**

Muskogee, Indian Territory, March 31, 1905.

Lewis E. Lindsay,
    Lindsay, Indian Territory.

Dear Sir:

    Referring to the affidavits recently forwarded of Juanita Lindsay and Benjamin W. Ralston to the birth of Lewis Murray Lindsay son of Lewis E. and Juanita Lindsay, August 6, 1903, it appears from our records that on January 13, 1904, there were received at this office the affidavits of Juanita Lindsay and Benjamin W. Ralston to the birth of James Murray Lindsay, son of Lewis E. and Juanita Lindsay, August 6, 1903.

    You are requested to state which is the correct name of the child referred to and under which name you desire to have him enrolled.

Respectfully,

SIGNED    *Tams Bixby*
Chairman.

---

**BIRTH AFFIDAVIT.**

### DEPARTMENT OF THE INTERIOR.
### COMMISSION TO THE FIVE CIVILIZED TRIBES.

---

    IN RE APPLICATION FOR ENROLLMENT, as a citizen of the Chocktaw[sic] Nation, of Lewis Murray Lindsay, born on the 6 day of August, 1903

Name of Father: Lewis E. Lindsay      a citizen of the Chocktaw Nation.
Name of Mother: Juanita Lindsay      a citizen of the Chocktaw Nation.

Postoffice    Lindsay, I.T.

---

**AFFIDAVIT OF MOTHER.**

UNITED STATES OF AMERICA, Indian Territory, }
    Southern      DISTRICT. }

    I, Juanita Lindsay, on oath state that I am 35 years of age and a citizen by Blood, of the Chocktaw Nation; that I am the lawful wife of Lewis Lindsay, who is a citizen, by Intermarriage of the Choctaw Nation;

## Applications for Enrollment of Choctaw Newborn
## Act of 1905   Volume IX

that a   male   child was born to me on   6   day of   August   , 1903; that said child has been named   Lewis Murray Lindsay   , and was living March 4, 1905.

*Signature*                                               Juanita Lindsay

Witnesses To ~~Mark~~:
{ Geo See
{ Robt. May

Subscribed and sworn to before me this 24th   day of   March   , 1905

Robt. May
Notary Public.

---

**AFFIDAVIT OF ATTENDING PHYSICIAN OR MID-WIFE.**

UNITED STATES OF AMERICA, Indian Territory, }
Southern                   DISTRICT.         }

I, Benj. W. Ralston M.D.   , a   Physician   , on oath state that I attended on Mrs.   Lindsay   , wife of   Lewis Lindsay   on the 6th   day of   August   , 1903; that there was born to her on said date a   male   child; that said child was living March 4, 1905, and is said to have been named   Lewis Murray Lindsay

*Signature*                                               Benj. W. Ralston M.D.

Witnesses To ~~Mark~~:
{ Geo See
{ Robt. May

Subscribed and sworn to before me this 24th   day of   March   , 1905

Robt. May
Notary Public.

---

Choc New Born 571
    Velma McClellan   b. 6-30-03
    Stelma McClellan   b. 6-30-03
    Ora M. McClellan   b. 12-27-04

# Applications for Enrollment of Choctaw Newborn
## Act of 1905 Volume IX

BIRTH AFFIDAVIT.

### DEPARTMENT OF THE INTERIOR.
### COMMISSION TO THE FIVE CIVILIZED TRIBES.

IN RE APPLICATION FOR ENROLLMENT, as a citizen of the Choctaw Nation, of Velma MClellan, born on the 30th day of June, 1903

Name of Father: Edmund MClellan     a citizen of the Choctaw Nation.

Name of Mother: Belle MClellan     a non citizen of the ——— Nation.

Postoffice    Nail P.O. I.T.

### AFFIDAVIT OF MOTHER.

UNITED STATES OF AMERICA, Indian Territory, }
Central     DISTRICT.

I, Belle MClellan, on oath state that I am 23 years of age and a non citizen by ———, of the ——— Nation; that I am the lawful wife of Edmund MClellan, who is a citizen, by Blood of the Choctaw Nation; that a Female child was born to me on 30th day of June, 1903; that said child has been named Velma MClellan, and was living March 4, 1905.

                                           Belle MClellan

Witnesses To Mark:

Subscribed and sworn to before me this ____ day of _____, 190__

                                           John R. Price
                                           Notary Public.

### AFFIDAVIT OF ATTENDING PHYSICIAN OR MID-WIFE.

UNITED STATES OF AMERICA, Indian Territory, }
Central     DISTRICT.

I, W.J. Melton, a Physician, on oath state that I attended on Mrs. Belle MClellan, wife of Edmund MClellan on the 30th day of June, 1903; that there was born to her on said date a Female child; that said child was living March 4, 1905, and is said to have been named Velma MClellan

                                           W.J. Melton, M.D.

# Applications for Enrollment of Choctaw Newborn
## Act of 1905 Volume IX

Witnesses To Mark:

{

Subscribed and sworn to before me this 21$^{st}$ day of March , 1905

C.H. Ewing
Notary Public.

---

**BIRTH AFFIDAVIT.**

### DEPARTMENT OF THE INTERIOR.
### COMMISSION TO THE FIVE CIVILIZED TRIBES.

---

IN RE APPLICATION FOR ENROLLMENT, as a citizen of the Choctaw Nation, of Velma M$^c$Lellan , born on the 30 day of June , 1903

Name of Father: Edmund M$^c$Lellan    a citizen of the Choctaw Nation.
Name of Mother: Belle M$^c$Lellan    a citizen of the U.S. Nation.

Postoffice    Nail P.O. Ind.Ter.

---

### AFFIDAVIT OF MOTHER.

UNITED STATES OF AMERICA, Indian Territory, }
Central      DISTRICT.

     I, Belle M$^c$Lellan , on oath state that I am 23 years of age and a citizen by ——— , of the United States Nation; that I am the lawful wife of Edmund M$^c$Lellan , who is a citizen, by Blood of the Choctaw Nation; that a Female child was born to me on 30 day of June , 1903; that said child has been named Velma M$^c$Lellan , and was living March 4, 1905.

Belle M$^c$Lellan

Witnesses To Mark:

{

Subscribed and sworn to before me this 22$^{nd}$ day of April, 1905

J.L. Rappolee
Notary Public.

# Applications for Enrollment of Choctaw Newborn
## Act of 1905   Volume IX

**AFFIDAVIT OF ATTENDING PHYSICIAN OR MID-WIFE.**

UNITED STATES OF AMERICA, Indian Territory, }
Central                    DISTRICT. }

I, W.J. Melton, a Physician, on oath state that I attended on Mrs. Belle M$^c$Lellan, wife of Edmund M$^c$Lellan on the 30 day of June, 1903; that there was born to her on said date a Female child; that said child was living March 4, 1905, and is said to have been named Velma M$^c$Lellan

W.J. Melton

Witnesses To Mark:
{

Subscribed and sworn to before me this 22 day of April, 1905

J.L. Rappolee
Notary Public.

---

7-3919

Muskogee, Indian Territory, April 5, 1905.

Edmund McLellan,
    Nail, Indian Territory.

Dear Sir:

    Receipt is hereby acknowledged of the affidavits of Belle McLellan and W. J. Melton to the birth of Velma McLellan, and Stelma McLellan, children of Edmund and Belle McLellan, June 30, 1903, also the affidavits of Belle McLellan and H. E. Rappolee to the birth of Ora M. McLellan, daughter of Edmund and Belle McLellan, December 27, 1904, and the same have been filed with our records as an application for the enrollment of said children.

Respectfully,

Commissioner in Charge.

---

# Applications for Enrollment of Choctaw Newborn
## Act of 1905 Volume IX

BIRTH AFFIDAVIT.

## DEPARTMENT OF THE INTERIOR.
## COMMISSION TO THE FIVE CIVILIZED TRIBES.

IN RE APPLICATION FOR ENROLLMENT, as a citizen of the Choctaw Nation, of Ora M. MClellan, born on the 27th day of December, 1904

Name of Father: Edmund MClellan     a citizen of the Choctaw Nation.

Name of Mother: Belle MClellan     a *non* citizen of the _____ Nation.

Postoffice    Nail P.O. I.T.

### AFFIDAVIT OF MOTHER.

UNITED STATES OF AMERICA, Indian Territory,
Central DISTRICT.

I, Belle MClellan, on oath state that I am 23 years of age and a *non* citizen by _____, of the _____ Nation; that I am the lawful wife of Edmund MClellan, who is a citizen, by Blood of the Choctaw Nation; that a Female child was born to me on 27th day of December, 1904; that said child has been named Ora M. MClellan, and was living March 4, 1905.

Belle Mclellan

Witnesses To Mark:

Subscribed and sworn to before me this ____ day of _____, 190_

John R. Price
Notary Public.

### AFFIDAVIT OF ATTENDING PHYSICIAN OR MID-WIFE.

UNITED STATES OF AMERICA, Indian Territory,
Central DISTRICT.

I, H. E. Rappolee, a Physician, on oath state that I attended on Mrs. Belle MClellan, wife of Edmund MClellan on the 27th day of December, 1904; that there was born to her on said date a Female child; that said child was living March 4, 1905, and is said to have been named Ora M. MClellan

H.E. Rappolee, M.D.

# Applications for Enrollment of Choctaw Newborn
## Act of 1905   Volume IX

Witnesses To Mark:

{

    Subscribed and sworn to before me this  21$^{st}$  day of    March    , 1905

                          C.H. Ewing
                              Notary Public.

---

**BIRTH AFFIDAVIT.**

### DEPARTMENT OF THE INTERIOR.
### COMMISSION TO THE FIVE CIVILIZED TRIBES.

---

**IN RE APPLICATION FOR ENROLLMENT,** as a citizen of the   Choctaw   Nation, of Ora M. M$^c$Lellan   , born on the   27   day of  December  , 1904

Name of Father:  Edmund M$^c$Lellan       a citizen of the  Choctaw   Nation.
Name of Mother:  Belle M$^c$Lellan       a citizen of the   U.S.   Nation.

                Postoffice   Nail P.O. Ind.Ter.

---

**AFFIDAVIT OF MOTHER.**

UNITED STATES OF AMERICA, Indian Territory, }
   Central           DISTRICT.  }

    I,  Belle M$^c$Lellan   , on oath state that I am  23   years of age and a citizen by ————— , of the  United States  Nation; that I am the lawful wife of   Edmund M$^c$Lellan  , who is a citizen, by Blood  of the   Choctaw   Nation; that a Female  child was born to me on  27   day of  December   , 1904; that said child has been named  Ora M M$^c$Lellan   , and was living March 4, 1905.

                        Belle M$^c$Lellan
Witnesses To Mark:

{

    Subscribed and sworn to before me this   22   day of   April, 1905

                          J.L. Rappolee
                          Notary Public.

# Applications for Enrollment of Choctaw Newborn
## Act of 1905   Volume IX

**AFFIDAVIT OF ATTENDING PHYSICIAN OR MID-WIFE.**

UNITED STATES OF AMERICA, Indian Territory,  
Central    DISTRICT.

I, H.E. Rappolee, a Physician, on oath state that I attended on Mrs. Belle M$^c$Lellan, wife of Edmund M$^c$Lellan on the 27 day of December, 1904; that there was born to her on said date a Female child; that said child was living March 4, 1905, and is said to have been named Ora M M$^c$Lellan

H.E. Rappolee

Witnesses To Mark:

Subscribed and sworn to before me this 22 day of April, 1905

J.L. Rappolee  
Notary Public.

---

**COPY**      Choctaw N.B. 571.

Muskogee, Indian Territory, April 28, 1905.

Edmund McLellan,  
  Nail, Indian Territory.

Dear Sir:

Receipt is hereby acknowledged of the affidavits of Belle McLellan and W. J. Melton to the birth of Stelma McLellan and Velma McLellan, twin children of Edmund and Belle McLellan, June 30, 1903; also the affidavits of Belle McLellan and H. E. Rappolee to the birth of Ora M. McLellan, daughter of Edmund and Belle McLellan, December 27, 1904, and the same have been filed in the matter of the enrollment of said children.

Receipt is also acknowledged of the marriage license and certificate between E. B. McLellan and Miss Bell[sic] Browder, which is offered in support of the application for the enrollment of the above named children, and the same has been filed with the record in this case.

Respectfully,  
SIGNED

*Tams Bixby*  
Chairman.

## Applications for Enrollment of Choctaw Newborn
## Act of 1905   Volume IX

N. B. 571

**COPY**

Muskogee, Indian Territory, April 10, 1905.

Edmund McLellan,
    Nail, Indian Territory.

Dear Sir:

There is inclosed you herewith for execution application for the enrollment of your infant children, Velma McLellan and Stelma McLellan, born June 30, 1903, and Ora M. McLellan, born December 27, 1904.

The affidavits heretofore forwarded to the Commission, show they claim through you. It is, therefore, necessary that you furnish either the original or a certified copy of the license and certificate of your marriage to their mother, Belle McLellan, returning same with the inclosed application.

In having these affidavits executed care should be exercised to see that all names are written in full, as they appear in the body of the affidavit, and in the event that either of the persons signing the affidavit are unable to write, signatures by mark must be attested by two witnesses. Each affidavit must be executed before a Notary Public and the notarial seal and signature of the officer must be attached to each separate affidavit.

Respectfully,
SIGNED
*T. B. Needles.*
Commissioner in Charge.

LM 10-55.

Applications for Enrollment of Choctaw Newborn
Act of 1905   Volume IX

A 1134

Mr   E.B. McLellan

AND

Miss Bell Browder

DEPARTMENT OF THE INTERIOR,
COMMISSION TO THE FIVE CIVILIZED TRIBES.
**FILED**

APR 27 1905

Tams Bixby CHAIRMAN.

## Marriage Certificate

Issued   April 22nd   1905.

Pat Henry   Clerk

By   Henry Wells   Deputy

## Marriage Certificate

STATE OF TEXAS            COUNTY OF

This Instrument Witnesseth that on the 5th day of August A.D. 1902 there was issued out of the office of the Clerk of the County Court of said County a License for the Marriage of

Mr E.B. McLellan

and Miss Bell Browder

and on the 6th day of August A.D. 1902

# Applications for Enrollment of Choctaw Newborn
## Act of 1905   Volume IX

said parties were legally united in Marriage by a properly authorized person, named in said License and due return thereof made to this office in the manner and form required by law, all of which is duly entered upon the Marriage Records of my office in Vol  N.  Page 269

**Witness** my hand and official seal at my office in Benham Texas on this the 22nd day of April A.D. 1905.

Pat Henry
Clerk County Court Fannin County Texas
By  Henry Wells
Deputy

---

BIRTH AFFIDAVIT.

### DEPARTMENT OF THE INTERIOR.
### COMMISSION TO THE FIVE CIVILIZED TRIBES.

---

IN RE APPLICATION FOR ENROLLMENT, as a citizen of the Choctaw Nation, of Stelma MClellan, born on the 30$^{th}$ day of June, 1903

Name of Father: Edmund MClellan          a citizen of the Choctaw Nation.

Name of Mother: Belle MClellan          a ^non citizen of the _____ Nation.

Postoffice  Nail P.O. I.T.

---

### AFFIDAVIT OF MOTHER.

UNITED STATES OF AMERICA, Indian Territory,  }
  Central               DISTRICT.

I, Belle MClellan, on oath state that I am 23 years of age and a ^non citizen by _____, of the _____ Nation; that I am the lawful wife of Edmund MClellan, who is a citizen, by Blood of the Choctaw Nation; that a

231

## Applications for Enrollment of Choctaw Newborn
## Act of 1905   Volume IX

Male   child was born to me on   30th   day of   June   , 1903; that said child has been named   Stelma MClellan   , and was living March 4, 1905.

Belle Mclellan

Witnesses To Mark:

Subscribed and sworn to before me this ........ day of ......................., 190....

John R. Price
Notary Public.

---

**AFFIDAVIT OF ATTENDING PHYSICIAN OR MID-WIFE.**

UNITED STATES OF AMERICA, Indian Territory,
Central    DISTRICT.

I,   W.J. Melton   , a   Physician   , on oath state that I attended on Mrs.   Belle MClellan   , wife of   Edmund MClellan   on the   30th   day of June, 1903; that there was born to her on said date a   Male   child; that said child was living March 4, 1905, and is said to have been named   Stelma MClellan

W.J. Melton M.D.

Witnesses To Mark:

Subscribed and sworn to before me this   21st   day of   March   , 1905

C.H. Ewing
Notary Public.

---

BIRTH AFFIDAVIT.

## DEPARTMENT OF THE INTERIOR.
## COMMISSION TO THE FIVE CIVILIZED TRIBES.

IN RE APPLICATION FOR ENROLLMENT, as a citizen of the   Choctaw   Nation, of   Stelma M[c]Lellan   , born on the   30   day of   June   , 1903

Name of Father: Edmund M[c]Lellan      a citizen of the   Choctaw   Nation.
Name of Mother: Belle M[c]Lellan       a citizen of the   U.S.   Nation.

Postoffice   Nail P.O. Ind.Ter.

# Applications for Enrollment of Choctaw Newborn
# Act of 1905  Volume IX

**AFFIDAVIT OF MOTHER.**

UNITED STATES OF AMERICA, Indian Territory, }
Central       DISTRICT.

I, Belle M$^c$Lellan, on oath state that I am 23 years of age and a citizen by ———, of the United States Nation; that I am the lawful wife of Edmund M$^c$Lellan, who is a citizen, by Blood of the Choctaw Nation; that a Male child was born to me on 30 day of June, 1903; that said child has been named Stelma M$^c$Lellan, and was living March 4, 1905.

Belle M$^c$Lellan

Witnesses To Mark:
{

Subscribed and sworn to before me this 22 day of April, 1905

J.L. Rappolee
Notary Public.

---

**AFFIDAVIT OF ATTENDING PHYSICIAN OR MID-WIFE.**

UNITED STATES OF AMERICA, Indian Territory, }
Central       DISTRICT.

I, W.J. Melton, a Physician, on oath state that I attended on Mrs. Belle M$^c$Lellan, wife of Edmund M$^c$Lellan on the 30 day of June, 1903; that there was born to her on said date a Male child; that said child was living March 4, 1905, and is said to have been named Stelma M$^c$Lellan

W.J. Melton

Witnesses To Mark:
{

Subscribed and sworn to before me this 22 day of April, 1905

J.L. Rappolee
Notary Public.

## Applications for Enrollment of Choctaw Newborn
## Act of 1905   Volume IX

Choc New Born 572
   Mary Margarite Oakes   b. 11-23-03

---

**BIRTH AFFIDAVIT.**

## DEPARTMENT OF THE INTERIOR.
## COMMISSION TO THE FIVE CIVILIZED TRIBES.

---

**IN RE APPLICATION FOR ENROLLMENT,** as a citizen of the       Choctaw       Nation, of Mary Margarite Oakes       , born on the 23$^{rd}$    day of   November   , 1903

Name of Father: Daniel W Oakes          a citizen of the   Choctaw   Nation.
Name of Mother: Mary A Oakes          a citizen of the   Choctaw   Nation.

Postoffice    Atlas, I.T.

---

**AFFIDAVIT OF MOTHER.**

UNITED STATES OF AMERICA, Indian Territory, }
   Central        DISTRICT.

I, Mary A. Oakes   , on oath state that I am   25   years of age and a citizen by   blood   , of the   Choctaw   Nation; that I am the lawful wife of   Daniel W. Oakes   , who is a citizen, by blood   of the   Choctaw   Nation; that a Female   child was born to me on   23$^{rd}$   day of   November   , 1903; that said child has been named   Mary Margarite Oakes   , and was living March 4, 1905.

                              Mary A Oakes
Witnesses To Mark:
{

Subscribed and sworn to before me this  29  day of    March    , 1905

                              H. Morris
                                 Notary Public.

---

**AFFIDAVIT OF ATTENDING PHYSICIAN OR MID-WIFE.**

UNITED STATES OF AMERICA, Indian Territory, }
   Central        DISTRICT.

I, Isabell Reynolds   , a   midwife   , on oath state that I attended on Mrs.   Mary A Oakes   , wife of   Daniel W Oakes   on the   23$^{rd}$   day of   November , 1903; that there was born to her on said date a   Female   child; that said child was living March 4, 1905, and is said to have been named   Mary Margarite Oakes

# Applications for Enrollment of Choctaw Newborn
## Act of 1905 Volume IX

Witnesses To Mark:
{ Mary Abnerson
  Alonzo Jeter

Isabell x Reynolds
(her mark)

Subscribed and sworn to before me this 29 day of March, 1905

H. Morris
Notary Public.

---

Choc New Born 572
    Magdaline Ludlow *(b. 9-4-1905)*
    Granted 2-21-07

---

23-572

Muskogee, Indian Territory, October 23, 1906.

Austin Ludlow,
    Ludlow, Indian Territory.

Dear Sir:

    In the matter of the application for the enrollment of Magdalene Ludlow, child of yourself and Josephine Ludlow, born September 4, 1905, you are advised that it appears that no physician or midwife was in attendance at the birth of this child. It will therefore be necessary that you forward the affidavits of two disinterested witnesses who know of the birth of this child, the date of her birth, the names of her parents, and that she was living March 4, 1906.

    This matter should receive your immediate attention in order that disposition may be made of the application for the enrollment of said child.

Respectfully,

Commissioner.

# Applications for Enrollment of Choctaw Newborn
## Act of 1905   Volume IX

23-572
23-855

Muskogee, Indian Territory, December 10, 1906.

A. W. James,
      Smithville, Indian Territory.

Dear Sir:

    Receipt is hereby acknowledged of your letter of November 22, 1906, transmitting affidavit of Ester Samuel Ludlow to the birth of Nellie Samuel Ludlow, child of Silward and Ester Samuel Ludlow, November 19, 1905; also affidavits of Josephene[sic] Ludlow and Lemsay Ludlow to the birth of Magdalene Ludlow, child of Austen and Josephene Ludlow, September 4, 1905, and the same have been filed in the matter of the enrollment of said children.

                              Respectfully,

                              Commissioner.

---

23-572

Muskogee, Indian Territory, December 12, 1906.

Austin Ludlow,
      Ludlow, Indian Territory.

Dear Sir:

    In the matter of the application for the enrollment of your child Magdalene Ludlow it appears from the affidavit of Josephene[sic] Ludlow executed before W. H. Martin June 4, 1906 that no one was present at the birth of this child, but yourself and your husband, while there was received at this office subsequently the affidavit of Lemsy Ludlow; that she acted as midwife at the birth of your child Magdalene Ludlow.

    You are requested to explain why it is stated in one affidavit that no one was present at the birth of this child while subsequently the affidavit of the midwife was forwarded.

                              Respectfully,

                              Commissioner.

# Applications for Enrollment of Choctaw Newborn
## Act of 1905   Volume IX

BIRTH AFFIDAVIT.

### DEPARTMENT OF THE INTERIOR,
### COMMISSIONER TO THE FIVE CIVILIZED TRIBES.

ENROLLMENT OF MINORS.   ACT OF CONGRESS, APPROVED APRIL 26, 1906.

IN RE APPLICATION FOR ENROLLMENT, as a citizen of the   Choctaw   Nation, of  Magdaline Ludlow  , born on the   4   day of  Sept  , 1905

Name of Father:  Austin Ludlow          a citizen of the  Choctaw   Nation.

*formerly Wilkin*

Name of Mother:  Josephine Ludlow       a citizen of the  Choctaw   Nation.

Tribal enrollment of father ............................ Tribal enrollment of mother ..........................

Postoffice   Ludlow I.T.

---

### AFFIDAVIT OF MOTHER.

UNITED STATES OF AMERICA, Indian Territory, }
Central                      District.         }

I,  Josephine Ludlow  , on oath state that I am  24  years of age and a citizen by blood , of the  Choctaw  Nation; that I am the lawful wife of  Austin Ludlow  , who is a citizen, by blood of the  Choctaw  Nation; that a  female  child was born to me on  4  day of  Sept  , 1905 , that said child has been named  Magdaline Ludlow  , and was living March 4, 1906. *that no one was present at the birth of the child except myself and my husband, Austin Ludlow*

                                                     her
                                 Josephine  x  Ludlow

WITNESSES TO MARK:             mark
{ *(Name Illegible)*
{ W^m L Martin

Subscribed and sworn to before me this   4  day of  June  , 1906.

                                 W.H. Martin
                                    Notary Public.

---

### AFFIDAVIT OF ATTENDING PHYSICIAN OR MID-WIFE.

UNITED STATES OF AMERICA, Indian Territory, }
Central                      District.         }

I,  Austin Ludlow husband of Josephine Ludlow formerly Wilkin, on oath state that I attended on  Josephine Ludlow  , wife of   myself    on the 4 day of Sept , 1905;

## Applications for Enrollment of Choctaw Newborn
## Act of 1905   Volume IX

that there was born to her on said date a   female   child; that said child was living March 4, 1906, and is said to have been named   Magdaline Ludlow

Austin Ludlow

WITNESSES TO MARK:
{

Subscribed and sworn to before me this   4   day of   June , 1906.

W.H. Martin<br>Notary Public.

BIRTH AFFIDAVIT.

### DEPARTMENT OF THE INTERIOR,
### COMMISSIONER TO THE FIVE CIVILIZED TRIBES.

ENROLLMENT OF MINORS.   ACT OF CONGRESS, APPROVED APRIL 26, 1906.

IN RE APPLICATION FOR ENROLLMENT, as a citizen of the   Choctaw   Nation, of   Magdaline Ludlow   , born on the   4   day of   Sept   , 1905

Name of Father: Austin Ludlow            a citizen of the   Choctaw   Nation.
Name of Mother: Josephine Ludlow & Wilken   a citizen of the   Choctaw   Nation.

Tribal enrollment of father   Roll No 5895   Tribal enrollment of mother   Roll No 6081

Postoffice   Ludlow Ind. Ter.

AFFIDAVIT OF MOTHER.

UNITED STATES OF AMERICA, Indian Territory, }
   Central               District.           }

I,   Josephene Ludlow   , on oath state that I am   28   years of age and a citizen by Choctaw   , of the   Choctaw   Nation; that I am the lawful wife of   Austin Ludlow   , who is a citizen, by   Blood   of the   Choctaw   Nation; that a   female   child was born to me on 4   day of   September   , 1906[sic] , that said child has been named   Magdaline Ludlow   , and was living March 4, 1906. *that no one was present at the birth of the child except myself and my husband, Austin Ludlow*

Josephine Ludlow

WITNESSES TO MARK:
{ Steven Bohanan
{ Silway Bohanan

# Applications for Enrollment of Choctaw Newborn
## Act of 1905   Volume IX

Subscribed and sworn to before me this   26   day of   Nov. , 1906.

*(Name Illegible)*
Notary Public.

---

### AFFIDAVIT OF ATTENDING PHYSICIAN OR MID-WIFE.

UNITED STATES OF AMERICA, Indian Territory, }
Central                           District. }

I,   Lemsay Ludlow   , a   midwife   on oath state that I attended on Josephine Ludlow  , wife of   Austin Ludlow   on the  4  day of  Sept , 1905; that there was born to her on said date a   female   child; that said child was living March 4, 1906, and is said to have been named   Magdaline Ludlow

Lemsay Ludlow

WITNESSES TO MARK:
{ Steven Bohanan
{ Silway Bohanan

Subscribed and sworn to before me this   26   day of   Nov. , 1906.

*(Name Illegible)*
Notary Public.

---

23-572

O.L.J.

## DEPARTMENT OF THE INTERIOR,
## COMMISSIONER TO THE FIVE CIVILIZED TRIBES.
-----

In the matter of the application for the enrollment of Magdaline Ludlow as a citizen by blood of the Choctaw Nation.

### DECISION.

It appears from the record herein that on June 4, 1906, application was made to the Commissioner to the Five Civilized Tribes for the enrollment of Magdaline Ludlow as a citizen by blood of the Choctaw Nation, under the provisions of the Act of Congress approved April 26, 1906 (34 Stats., 137).

It further appears from the record herein and from the records in the possession of this office that said applicant was born on September 4, 1905, and is the daughter of Austin Ludlow whose name appears opposite No. 5895 upon the final roll of citizens by blood of the Choctaw Nation approved by the Secretary of the Interior January 16, 1903, and Josephine Ludlow whose name as Josephine Wilkin appears as No. 6081 upon the

## Applications for Enrollment of Choctaw Newborn
## Act of 1905   Volume IX

final roll of citizens by blood of the Choctaw Nation approved by the Secretary of the Interior January 17, 1903; and that said applicant was living on March 4, 1906.

I am, therefore, of the opinion that Magdaline Ludlow should be enrolled as a citizen by blood of the Choctaw Nation, under the provisions of the Act of Congress approved April 26, 1906 (34 Stats., 137), and it is so ordered.

Tams Bixby   Commissioner.

Muskogee, Indian Territory.
FEB 18 1907

**COPY**

23-572

Muskogee, Indian Territory, February 25, 1907.

Austin Ludlow,
    Ludlow, Indian Territory.

Dear Sir:-

Inclosed herewith you will find a copy of the decision of the Commissioner to the Five Civilized Tribes, rendered February 18, 1907, granting the application for the enrollment of Magdaline Ludlow as a citizen by blood of the Choctaw Nation.

You are hereby advised that the name of Magdaline Ludlow has been placed upon a schedule of Choctaw freedmen to be submitted to the Secretary of the Interior for his approval. You will be notified of Departmental action thereon.

Respectfully,

SIGNED

*Tams Bixby*
Commissioner.

Incl. 23-572
Registered.

# Applications for Enrollment of Choctaw Newborn
## Act of 1905  Volume IX

**COPY**

23-572

Muskogee, Indian Territory, February 25, 1907.

Mansfield, McMurray & Cornish,
    Attorneys for the Choctaw and Chickasaw Nations.
      South McAlester, Indian Territory.

Gentlemen:-

    Inclosed herewith you will find a copy of the decision of the Commissioner to the Five Civilized Tribes, rendered February 18, 1907, granting the application for the enrollment of Magdaline Ludlow as a citizen by blood of the Choctaw Nation.

    You are hereby advised that the name of Magdaline Ludlow has been placed upon a schedule of Choctaw freedmen to be submitted to the Secretary of the Interior for his approval. You will be notified of Departmental action thereon.

                    Respectfully,

                    SIGNED  *Tams Bixby*
                           Commissioner.

Incl. 23-572
Registered.

---

Choc New Born 573
    Durie McClish   b. 12-15-04

                             7-3180

Muskogee, Indian Territory, April 5, 1905.

Lorden McClish,
    Wilburton, Indian Territory.

Dear Sir:

    Receipt is hereby acknowledged of the affidavits of Sissy McClish and John J. Gill to the birth of Durie McClish, son of Lorden and Sissy McClish, December 15, 1904, and the same have been filed with our records as an application for the enrollment of said child.

### Applications for Enrollment of Choctaw Newborn
### Act of 1905 Volume IX

Respectfully,

Commissioner in Charge.

## AFFIDAVIT OF ATTENDING PHYSICIAN OR MIDWIFE

UNITED STATES OF AMERICA
INDIAN TERRITORY
Central DISTRICT

I, Dr. J.J. Gill a Physician on oath state that I attended on Mrs. M$^c$Clish wife of Lorden M$^c$Clish on the 15 day of December, 1904, that there was born to her on said date a male child, that said child is now living, and is said to have been named Durie M$^c$Clish

Jno J Gill    *M.D.*

Subscribed and sworn to before me this, the 14 day of Feb 1905

J F Maxey    Notary Public.

WITNESSETH:
Must be two witnesses who are citizens
- Willis Hancock
- Ellen Thompson

We hereby certify that we are well acquainted with Dr. John J Gill a Physician and know him to be reputable and of good standing in the community.

*(Name Illegible)*

B.A. Welch

# Applications for Enrollment of Choctaw Newborn
## Act of 1905   Volume IX

**NEW-BORN AFFIDAVIT.**

Number..........

### ...Choctaw Enrolling Commission...

IN THE MATTER OF THE APPLICATION FOR ENROLLMENT, as a citizen of the Choctaw Nation, of Durie M$^c$Clish

born on the 15 day of __December__ 190 4

Name of father   Lorden M$^c$Clish          a citizen of   Choctaw
Nation final enrollment No.  9037
Name of mother   Sissie M$^c$Clish          a citizen of   Choctaw
Nation final enrollment No.  9203

Postoffice   Red Oak I.T.

### AFFIDAVIT OF MOTHER.

UNITED STATES OF AMERICA
INDIAN TERRITORY
Central   DISTRICT

I   Sissie M$^c$Clish   , on oath state that I am 19 years of age and a citizen by blood of the Choctaw Nation, and as such have been placed upon the final roll of the Choctaw Nation, by the Honorable Secretary of the Interior my final enrollment number being 9203 ; that I am the lawful wife of Lorden M$^c$Clish , who is a citizen of the Choctaw Nation, and as such has been placed upon the final roll of said Nation by the Honorable Secretary of the Interior, his final enrollment number being 9031 and that a Male child was born to me on the 15 day of December 190 4; that said child has been named Durie M$^c$Clish , and is now living.

Sissie M$^c$Clish

Witnesseth.
Must be two Witnesses who are Citizens.
Willis Hancock
Ellen x Thompson
her mark

Subscribed and sworn to before me this 14 day of Feb 190 5

J F Maxey
Notary Public.

My commission expires: Jan 1907

## Applications for Enrollment of Choctaw Newborn
## Act of 1905 Volume IX

BIRTH AFFIDAVIT.

### DEPARTMENT OF THE INTERIOR.
### COMMISSION TO THE FIVE CIVILIZED TRIBES.

IN RE APPLICATION FOR ENROLLMENT, as a citizen of the Choctaw Nation, of Durie McClish , born on the 15th day of December , 1904

Name of Father: Lorden McClish    a citizen of the Choctaw Nation.
Name of Mother: Sissy McClish    a citizen of the Choctaw Nation.

Postoffice    Wilburton, Ind. Ter.

#### AFFIDAVIT OF MOTHER.

UNITED STATES OF AMERICA, Indian Territory,  
    Central     DISTRICT.

I, Sissy M$^c$Clish , on oath state that I am 19 years of age and a citizen by blood , of the Choctaw Nation; that I am the lawful wife of Lorden M$^c$Clish, who is a citizen, by blood of the Choctaw Nation; that a male child was born to me on 15 day of December , 1904; that said child has been named Durie M$^c$Clish , and was living March 4, 1905.

                                    Sissy McClish

Witnesses To Mark:

Subscribed and sworn to before me this 31 day of March , 1905

                                    J.D. Yandell
                                         Notary Public.

#### AFFIDAVIT OF ATTENDING PHYSICIAN OR MID-WIFE.

UNITED STATES OF AMERICA, Indian Territory,  
    Central     DISTRICT.

I, John J Gill , a Physician , on oath state that I attended on Mrs. Sissy M$^c$Clish , wife of Lorden M$^c$Clish on the 15 day of December, 1904; that there was born to her on said date a male child; that said child was living March 4, 1905, and is said to have been named Durie M$^c$Clish

                                    Jno J Gill, M.D.

Witnesses To Mark:

## Applications for Enrollment of Choctaw Newborn
## Act of 1905   Volume IX

Subscribed and sworn to before me this 31 day of    March    , 1905

                                 J.D. Yandell
                                         Notary Public.

---

Choc New Born 574
      Jimmey Coone   b. 9-28-04

### *Affidavit of Attending Physician or Midwife*

UNITED STATES OF AMERICA,
   INDIAN TERRITORY,
    Central      DISTRICT

    I,     J M Parsons       a       Physician
on oath state that I attended on Mrs.  Viney Coon     wife of   Albert Coon
on the  $28^{th}$    day of  Sept  , 190 4, that there was born to her on said date a   male   child, that said child is now living, and is said to have been named   James Coon

                              J M Parsons              M. D.

    Subscribed and sworn to before me this the   $16^{th}$   day of   Jan    1905

                              W A Shoney
                                     Notary Public.

WITNESSETH:
  Must be two witnesses   { S.L. Bacon
  who are citizens and
  know the child.               H.L. Gooding

    We hereby certify that we are well acquainted with     J M Parsons
a   Physician          and know      him     to be reputable and of good standing in the community.

                        Must be two citizen { S.L. Bacon
                        witnesses.                H.L. Gooding

# Applications for Enrollment of Choctaw Newborn
## Act of 1905   Volume IX

BIRTH AFFIDAVIT.

**DEPARTMENT OF THE INTERIOR.**
**COMMISSION TO THE FIVE CIVILIZED TRIBES.**

IN RE APPLICATION FOR ENROLLMENT, as a citizen of the  Choctaw  Nation, of  Jimmey Coon[sic]  , born on the 28$^{th}$ day of Sept , 1904

Name of Father: ........................................ a citizen of the  ~~Choctaw~~  Nation.
Name of Mother:  Viney Coone  citizen of the  Choctaw  Nation.

Postoffice  Soper, I.T.

**AFFIDAVIT OF MOTHER.**

UNITED STATES OF AMERICA, Indian Territory,
Central   DISTRICT.

I,  Viney Coone  , on oath state that I am  30 years  years of age and a citizen by  Blood  , of the  Choctaw  Nation; that I am the lawful wife of ——————— , who is a citizen, by ——— of the ——————— Nation; that a  male  child was born to me on  28$^{th}$  day of  September  , 1904; that said child has been named  Jimmey Coone  , and was living March 4, 1905.

                                  her
                        Viney x Coone
Witnesses To Mark:                 mark
  R.C. Bills
  S.S. Markham

Subscribed and sworn to before me this  31$^{st}$ day of  March  , 1905

*My commission expires*         WE Larecy
*July 9$^{th}$, 1908.*            Notary Public.

**AFFIDAVIT OF ATTENDING PHYSICIAN OR MID-WIFE.**

UNITED STATES OF AMERICA, Indian Territory,
Central   DISTRICT.

I,  John M Parsons  , on oath state that I attended on Mrs.  Viney Coone  , wife of ——— on the 28$^{th}$ day of Sept , 1904; that there was born to her on said date a  male  child; that said child was living March 4, 1905, and is said to have been named Jimmey Coone

                        John M Parsons

# Applications for Enrollment of Choctaw Newborn
## Act of 1905 Volume IX

Witnesses To Mark:
{

Subscribed and sworn to before me this 31ˢᵗ day of March , 1905

*My commission expires*
*July 9ᵗʰ, 1908.*

WE Larecy
Notary Public.

---

## NEW-BORN AFFIDAVIT.

Number..............

### ...Choctaw Enrolling Commission...

IN THE MATTER OF THE APPLICATION FOR ENROLLMENT, as a citizen of the Choctaw Nation, of James Coon

born on the 28ᵗʰ day of ___Sept___ 190 4

Name of father    Albert Coon         a citizen of    white
Nation final enrollment No. ———
Name of mother    Viney Coon          a citizen of    Choctaw
Nation final enrollment No. 4001

Postoffice    Soper I.T.

### AFFIDAVIT OF MOTHER.

UNITED STATES OF AMERICA
INDIAN TERRITORY
   Central    DISTRICT

I    Viney Coon    , on oath state that I am 35 years of age and a citizen by blood of the Choctaw Nation, and as such have been placed upon the final roll of the Choctaw Nation, by the Honorable Secretary of the Interior my final enrollment number being    4001 ; that I am the lawful wife of    Albert Coone[sic]    , who is a citizen of the    white    Nation, and as such has been placed upon the final roll of said Nation by the Honorable Secretary of the Interior, his final enrollment number being    ——— and that a    Male    child was born to me on the    28 day of    Sept    190 4; that said child has been named    James Coon    , and is now living.

                                    her
                        Viney Coon x
Witnesseth.                         mark
   Must be two  } S.L. Bacon
   Witnesses who }
   are Citizens.    H.L. Gooding

## Applications for Enrollment of Choctaw Newborn
## Act of 1905   Volume IX

Subscribed and sworn to before me this   16   day of   Jan     190 5

                                                               W A Shoney
                                                                       Notary Public.

My commission expires:
Jan 10, 1909

---

**BIRTH AFFIDAVIT.**

## DEPARTMENT OF THE INTERIOR.
## COMMISSION TO THE FIVE CIVILIZED TRIBES.

---

     IN RE APPLICATION FOR ENROLLMENT, as a citizen of the   Choctaw   Nation, of Jimmey Coon   , born on the   28th   day of   Sept.   , 1904

Name of Father: ..................................................  a citizen of the ........................... Nation.
Name of Mother:  Viney Coone                a citizen of the   Choctaw   Nation.

                                Postoffice     Soper, I. T.

---

### AFFIDAVIT OF MOTHER.

UNITED STATES OF AMERICA, Indian Territory, }
    Central                    DISTRICT.

     I,   Viney Coone       , on oath state that I am   30 years   years of age and a citizen by   blood   , of the   Choctaw   Nation; that I am the lawful wife of --------------------- , who is a citizen, by ------------- of the ............................ Nation; that a   male   child was born to me on   28th   day of   September   , 1904; that said child has been named  Jimmey Coone   , and was living March 4, 1905.

                                            her
                                       Viney  x  Coone
Witnesses To Mark:                          mark
(SEAL) R. C. Bills
       S. S. Markham

     Subscribed and sworn to before me this   31st   day of   March     , 1905

My commission expires                       W. E. Laricy[sic]
  July 9th, 1908.                          Notary Public.

# Applications for Enrollment of Choctaw Newborn
# Act of 1905  Volume IX

**AFFIDAVIT OF ATTENDING PHYSICIAN OR MID-WIFE.**

UNITED STATES OF AMERICA, Indian Territory, }
　　Central　　　　　　　　DISTRICT.

　　I,　John M. Parsons　　　, a........................, on oath state that I attended on Mrs. Vinie[sic] Coone　, wife of ------------------ on the 28th day of Sept., 190_; that there was born to her on said date a　male　child; that said child was living March 4, 1905, and is said to have been named Jimmey Coone

(SEAL)　　　　　　　　　　　　　　(Signed) John M. Parsons
Witnesses To Mark:
{　My commission expires
　　　July 9th, 1908.
　　Subscribed and sworn to before me this　31st day of　March　, 1905

　　　　　　　　　　　　　　W.E. Laricy
　　　　　　　　　　　　　　　　Notary Public.

---

　　This is to certify that I am the officer having custody of the records pertaining to the enrollment of the members of the Choctaw, Chickasaw, Cherokee, Creek and Seminole Tribes of Indians, and the disposition of the land of said tribes, and that the above and foregoing is a true and correct copy of birth affidavit of Jimmey Coone, Choctaw New Born Roll No. 438, on file in this office.

Muskogee, Oklahoma,
　　November 11, 1909.

---

Choc New Born 575
　　Calvin Thompson  b. 1-17-03

# Applications for Enrollment of Choctaw Newborn
## Act of 1905   Volume IX

COMMISSIONERS:
TAMS BIXBY,
THOMAS B. NEEDLES,
C.R. BRECKINBRIDGE.

WM. O. BEALL
Secretary

**DEPARTMENT OF THE INTERIOR,**
**COMMISSIONER TO THE FIVE CIVILIZED TRIBES.**

ADDRESS ONLY THE
COMMISSION TO THE FIVE CIVILIZED TRIBES.

$W^m O.B.$

REFER IN REPLY TO THE FOLLOWING:

7-NB-575.

Muskogee, Indian Territory, May 26, 1905.

Wilburn Thompson,
    Atoka, Indian Territory.
Dear Sir:

    There is enclosed you herewith for execution application for the enrollment of your infant child, Calvin Thompson.

    In the affidavits filed in this office on the 6th ultimo, the date of the child's birth is given as January 17, 1903, while in those filed on the 26th ultimo, the mother gives the date of birth as February 17, 1903, and the midwife gives it as January 17, 1903. In the enclosed application the date of birth is left blank. Please insert the correct date and, when the application is properly executed, return it to this office.

    In having these affidavits executed care should be exercised to see that all names are written in full, as they appear in the body of the affidavit, and in the event that either of the persons signing the affidavit are unable to write, signatures by mark must be attested by two witnesses. Each affidavit must be executed before a Notary Public and the notarial seal and signature of the officer must be attached to each separate affidavit.

                          Respectfully,

                            Tams Bixby

VR 26-3.                                        Chairman.

---

*(The above letter given again.)*

---

## Applications for Enrollment of Choctaw Newborn
## Act of 1905   Volume IX

7-NB 575

Muskogee, Indian Territory, April 20, 1905.

Wilburn Thompson,
    Atoka, Indian Territory.

Dear Sir:

    Receipt is hereby acknowledged of your letter without date giving the names of the parents of Amanda Thompson and her roll number.

    This information has been made a matter of record.

Respectfully,

Chairman.

---

N. B. 575

**COPY**

Muskogee, Indian Territory, April 8, 1905.

Wilburn Thompson,
    Atoka, Indian Territory.

Dear Sir:

    Referring to the affidavits heretofore forwarded, relative to the birth of Calvin Thompson, born January 17, 1903, it is stated in the affidavit of the mother, Amanda Thompson, that she is a citizen by blood of the Choctaw Nation.

    If this is correct you are requested to state when, where and under what name she was listed for enrollment, the names of her parents and other members of her family for whom application was made at the same time, and if she has selected her allotment, give her roll number as the same appears upon her allotment certificate.

Respectfully,
SIGNED
*T. B. Needles.*
Commissioner in Charge.

7-4174 R 11716
Name of father *Alfred Bacon*
Name of mother *Bicy Wilson*

---

Applications for Enrollment of Choctaw Newborn
Act of 1905   Volume IX

# NEW BORN AFFIDAVIT

No _____

## CHOCTAW ENROLLING COMMISSION

IN THE MATTER OF THE APPLICATION FOR ENROLLMENT as a citizen of the Choctaw Nation, of Calvin Thompson born on the $17^{th}$ day of January 190 3

Name of father  Wilburn Thompson  a citizen of  Choctaw  Nation, final enrollment No. 11976  *Thompson*

Name of mother  Mandy Jones *now*  a citizen of  Choctaw  Nation, final enrollment No. 11716

Atoka I.T.  Postoffice.

### AFFIDAVIT OF MOTHER

UNITED STATES OF AMERICA }
INDIAN TERRITORY }
DISTRICT    Central    }

I   Mandy Jones, now Thompson  , on oath state that I am  19  years of age and a citizen by   blood   of the   Choctaw   Nation, and as such have been placed upon the final roll of the  Choctaw  Nation, by the Honorable Secretary of the Interior my final enrollment number being   11716  ; that I am the lawful wife of  Wilburn Thompson , who is a citizen of the   Choctaw   Nation, and as such has been placed upon the final roll of said Nation by the Honorable Secretary of the Interior, his final enrollment number being  11976  and that a   male   child was born to me on the   $17^{th}$  day of January 190 3; that said child has been named  Calvin Thompson  , and is now living.

                                her
WITNESSETH:        Mandy x Thompson
Must be two witnesses { Wallace Thompson
who are citizens      { Elias Harris

Subscribed and sworn to before me this, the  $22^{d}$  day of   February  , 190 5

A.E. Folsom
Notary Public.

My Commission Expires:
Jan 9 - 1909

## Applications for Enrollment of Choctaw Newborn
## Act of 1905    Volume IX

*Affidavit of Attending Physician or Midwife*

UNITED STATES OF AMERICA,  
INDIAN TERRITORY,  
Central    DISTRICT

I, Isabell Johnson    a    Mid wife on oath state that I attended on Mrs. Mandy Jones now Thompson    wife of Wilburn Thompson on the    17th    day of January    , 190 3, that there was born to her on said date a male    child, that said child is now living, and is said to have been named    Calvin Thompson

Isabell Johnson    Mid Wife.

Subscribed and sworn to before me this the    22    day of    February    1905

A.E. Folsom  
Notary Public.

WITNESSETH:  
Must be two witnesses who are citizens and know the child.  
{ Wallace Thompson  
Elias Harris

We hereby certify that we are well acquainted with    Isabell Johnson a    mid wife    and know    her    to be reputable and of good standing in the community.

Must be two citizen witnesses.  
{ Wallace Thompson  
Elias Harris

DEPARTMENT OF THE INTERIOR,  
COMMISSION TO THE FIVE CIVILIZED TRIBES.

In the Matter of the Enrollment of Calvin Thompson, as a citizen by blood of the Choctaw Nation, Indian Territory:-

Comes now Wilburn Thompson, of lawful age, and being by me first duly sworn deposes and says:-

That Calvin Thompson, my minor child, was born on the 17th day of January, 1903, and the mother of said child is Amanda Thompson, nee Jones. That the midwife who was present at the time of the birth of said child has gone to some other country, and here[sic] whereabouts at this time are unknown to me. That said child was a male child, is now living and is named Calvin Thompson, and he offers this, his affidavit, in support of said application in lieu of the usual form, subscribed and attested by the mid-wife.

Wilburn Thompson

# Applications for Enrollment of Choctaw Newborn
## Act of 1905   Volume IX

Subscribed in my presence and sworn to before me, this 1st day of June, 1905.

                EA Newman
                Notary Public.

BIRTH AFFIDAVIT.

## DEPARTMENT OF THE INTERIOR.
## COMMISSION TO THE FIVE CIVILIZED TRIBES.

IN RE APPLICATION FOR ENROLLMENT, as a citizen of the Choctaw Nation, of Calvin Thompson, born on the 17$^{th}$ day of January, 1903

Name of Father: Wilburn Thompson   a citizen of the Choctaw Nation.
Name of Mother: Amanda Thompson (nee Jones) a citizen of the Choctaw Nation.

                Postoffice   Atoka Ind Ter

### AFFIDAVIT OF MOTHER.

UNITED STATES OF AMERICA, Indian Territory,
................................................DISTRICT.

I, Amandy Thompson (Jones), on oath state that I am 19 years of age and a citizen by blood, of the Choctaw Nation; that I am the lawful wife of Wilburn Thompson, who is a citizen, by blood of the Choctaw Nation; that a male child was born to me on 17$^{th}$ day of January, 1903; that said child has been named Calvin Thompson, and was living March 4, 1905.

                      her
              Amanda x Thompson
Witnesses To Mark:      mark
  { Chas Moses
    Wilson Jones

Subscribed and sworn to before me this 1$^{st}$ day of June, 1905

                EA Newman
                  Notary Public.

# Applications for Enrollment of Choctaw Newborn
## Act of 1905   Volume IX

**AFFIDAVIT OF ATTENDING PHYSICIAN OR MID-WIFE.**

UNITED STATES OF AMERICA, Indian Territory, }
................................................ DISTRICT. }

I,................................., a..........................., on oath state that I attended on Mrs. Amanda Thompson, wife of Wilburn Thompson on the ........ day of ........................................., 1......; that there was born to her on said date a male child; that said child was living March 4, 1905, and is said to have been named Calvin Thompson

Witnesses To Mark:

{ ...................................
{ ...................................

Subscribed and sworn to before me this ........ day of ..........., 1905.

........................................................
Notary Public.

---

BIRTH AFFIDAVIT.

### DEPARTMENT OF THE INTERIOR.
### COMMISSION TO THE FIVE CIVILIZED TRIBES.

---

**IN RE APPLICATION FOR ENROLLMENT**, as a citizen of the Choctaw Nation, of Calvin Thompson, born on the 17 day of January, 1903

Name of Father: Wilburn Thompson    a citizen of the Choctaw Nation.
Name of Mother: Amanda Thompson nee Jones    a citizen of the Choctaw Nation.

Postoffice    Atoka, I. T.

---

**AFFIDAVIT OF MOTHER.**

UNITED STATES OF AMERICA, Indian Territory, }
      Central      DISTRICT. }

I, Amandy Thompson, on oath state that I am 19 years of age and a citizen by blood, of the Choctaw Nation; that I am the lawful wife of Wilburn Thompson, who is a citizen, by blood of the Choctaw Nation; that a male child was born to me on 17th day of January, 1903; that said child has been named Calvin Thompson, and was living March 4, 1905.

                      her
            Amanda  x  Thompson
                     mark

## Applications for Enrollment of Choctaw Newborn
## Act of 1905   Volume IX

Witnesses To Mark:
{ Arthur O Archer
{ Richard Shanafelt

Subscribed and sworn to before me this 1$^{st}$ day of April , 1905

W.H. Angell
Notary Public.

---

**AFFIDAVIT OF ATTENDING PHYSICIAN OR MID-WIFE.**

UNITED STATES OF AMERICA, Indian Territory, }
  Central          DISTRICT. }

I, Isabell Johnson , a midwife , on oath state that I attended on Mrs. Amanda Thompson , wife of Wilburn Thompson on the 17$^{th}$ day of January , 1903 ; that there was born to her on said date a male child; that said child was living March 4, 1905, and is said to have been named Calvin Thompson

　　　　　　　　　　　　　　　　　　　　her
　　　　　　　　　　　　　　Isabell x Johnson
　　　　　　　　　　　　　　　　　mark

Witnesses To Mark:
{ Arthur O Archer
{ Richard Shanafelt

Subscribed and sworn to before me this 1$^{st}$ day of April , 1905

W.H. Angell
Notary Public.

---

Choc New Born 576
　　Zelma McClish   b. 10-12-04

# Applications for Enrollment of Choctaw Newborn
## Act of 1905   Volume IX

7-3101

Muskogee, Indian Territory, April 5, 1905.

Ross McClish,
    Wilburton, Indian Territory.

Dear Sir:

    Receipt is hereby acknowledged of the affidavits of Minnie McClish and E. L. Evins to the birth of Zelma McClish, daughter of Ross and Minnie McClish, October 12, 1904, and the same have been filed with our records as an application for the enrollment of said child.

                      Respectfully,

                                        Commissioner in Charge.

---

7-NB-576.

**COPY**

Muskogee, Indian Territory, April 25, 1905.

Ross McClish,
    Wilburton, Indian Territory.

Dear Sir:

    Receipt is hereby acknowledged of your letter of April 17th, enclosing marriage license and certificate between Ross McClish and Minnie Mosteller, which you offer in support of the application for the enrollment of your child, Zelma McClish, and the same have been filed with the records in this case.

                      Respectfully,
                      SIGNED

                            *Tams Bixby*
                            Chairman.

# Applications for Enrollment of Choctaw Newborn
## Act of 1905   Volume IX

**COPY**

N. B. 576

Muskogee, Indian Territory, April 8, 1905.

Ross McClish,
    Wilburton, Indian Territory.

Dear Sir:

    You are hereby advised that before the application for the enrollment of Zelma McClish can be finally disposed of, it will be necessary for you to furnish the Commission with either the original or a certified copy of the license and certificate of your marriage to Minnie McClish.

    Please attend to this matter at once.

        Respectfully,
        SIGNED
        *T. B. Needles.*
        Commissioner in Charge.

---

7 NB 576

Muskogee, Indian Territory, June 16, 1905.

Ross McClish,
    Wilburton, Indian Territory.

Dear Sir:

    Receipt is hereby acknowledged of your letter of June 13, 1905, asking the status of the enrollment of your child.

    In reply to your letter you are advised that the name of your child Zelma McClish is being placed upon a schedule of citizens by blood of the Choctaw Nation prepared for forwarding to the Secretary of the Interior. You will be n notified when her enrollment is approved by the Department.

        Respectfully,

        Chairman.

## Applications for Enrollment of Choctaw Newborn
## Act of 1905 Volume IX

DEPARTMENT OF THE INTERIOR,
Commission to the Five Civilized Tribes.

**FILED**

APR 24 1905

Tams Bixby    CHAIRMAN.

No. 3641

### Certificate of Record of Marriages.

UNITED STATES OF AMERICA,
INDIAN TERRITORY,  } SCT:
................. DISTRICT.

I, ................., Clerk of the United States Court in the Indian Territory and District aforesaid, do hereby CERTIFY, that the License for and Certificate of the Marriage of

Mr. ......................................... and

M......................................... was

filed in my office in said Territory and District the ......... day of ................. A.D.,190..... and duly recorded in Book 10 of Marriage Record, Page 524

WITNESS my hand and seal of said Court, at ................., this ......... day of ................., A.D. 190.....

................. Clerk.
By ................. Deputy.

No. 3641    FORM NO. 598.

# MARRIAGE LICENSE.

UNITES STATES OF AMERICA,
THE INDIAN TERRITORY,  } ss:
Central    DISTRICT.

To any Person Authorized by Law to Solemnize Marriage—Greeting:

You are hereby commanded to solemnize the Rite and publish the Banns of Matrimony between Mr. Ross McClish of Wilburton in the Indian Territory, aged 24 years, and Miss Minnie Mosteller of Wilburton in

259

## Applications for Enrollment of Choctaw Newborn
## Act of 1905   Volume IX

the Indian Territory, aged   17   years, according to law, and do you officially sign and return this License to the parties therein named.

WITNESS my hand and official seal, this   14   day of   July   A. D. 190 3

EJ Fannin
*Clerk of the United States Court.*

WC Donnelly
*Deputy*

## CERTIFICATE OF MARRIAGE.

UNITES STATES OF AMERICA,
THE INDIAN TERRITORY,   } ss:   I,   W M Colwell
................................ DISTRICT.       a   Baptist Minister

do hereby CERTIFY, that on the   19   day of   July   A, D. 190 3  ; I did duly and according to law, as commanded in the foregoing License, solemnize the Rite and publish the BANNS OF MATRIMONY between the parties therein named.

Witness my hand this the 19   day of   July   , A. D. 190 3

My credentials are recorded in the office of the Clerk of the United States Court in the Indian Territory, Central District, Book   R   Page   202

W.M. Colwell
a   Gospel Minister

**BIRTH AFFIDAVIT.**

### DEPARTMENT OF THE INTERIOR.
### COMMISSION TO THE FIVE CIVILIZED TRIBES.

**IN RE APPLICATION FOR ENROLLMENT,** as a citizen of the   Choctaw   Nation, of Zelma M$^c$Clish   , born on the   12   day of   October   , 1904

Name of Father:  Ross M$^c$Clish     a citizen of the   Choctaw   Nation.
Name of Mother:  Minnie M$^c$Clish     a citizen of the   Choctaw   Nation.

Postoffice   Wilburton Ind. Tery.

# Applications for Enrollment of Choctaw Newborn
## Act of 1905   Volume IX

**AFFIDAVIT OF MOTHER.**

UNITED STATES OF AMERICA, Indian Territory,  
Central DISTRICT.

I, Minnie M$^c$Clish, on oath state that I am Eighteen years of age and a citizen by Intermarriage, of the Choctaw Nation; that I am the lawful wife of Ross McClish, who is a citizen, by Blood of the Choctaw Nation; that a Female child was born to me on 12 day of October, 1904; that said child has been named Zelma M$^c$Clish, and was living March 4, 1905.

                                              her  
                                   Minnie x M$^c$Clish  

Witnesses To Mark:                    mark  
{ Clifford Perry  
  J C Kistler

Subscribed and sworn to before me this 31 day of March, 1905

                                  W.P. M$^c$Ginnis  
                                      Notary Public.

---

**AFFIDAVIT OF ATTENDING PHYSICIAN OR MID-WIFE.**

UNITED STATES OF AMERICA, Indian Territory,  
Central DISTRICT.

I, E.L. Evins M.D., a Physician, on oath state that I attended on Mrs. Minnie M$^c$Clish, wife of Ross M$^c$Clish on the 12$^{th}$ day of October, 1904; that there was born to her on said date a Female child; that said child was living March 4, 1905, and is said to have been named Zelma M$^c$Clish

                                   E.L. Evins M.D.  
Witnesses To Mark:  
{

Subscribed and sworn to before me this 31 day of March, 1905

                                  W.P. M$^c$Ginnis  
                                     Notary Public.

Commission Expires March 17, 1909

## Applications for Enrollment of Choctaw Newborn
## Act of 1905  Volume IX

<u>Choc New Born 577</u>
  Charley Allen Lewis  b.  10-14-03

                  7-3166

          Muskogee, Indian Territory, April 5, 1905.

R. W. Higgins,
  Attorney at Law,
    Hartshorne, Indian Territory.

Dear Sir:

  Receipt is hereby acknowledged of your letter of March 31, 1905, enclosing affidavits of Ruthie Lewis and W. H. Cleckler to the birth of Charley Allen Lewis, son of Thomas and Ruthie Lewis, October 14, 1903, and the same have been filed with our records as an application for the enrollment of said child.

       Respectfully,

              Commissioner in Charge.

## AFFIDAVIT OF ATTENDING PHYSICIAN OR MIDWIFE

UNITED STATES OF AMERICA
INDIAN TERRITORY
 Central   DISTRICT
       *W. H. Cleckler*
  I, W.H. Cleckler   a   Physician
on oath state that I attended on Mrs.  T.B. Lewis wife of  Thomas B. Lewis

on the  14$^{th}$ day of  October , 190 3 , that there was born to her on said date a boy child, that said child is now living, and is said to have been named Charley Allen Lewis

             W H Cleckler

    Subscribed and sworn to before me this, the  3$^{rd}$   day of
    Jan  190 5

WITNESSETH:         Gerald Reidt   Notary Public.
 Must be two witnesses { J D Chastain  My comm exp Jan 7-1908
 who are citizens
        Henry C Freeney

## Applications for Enrollment of Choctaw Newborn
## Act of 1905  Volume IX

We hereby certify that we are well acquainted with   W.H. Cleckler a   physician   and know   him   to be reputable and of good standing in the community.

    J.D. Chastain        Wm J Hulsey

    Henry C Freeney        Isaac D. Patterson

**NEW-BORN AFFIDAVIT.**

Number............

...Choctaw Enrolling Commission...

IN THE MATTER OF THE APPLICATION FOR ENROLLMENT, as a citizen of the Choctaw   Nation, of   Charley Allen Lewis

born on the  14<sup>th</sup>  day of ____October____ 190 4

Name of father   Thomas B Lewis      a citizen of   Choctaw
Nation final enrollment No.  ~~10939~~  740
Name of mother   Ruthie Lewis      a citizen of   Choctaw
Nation final enrollment No.  14355

    Postoffice   Hartshorne, I T

**AFFIDAVIT OF MOTHER.**

UNITED STATES OF AMERICA
INDIAN TERRITORY
Central   DISTRICT

I   Ruthie Lewis   , on oath state that I am 26   years of age and a citizen by  birth   of the   Choctaw   Nation, and as such have been placed upon the final roll of the   Choctaw   Nation, by the Honorable Secretary of the Interior my final enrollment number being   14355  ; that I am the lawful wife of   Thomas B Lewis   , who is a citizen of the   Choctaw  *By Intermarriage*  Nation, and as such has been placed upon the final roll of said Nation by the Honorable Secretary of the Interior, his final enrollment number being   740   and that a   boy   child was born to me on the   14<sup>th</sup>   day of   October   190 3; that said child has been named   Charley Allen Lewis   , and is now living.

         Ruthie Lewis

Witnesseth.
Must be two Witnesses who are Citizens.   } J D Chastain

     Henry C Freeney

## Applications for Enrollment of Choctaw Newborn
## Act of 1905   Volume IX

Subscribed and sworn to before me this 3rd   day of   Jan   1905

Gerald Reidt<br>Notary Public.

My commission expires:
Jan 7 - 1908

---

**BIRTH AFFIDAVIT.**

### DEPARTMENT OF THE INTERIOR.
### COMMISSION TO THE FIVE CIVILIZED TRIBES.

---

**IN RE APPLICATION FOR ENROLLMENT,** as a citizen of the   Choctaw   Nation, of   Charley Allen Lewis   , born on the   14   day of   Oct   , 1903

Name of Father: Thomas B Lewis   a citizen of the   Choctaw   Nation. *by intermarriage*
Name of Mother: Ruthie Lewis   a citizen of the   Choctaw   Nation.

Postoffice   Hartshorne I.T.

---

**AFFIDAVIT OF MOTHER.**

UNITED STATES OF AMERICA, Indian Territory,
Central   DISTRICT.

I,   Ruthie Lewis   , on oath state that I am   27   years of age and a citizen by blood  , of the   Choctaw   Nation; that I am the lawful wife of   Thomas B Lewis   , who is a citizen, by   marriage   of the   Choctaw   Nation; that a   male   child was born to me on   14   day of   Oct   , 1903; that said child has been named   Charley Allen Lewis   , and was living March 4, 1905.

Ruthie Lewis

Witnesses To Mark:

Subscribed and sworn to before me this 29   day of   March   , 1905

Robert W Higgins<br>Notary Public.

## Applications for Enrollment of Choctaw Newborn
## Act of 1905   Volume IX

**AFFIDAVIT OF ATTENDING PHYSICIAN OR MID-WIFE.**

UNITED STATES OF AMERICA, Indian Territory,
Central                                DISTRICT.

I,   WH Cleckler   , a   physician   , on oath state that I attended on Mrs.   Ruthie Lewis   , wife of   Thomas B Lewis   on the   14   day of   Oct   , 1903; that there was born to her on said date a   male   child; that said child was living March 4, 1905, and is said to have been named Charley Allen Lewis

W.H. Cleckler M.D.

Witnesses To Mark:

Subscribed and sworn to before me this   29   day of   March   , 1905

Robert W Higgins
Notary Public.

---

Choc New Born 578
　　　William A. Featherston  b. 1-22-03

7-3226

Muskogee, Indian Territory, April 6, 1905.

McKennon & Dean,
　　　Attorneys at Law,
　　　　　South McAlester, Indian Territory.

Gentlemen:

　　Receipt is hereby acknowledged of your letter of March 31, 1905, enclosing affidavits of Mittie A. Featherston and N. R. Nawlin to the birth of William A. Featherston, son of Lucius C. and Mittie A. Featherston, January 22, 1903, and the same have been filed with our records as an application for the enrollment of said child.

Respectfully,

Commissioner in Charge.

# Applications for Enrollment of Choctaw Newborn
## Act of 1905 Volume IX

7-NB-578.

Muskogee, Indian Territory, July 7, 1905.

L. C. Featherston,
    Featherston, Indian Territory.

Dear Sir:

    Receipt is hereby acknowledged of your letter of July 1, 1905, asking if you may now file for your youngest son William A. Featherston.

    In reply to your letter you are advised that the name of your son William A. Featherston has been placed upon a schedule of citizens by blood of the Choctaw Nation prepared for forwarding to the Secretary of the Interior, but this office has not yet been notified of Departmental action thereon. You will be advised when the enrollment of your son is approved by the Secretary of the Interior and pending his approval no selection of allotment could be made in his behalf.

                      Respectfully,

                                    Commissioner.

## AFFIDAVIT OF ATTENDING PHYSICIAN OR MIDWIFE

UNITED STATES OF AMERICA
INDIAN TERRITORY
    Central    DISTRICT

    I, Mrs J.S. Boatright a citizen of U.S. on oath state that I attended on Mrs. Mittie A. Featherston wife of Lucius C Featherston on the 22$^{nd}$ day of Jan , 190 3, that there was born to her on said date a male child, that said child is now living, and is said to have been named William A. Featherston

                      Mattie Boatright    Mid M$\cancel{D}$.

WITNESSETH:
Must be two witnesses who are citizens and know the child.
{ David Jackson
  Nicholas Nail

        Subscribed and sworn to before me this, the 6 day of
~~Jan~~ Feb    190 5

                        J C Hubert    Notary Public.
                        My commission expires Nov 25 1908

## Applications for Enrollment of Choctaw Newborn
## Act of 1905 Volume IX

We hereby certify that we are well acquainted with Mattie Boatright a Mid Wife and know her to be reputable and of good standing in the community.

Bessie Crosby

Mrs Montgomery

**NEW-BORN AFFIDAVIT.**

Number............

**...Choctaw Enrolling Commission...**

IN THE MATTER OF THE APPLICATION FOR ENROLLMENT, as a citizen of the Choctaw Nation, of William A Featherston

born on the 22 day of Jan 190 3

Name of father   Lucius C Featherston          a citizen of  Choctaw by Ind M.
Nation final enrollment No. 301
Name of mother   Mittie A Featherston          a citizen of  Choctaw
Nation final enrollment No. 9313

Postoffice   Featherston

**AFFIDAVIT OF MOTHER.**

UNITED STATES OF AMERICA
INDIAN TERRITORY
Central   DISTRICT

I   Mittie A Featherston   , on oath state that I am 31 years of age and a citizen by Blood of the Choctaw Nation, and as such have been placed upon the final roll of the Choctaw Nation, by the Honorable Secretary of the Interior my final enrollment number being 9313 ; that I am the lawful wife of Lucius C Featherston , who is a citizen of the Choctaw Nation, and as such has been placed upon the final roll of said Nation by the Honorable Secretary of the Interior, his final enrollment number being 301 and that a Male child was born to me on the 22 day of Jan 190 3; that said child has been named William A Featherston , and is now living.

Mittie A Featherston

Witnesseth.

Must be two Witnesses who are Citizens.   A.L. Hancock

Lewis Carnes

## Applications for Enrollment of Choctaw Newborn
## Act of 1905   Volume IX

Subscribed and sworn to before me this 13th day of February 190 5

WB McMullan
Notary Public.
My commission expires: June 1st 1905                     Bexar County Texas

---

**BIRTH AFFIDAVIT.**

### DEPARTMENT OF THE INTERIOR.
### COMMISSION TO THE FIVE CIVILIZED TRIBES.

---

**IN RE APPLICATION FOR ENROLLMENT,** as a citizen of the Choctaw Nation, of William A Featherston, born on the 22 day of Jan, 1903

Name of Father: Lucius C Featherston    a citizen of the Choctaw Nation.
Name of Mother: Mittie A Featherston    a citizen of the Choctaw Nation.

Postoffice   Featherston, Ind. Ty.

---

**AFFIDAVIT OF MOTHER.**

UNITED STATES OF AMERICA, Indian Territory, }
............................................ DISTRICT. }

I, Mittie A Featherston, on oath state that I am thirty-one years of age and a citizen by blood, of the Choctaw Nation; that I am the lawful wife of Lucius C Featherston, who is a citizen, by marriage of the Choctaw Nation; that a male child was born to me on 22 day of Jan, 1903; that said child has been named William A Featherston, and was living March 4, 1905.

Mittie A Featherston

Witnesses To Mark:
{

Subscribed and sworn to before me this 28th day of March, 1905

WB McMullan
Notary Public.
Bexar Co Texas
My commission expires June 1st 1905

# Applications for Enrollment of Choctaw Newborn
# Act of 1905 Volume IX

## AFFIDAVIT OF ATTENDING PHYSICIAN OR MID-WIFE.

UNITED STATES OF AMERICA, Indian Territory,
Western          DISTRICT.

I,   N.R. Nawlin  , a   physician  , on oath state that I attended on Mrs.   Mittie A Featherston  , wife of   Lucius C Featherston   on the 22$^{nd}$  day of  January , 1903; that there was born to her on said date a   male   child; that said child was living March 4, 1905, and is said to have been named   William A Featherston

N.R. Nawlin

Witnesses To Mark:

Subscribed and sworn to before me this  31$^{st}$  day of  March  , 1905

Frank W. Rushing
My Commission Expires Jan. 30, 1909.                    Notary Public.

---

Choc New Born 579
    Andre[sic] L. Bullard  b. 5-18-03

## AFFIDAVIT OF ATTENDING PHYSICIAN OR MIDWIFE

UNITED STATES OF AMERICA
INDIAN TERRITORY
   Western    DISTRICT

I,   (Illegible) Gillian    a    Mid Wife on oath state that I attended on Mrs.   Villey Bullard   wife of   Andrew C Bullard   on the   18$^{th}$   day of   May   , 190 3, that there was born to her on said date a   male   child, that said child is now living, and is said to have been named   Andrew C[sic] Bullard

Mary F Gillian    $m.D.$

Subscribed and sworn to before me this, the   21$^{st}$    day of   January    190 5

Guy A Curry    Notary Public.

## Applications for Enrollment of Choctaw Newborn
## Act of 1905   Volume IX

WITNESSETH:

Must be two witnesses who are citizens { John L Herron

David Coley

We hereby certify that we are well acquainted with  (Illegible) Gillian a  midwife  and know  her  to be reputable and of good standing in the community.

John Herron _____

David Coley _____

**NEW-BORN AFFIDAVIT.**

Number..............

...Choctaw Enrolling Commission...

IN THE MATTER OF THE APPLICATION FOR ENROLLMENT, as a citizen of the Choctaw   Nation, of   Andrew L Bullard

born on the  18$^{th}$  day of __May__  190 3

Name of father   Andrew C Bullard        a citizen of   Choctaw
Nation final enrollment No.   653
Name of mother   Villey Bullard           a citizen of   Choctaw
Nation final enrollment No.   8689

Postoffice   Quinton I.T.

**AFFIDAVIT OF MOTHER.**

UNITED STATES OF AMERICA
INDIAN TERRITORY
  Western    DISTRICT

I   Villey Bullard            , on oath state that I am   25   years of age and a citizen by  blood  of the  Choctaw   Nation, and as such have been placed upon the final roll of the   Choctaw  Nation, by the Honorable Secretary of the Interior my final enrollment number being   8689  ; that I am the lawful wife of   Andrew C Bullard  , who is a citizen of the   Choctaw   Nation, and as such has been placed upon the final roll of said Nation by the Honorable Secretary of the Interior, his final enrollment number being ——— and that a   Male   child was born to me on the 18$^{th}$   day of   May    190 3; that said child has been named   Andrew L Bullard   , and is now living.

Villey Bullard

# Applications for Enrollment of Choctaw Newborn
## Act of 1905 Volume IX

Witnesseth.

<small>Must be two Witnesses who are Citizens.</small> } Jo h[sic] L Herron

David Coley

Subscribed and sworn to before me this 21<sup>st</sup> day of Jan 190 5

Guy a Curry
Notary Public.

My commission expires:
Apr 27 - 1907

---

United States of America,
Indian Territory, SS
Western District.

I, Andrew C. Bullard, husband of Villey M. Bullard, being first duly sworn, do hereby state that the correct name of my wife is Villey M. Bullard, and that the name Villa M. Bullard, as it appears in the body off the affidavit to the birth of our son, Andrew L. Bullard, is incorrect, having been placed there by the Notary Public before whom the affidavit was acknowledged, through error.

Andrew C Bullard

Subscribed and sworn to before me this April 5, 1905.

JB Campbell
Notary Public.

---

**BIRTH AFFIDAVIT.**

### DEPARTMENT OF THE INTERIOR.
### COMMISSION TO THE FIVE CIVILIZED TRIBES.

---

**IN RE APPLICATION FOR ENROLLMENT,** as a citizen of the Choctaw Nation, of Andrew L. Bullard , born on the 18 day of May , 1903

Name of Father: Andrew C. Bullard    a citizen of the Choctaw Nation.
Name of Mother: Villa M. Bullard    a citizen of the Choctaw Nation.

Postoffice Quinton Ind. T.

# Applications for Enrollment of Choctaw Newborn
# Act of 1905   Volume IX

### AFFIDAVIT OF MOTHER.

UNITED STATES OF AMERICA, Indian Territory, }
Western      DISTRICT.

I,   Villa M. Bullard   , on oath state that I am   25   years of age and a citizen by   Blood   , of the   Choctaw   Nation; that I am the lawful wife of   Andrew C. Bullard   , who is a citizen, by Intermarriage   of the   Choctaw   Nation; that a   male   child was born to me on   18   day of   May   , 1903; that said child has been named   Andrew L. Bullard   , and was living March 4, 1905.

Witnesses To Mark:
{

Villey M Bullard

Subscribed and sworn to before me this   4   day of   April   , 1905

J. M. White
Notary Public.

---

### AFFIDAVIT OF ATTENDING PHYSICIAN OR MID-WIFE.

UNITED STATES OF AMERICA, Indian Territory, }
Western      DISTRICT.

I,   J. D. Clarkson   , a   Physician   , on oath state that I attended on Mrs.   Villa M. Bullard   , wife of   Andrew C. Bullard   on the 18 day of May , 1903; that there was born to her on said date a   Male   child; that said child was living March 4, 1905, and is said to have been named   Andrew L. Bullard

Witnesses To Mark:
{

J D Clarkson M.D.

Subscribed and sworn to before me this   3   day of   April   , 1905

J. M. White
Notary Public.

---

Choc New Born 580
Frederick Arthur Burton   b. 8-3-04

# Applications for Enrollment of Choctaw Newborn
## Act of 1905   Volume IX

United States of America,
Indian Territory,          SS.
Western District.

    I, Julia A. Folsom, on oath state that I am the mother of Lela M. Burton who makes affidavit to the birth of her child, Frederick Arthur Burton in the matter of his enrollment as a citizen by blood of the Choctaw Nation; that the maiden name of the said Lela M. Burton was Lela M. Kincade, and that since the time she was listed for enrollment she has married H. E. Burton, a non-citizen.

                        Julia A Folsom

Subscribed and sworn to before me this 5th day of April 1905.

                        Edward Merrick
                        Notary Public.

---

**BIRTH AFFIDAVIT.**

### DEPARTMENT OF THE INTERIOR.
### COMMISSION TO THE FIVE CIVILIZED TRIBES.

    **IN RE APPLICATION FOR ENROLLMENT,** as a citizen of the    Choctaw    Nation, of Frederick Arthur Burton    , born on the 3   day of   August  , 1904

Name of Father: H. E. Burton        a citizen of the United States Nation.
Name of Mother: Lela M. Burton      a citizen of the   Choctaw   Nation.

                  Postoffice    Poteau, I.T.

---

**AFFIDAVIT OF MOTHER.**

UNITED STATES OF AMERICA, Indian Territory,
    Central        DISTRICT.

    I,   Lela M. Burton    , on oath state that I am   16    years of age and a citizen by   Blood   , of the   Choctaw    Nation; that I am the lawful wife of H. E. Burton  , who is a citizen, ~~by~~ _____ of the    United States ~~Nation~~; that a   male   child was born to me on    3    day of    August    , 1904; that said child has been named Frederick Arthur Burton    , and was living March 4, 1905.

                        Lela M. Burton

Witnesses To Mark:

# Applications for Enrollment of Choctaw Newborn
## Act of 1905 Volume IX

Subscribed and sworn to before me this 30 day of March, 1905

My Commission expires W.H. Harrison
March 8-1907 Notary Public.

### AFFIDAVIT OF ATTENDING PHYSICIAN OR MID-WIFE.

UNITED STATES OF AMERICA, Indian Territory,
Central DISTRICT.

I, M.A. Nolan, a mid-wife, on oath state that I attended on Mrs. Lela M Burton, wife of H.E. Burton on the 3 day of August, 1904; that there was born to her on said date a male child; that said child was living March 4, 1905, and is said to have been named Frederick Arthur Burton

M.A. Nolan

Witnesses To Mark:

Subscribed and sworn to before me this 30 day of March, 1905

My Commission expires W.H. Harrison
March 8-1907 Notary Public.

---

Choc New Born 581
John Henry Falconer b. 12-21-04

## AFFIDAVIT OF ATTENDING PHYSICIAN OR MIDWIFE

UNITED STATES OF AMERICA
INDIAN TERRITORY
Central DISTRICT

I, E.L. Collins a Physician on oath state that I attended on Mrs. Ida L Falconer wife of Henry Falconer on the 21$^{st}$ day of December, 1904, that there was born to her on said date a male child, that said child is now living, and is said to have been named John Henry Falconer

E.L. Collins  *M.D.*

# Applications for Enrollment of Choctaw Newborn
## Act of 1905   Volume IX

Subscribed and sworn to before me this, the   11$^{th}$   day of February   190 5

WITNESSETH:   Jno H Gooding   Notary Public.
Must be two witnesses { EG Goodnight   My com ex 1/19/1908
who are citizens    Rena Trahan

We hereby certify that we are well acquainted with   E.L. Collins M.D. a   Physician   and know   him   to be reputable and of good standing in the community.

EG Goodnight   _____

Rena Trahan   _____

**NEW-BORN AFFIDAVIT.**

Number...............

## ...Choctaw Enrolling Commission...

IN THE MATTER OF THE APPLICATION FOR ENROLLMENT, as a citizen of the Choctaw   Nation, of   John Henry Falconer

born on the   21   day of   December   190 4

Name of father   Henry Falconer   a citizen of   Choctaw
Nation final enrollment No.   7212
Name of mother   Ida L Falconer   a citizen of   Choctaw
Nation final enrollment No.   14335

Postoffice   Spiro I.T.

**AFFIDAVIT OF MOTHER.**

UNITED STATES OF AMERICA
INDIAN TERRITORY
Central   DISTRICT

I   Ida L Falconer   , on oath state that I am   30   years of age and a citizen by   blood   of the   Choctaw   Nation, and as such have been placed upon the final roll of the   Choctaw   Nation, by the Honorable Secretary of the Interior my final enrollment number being   14335   ; that I am the lawful wife of   Henry Falconer   , who is a citizen of the   Choctaw   Nation, and as such has been placed upon the final roll of said Nation by the Honorable Secretary of the Interior, his final enrollment number being   7212   and that a   Male   child was born to me on

## Applications for Enrollment of Choctaw Newborn
## Act of 1905  Volume IX

the  21  day of  December  190 4; that said child has been named  John Henry Falconer  , and is now living.

Ida L Falconer

Witnesseth.
Must be two Witnesses who are Citizens.  } E H Hickman
John Taylor

Subscribed and sworn to before me this  27  day of  Feb  190 5

W E Harrell
Notary Public.

My commission expires:  Aug 6-1908

---

BIRTH AFFIDAVIT.

### DEPARTMENT OF THE INTERIOR.
### COMMISSION TO THE FIVE CIVILIZED TRIBES.

---

IN RE APPLICATION FOR ENROLLMENT, as a citizen of the  Choctaw  Nation, of John Henry Falconer  , born on the 21st  day of  December  , 1904

Name of Father: Henry Falconer       a citizen of the  Choctaw  Nation.
Name of Mother: Ida L Falconer       a citizen of the  Choctaw  Nation.

Postoffice  Spiro, Ind. Ter.

---

### AFFIDAVIT OF MOTHER.

UNITED STATES OF AMERICA, Indian Territory,
Central      DISTRICT.

I,  Ida L Falconer  , on oath state that I am  30  years of age and a citizen by  blood  , of the  Choctaw  Nation; that I am the lawful wife of  Henry Falconer  , who is a citizen, by  blood  of the  Choctaw  Nation; that a male  child was born to me on  21st  day of  December  , 1904; that said child has been named  John Henry Falconer  , and was living March 4, 1905.

Ida L Falconer

Witnesses To Mark:

# Applications for Enrollment of Choctaw Newborn
## Act of 1905 Volume IX

Subscribed and sworn to before me this 30th day of March, 1905

Wirt Franklin
Notary Public.

---

### AFFIDAVIT OF ATTENDING PHYSICIAN OR MID-WIFE.

UNITED STATES OF AMERICA, Indian Territory, }
Central DISTRICT. }

I, E L Collins, a physician, on oath state that I attended on Mrs. Ida L Falconer, wife of Henry Falconer on the 21st day of December, 1904; that there was born to her on said date a male child; that said child was living March 4, 1905, and is said to have been named John Henry Falconer

E.L. Collins
Witnesses To Mark:

{ Subscribed and sworn to before me this 30th day of March, 1905

Wirt Franklin
Notary Public.

---

Choc New Born 582
Emmet Tobler b. 2-9-05

BIRTH AFFIDAVIT.
### DEPARTMENT OF THE INTERIOR.
### COMMISSION TO THE FIVE CIVILIZED TRIBES.

IN RE APPLICATION FOR ENROLLMENT, as a citizen of the Choctaw Nation, of Emmet Tobler, born on the 9th day of February, 1905

Name of Father: Albert Tobler   a citizen of the United States Nation.
Name of Mother: Annie E Tobler   a citizen of the Choctaw Nation.

Postoffice   Spiro, Ind. Ter.

## Applications for Enrollment of Choctaw Newborn
## Act of 1905   Volume IX

### AFFIDAVIT OF MOTHER.

UNITED STATES OF AMERICA, Indian Territory,　}
　　Central　　　　　　　DISTRICT.

I,　Annie E. Tobler　, on oath state that I am　21　years of age and a citizen by　blood　, of the　Choctaw　Nation; that I am the lawful wife of　Albert Tobler　, who is a citizen, by ............... of the　United States　Nation; that a male　child was born to me on　9th　day of　February　, 1905; that said child has been named　Emmet Tobler　, and was living March 4, 1905.

　　　　　　　　　　　　　　　　　　　　Annie E Tobler
Witnesses To Mark:
{

　　Subscribed and sworn to before me this　30th　day of　March　, 1905

　　　　　　　　　　　　　　　　Wirt Franklin
　　　　　　　　　　　　　　　　　Notary Public.

---

### AFFIDAVIT OF ATTENDING PHYSICIAN OR MID-WIFE.

UNITED STATES OF AMERICA, Indian Territory,　}
　　Central　　　　　　　DISTRICT.

I,　W.O. Hartshorne　, a　physician　, on oath state that I attended on Mrs.　Annie E. Tobler　, wife of　Albert Tobler　on the 9th　day of　February　, 1905; that there was born to her on said date a　male　child; that said child was living March 4, 1905, and is said to have been named Emmet Tobler

　　　　　　　　　　　　　　　　　　　　W.O. Hartshorne
Witnesses To Mark:
{

　　Subscribed and sworn to before me this　30th　day of　March　, 1905

　　　　　　　　　　　　　　　　Wirt Franklin
　　　　　　　　　　　　　　　　　Notary Public.

---

Choc New Born 583
　　Loise Thomas   b. 5-22-04

# Applications for Enrollment of Choctaw Newborn
## Act of 1905   Volume IX

Choctaw 347

Muskogee, Indian Territory, April 6, 1905.

C. M. Thomas,
   Cumberland, Indian Territory.

Dear Sir:

Receipt is hereby acknowledged of the affidavits of Mary J. Moore Thomas and W. N Dean to the birth of Loise Thomas, daughter of C. M. and Mary J. Moore Thomas, May 22, 1904, and the same have been filed with our records as an application for the enrollment of said child.

Respectfully,

Commissioner in Charge.

---

**BIRTH AFFIDAVIT.**

**DEPARTMENT OF THE INTERIOR.**
**COMMISSION TO THE FIVE CIVILIZED TRIBES.**

---

**IN RE APPLICATION FOR ENROLLMENT,** as a citizen of the   Choctaw   Nation, of Loise Thomas   , born on the 22   day of May   , 1904

*by intermarriage*

Name of Father: C. M. Thomas          a citizen of the   Choctaw   Nation.
Name of Mother: Mary J (Moore) Thomas   a citizen of the   Choctaw   Nation.
*daughter of Thomas D & Nancy M. Moore*

Postoffice   Cumberland, I.T.

---

**AFFIDAVIT OF MOTHER.**

UNITED STATES OF AMERICA, Indian Territory, }
   Southern         DISTRICT.                }

I,   Mrs Mary J (Moore) Thomas   , on oath state that I am   18   years of age and a citizen by   blood   , of the   Choctaw   Nation; that I am the lawful wife of C. M. Thomas   , who is a citizen, by   intermarriage   of the   Choctaw   Nation; that a   Female   child was born to me on   22"   day of May   , 1904; that said child has been named   Loise Thomas   , and was living March 4, 1905.

Mary J Moore Thomas

Witnesses To Mark:

## Applications for Enrollment of Choctaw Newborn
## Act of 1905   Volume IX

Subscribed and sworn to before me this  27   day of     March       , 1905

                                    J Frank Adams
                                    Notary Public.

**AFFIDAVIT OF ATTENDING PHYSICIAN OR MID-WIFE.**

UNITED STATES OF AMERICA, Indian Territory, }
   Southern               DISTRICT.   }

    I,   W.N. Dean         , a    Physician      , on oath state that I attended on Mrs.   Mary J (Moore) Thomas        , wife of    C.M. Thomas      on the  22  day of  May     , 1904; that there was born to her on said date a     Female     child; that said child was living March 4, 1905, and is said to have been named   Loise Thomas

                                    W.N. Dean M.D.
Witnesses To Mark:

{ Subscribed and sworn to before me this  27   day of    March      , 1905

                                    J Frank Adams
                                    Notary Public.

---

<u>Choc New Born 584</u>
    Adley Vy Lynn   b. 6-19-04

                                                  Choctaw N. B. 584.
                        **COPY**

                    Muskogee, Indian Territory, April 19, 1905.

Henry Lee Lynn,
    Madill, Indian Territory.

Dear Sir:

    Receipt is hereby acknowledged of the affidavits of Minnie Lee Lynn and Thos. A. Blaylock to the birth of Adley Vy Lynn, daughter of Henry Lee and Minnie Lee Lynn, June 19, 1904, and the same have been filed with our records in the matter of the enrollment of said child.

# Applications for Enrollment of Choctaw Newborn
# Act of 1905  Volume IX

Respectfully,

SIGNED

*Tams Bixby*
Chairman.

---

COPY

N. B. 584

Muskogee, Indian Territory, April 10, 1905.

Henry Lee Lynn,
　　Madill, Indian Territory.

Dear Sir:

There is inclosed you herewith for execution application for the enrollment of your infant child, Adley Vy Lynn, born June 19, 1904.

In the affidavit of the attending physician heretofore filed with the Commission the date of the birth of said child is given as June 19, 1905, which is evidently a mistake. It is, therefore, necessary that application be re-executed.

In having these affidavits executed care should be exercised to see that all names are written in full, as they appear in the body of the affidavit, and in the event that either of the persons signing the affidavit are unable to write, signatures by mark must be attested by two witnesses. Each affidavit must be executed before a Notary Public and the notarial seal and signature of the officer must be attached to each separate affidavit.

Respectfully,

SIGNED

*T. B. Needles.*
Commissioner in Charge.

LM 10-54

## Applications for Enrollment of Choctaw Newborn
## Act of 1905 Volume IX

**BIRTH AFFIDAVIT.**

### DEPARTMENT OF THE INTERIOR.
### COMMISSION TO THE FIVE CIVILIZED TRIBES.

IN RE APPLICATION FOR ENROLLMENT, as a citizen of the Choctaw Nation, of Adley Vy Lynn, born on the 19th day of June, 1904

Name of Father: Henry Lee Lynn          a citizen of the United States Nation.
                        *(nee Cummings)*
Name of Mother: Minnie Lee Lynn          a citizen of the Choctaw Nation.

Postoffice   Madill, Ind Territory

**AFFIDAVIT OF MOTHER.**

UNITED STATES OF AMERICA, Indian Territory,
Southern                DISTRICT.

I, Minnie Lee Lynn, on oath state that I am Twenty eight years of age and a citizen by blood, of the Choctaw Nation; that I am the lawful wife of Henry Lee Lynn, who is a citizen, by _____ of the United States Nation; that a female child was born to me on 19th day of June, 1904; that said child has been named Adley Vy Lynn, and was living March 4, 1905.

Minnie Lee Lynn

Witnesses To Mark:

Subscribed and sworn to before me this 27" day of March, 1905

*(Name Illegible)*
Notary Public.

**AFFIDAVIT OF ATTENDING PHYSICIAN OR MID-WIFE.**

UNITED STATES OF AMERICA, Indian Territory,
Southern                DISTRICT.

I, Thos A Blaylock, a Physician, on oath state that I attended on Mrs. Minnie Lee Lynn, wife of Henry Lee Lynn on the 19th day of June, 1905[sic]; that there was born to her on said date a _____ child; that said child was living March 4, 1905, and is said to have been named Adley Vy Lynn

Thos A Blaylock M.D.

# Applications for Enrollment of Choctaw Newborn
## Act of 1905   Volume IX

Witnesses To Mark:

{

    Subscribed and sworn to before me this   19" day of   June   , 1905

*(Name Illegible)*
Notary Public.

---

**BIRTH AFFIDAVIT.**

## DEPARTMENT OF THE INTERIOR.
## COMMISSION TO THE FIVE CIVILIZED TRIBES.

---

    **IN RE APPLICATION FOR ENROLLMENT,** as a citizen of the    Choctaw    Nation, of Adley Vy Lynn   , born on the   19th   day of   June   , 1904

Name of Father: Henry Lee Lynn    a citizen of the United States Nation.
Name of Mother: Minnie Lee Lynn Cummings   a citizen of the   Choctaw   Nation.

                  Postoffice   Madill, Ind Ter

---

**AFFIDAVIT OF MOTHER.**

**UNITED STATES OF AMERICA, Indian Territory,**
  Southern            **DISTRICT.**

    I,   Minnie Lee Lynn   (Cummings)   , on oath state that I am   28   years of age and a citizen by   Blood   , of the   Choctaw   Nation; that I am the lawful wife of Henry Lee Lynn   , who is a citizen, by ——— of the   United States   Nation; that a   Female   child was born to me on   19"   day of   June   , 1904; that said child has been named   Adley Vy Lynn   , and was living March 4, 1905.

                  Minnie Lee Lynn

Witnesses To Mark:

{

    Subscribed and sworn to before me this   14   day of   April   , 1905

*(Name Illegible)*
Notary Public.

# Applications for Enrollment of Choctaw Newborn
# Act of 1905  Volume IX

### AFFIDAVIT OF ATTENDING PHYSICIAN OR MID-WIFE.

UNITED STATES OF AMERICA, Indian Territory,
Southern          DISTRICT.

I,  Thos A Blaylock  , a  Physician  , on oath state that I attended on Mrs.  Minnie Lee Lynn  , wife of  Henry Lee Lynn  on the  19th day of June , 1904; that there was born to her on said date a  Female  child; that said child was living March 4, 1905, and is said to have been named  Adley Vy Lynn

Thos A Blaylock M.D.

Witnesses To Mark:

Subscribed and sworn to before me this  14  day of  April  , 1905

*(Name Illegible)*
Notary Public.

---

Choc New Born 585
   Ethel Dobyns   b. 2-12-05
   Annie Belle Dobyns   b. 1-29-03

---

$W^m O.B.$

COMMISSIONERS:
TAMS BIXBY,
THOMAS B. NEEDLES,
C.R. BRECKINBRIDGE.

WM. O. BEALL
Secretary

**DEPARTMENT OF THE INTERIOR,**
**COMMISSIONER TO THE FIVE CIVILIZED TRIBES.**

REFER IN REPLY TO THE FOLLOWING:

Choctaw 3925.

ADDRESS ONLY THE
COMMISSION TO THE FIVE CIVILIZED TRIBES

Muskogee, Indian Territory, April 6, 1905.

Oscar Dobyns,
   Madill, Indian Territory.

Dear Sir:

Receipt is hereby acknowledged of the affidavits of Joanna Dobyns and E. F. Lewis to the birth of Ethel Dobyns, daughter of Oscar and Joanna Dobyns, February 12, 1905, and the same have been filed with our records as an application for the enrollment of said child.

# Applications for Enrollment of Choctaw Newborn
## Act of 1905   Volume IX

Respectfully,

T.B. Needles
Commissioner in Charge.

COMMISSIONERS:
TAMS BIXBY,
THOMAS B. NEEDLES,
C.R. BRECKINBRIDGE.

WM. O. BEALL
Secretary

**DEPARTMENT OF THE INTERIOR,
COMMISSIONER TO THE FIVE CIVILIZED TRIBES.**

ADDRESS ONLY THE
COMMISSION TO THE FIVE CIVILIZED TRIBES.

$W^m O.B.$

REFER IN REPLY TO THE FOLLOWING:

Choctaw 3925.

Muskogee, Indian Territory, April 12, 1905.

Oscar Dobyns,
    Madill, Indian Territory.

Dear Sir:

    Receipt is hereby acknowledged of the affidavits of Joanna Dobyns and W. L. Davis to the birth of Annie Belle Dobyns, daughter of Oscar and Joanna Dobyns, January 29, 1904, and the same have been filed with our records as an application for the enrollment of said child.

Respectfully,

T.B. Needles
Commissioner in Charge.

**COPY**   Choctaw N.B. 585.

Muskogee, Indian Territory, April 21, 1905.

Oscar Dobyns,
    Kingston, Indian Territory.

Dear Sir:

    Receipt is hereby acknowledged of your letter of April 17, asking if birth certificates for the enrollment of your two children have been received.

    In reply to your letter you are informed that the affidavits heretofore forwarded to the birth of Ethel and Annie Belle Dobyns have been filed with our records as an application for the enrollment of said children.

# Applications for Enrollment of Choctaw Newborn
## Act of 1905  Volume IX

Respectfully,
SIGNED

*Tams Bixby*
Chairman.

---

BIRTH AFFIDAVIT.

### DEPARTMENT OF THE INTERIOR.
### COMMISSION TO THE FIVE CIVILIZED TRIBES.

---

IN RE APPLICATION FOR ENROLLMENT, as a citizen of the Choctaw Nation, of Annie Belle Dobyns, born on the $29^{th}$ day of Jan, 1903

Name of Father: Oscar Dobyns     a citizen of the ——— Nation.
Name of Mother: Joanna Dobyns     a citizen of the Choctaw Nation.

Postoffice    Madill I.T.

---

### AFFIDAVIT OF MOTHER.

UNITED STATES OF AMERICA, Indian Territory,  }
Southern      DISTRICT.

I, Joanna Dobyns, on oath state that I am 26 years of age and a citizen by blood, of the Choctaw Nation; that I am the lawful wife of Oscar Dobyns, who is a citizen, by intermarriage of the Choctaw Nation; that a female child was born to me on $29^{th}$ day of Jan, 1903; that said child has been named Annie Belle Dobyns, and was living March 4, 1905.

Joanna Dobyns

Witnesses To Mark:
{

Subscribed and sworn to before me this $1^{st}$ day of April, 1905

D.P. Johnston
Notary Public.

---

### AFFIDAVIT OF ATTENDING PHYSICIAN OR MID-WIFE.

UNITED STATES OF AMERICA, Indian Territory,  }
Southern      DISTRICT.

I, W.L. Davis, a Physician, on oath state that I attended on Mrs. Joanna Dobyns, wife of Oscar Dobyns on the $29^{th}$ day of Jan,

## Applications for Enrollment of Choctaw Newborn
## Act of 1905   Volume IX

1903; that there was born to her on said date a   female   child; that said child was living March 4, 1905, and is said to have been named  Annie Belle Dobyns

W.L. Davis M.D.

Witnesses To Mark:

{

    Subscribed and sworn to before me this 1st day of   April   , 1905

D.P. Johnston<br>Notary Public.

---

BIRTH AFFIDAVIT.

### DEPARTMENT OF THE INTERIOR.
### COMMISSION TO THE FIVE CIVILIZED TRIBES.

---

**IN RE APPLICATION FOR ENROLLMENT,** as a citizen of the   Choctaw   Nation, of Ethel Dobyns   , born on the   12th   day of   Feb   , 1905

Name of Father:  Oscar Dobyns         a citizen of the   ———   Nation.
Name of Mother:  Joanna Dobyns        a citizen of the   Choctaw   Nation.

Postoffice   Madill I.T.

---

**AFFIDAVIT OF MOTHER.**

UNITED STATES OF AMERICA, Indian Territory, }
    Southern         DISTRICT. }

    I, Joanna Dobyns   , on oath state that I am   26   years of age and a citizen by   blood   , of the   Choctaw   Nation; that I am the lawful wife of   Oscar Dobyns   , who is a citizen, by   intermarriage   of the   Choctaw   Nation; that a   female   child was born to me on   12th   day of   Feb   , 1905; that said child has been named   Ethel Dobyns   , and was living March 4, 1905.

Joanna Dobyns

Witnesses To Mark:

{

    Subscribed and sworn to before me this  30th   day of   March   , 1905

D.P. Johnston<br>Notary Public.

# Applications for Enrollment of Choctaw Newborn
## Act of 1905 Volume IX

### AFFIDAVIT OF ATTENDING PHYSICIAN OR MID-WIFE.

UNITED STATES OF AMERICA, Indian Territory,
Southern DISTRICT.

I, E.F. Lewis, a Physician, on oath state that I attended on Mrs. Joanna Dobyns, wife of Oscar Dobyns on the 12$^{th}$ day of Feb, 1905; that there was born to her on said date a female child; that said child was living March 4, 1905, and is said to have been named Ethel Dobyns

E.F. Lewis

Witnesses To Mark:

Subscribed and sworn to before me this 30$^{th}$ day of March, 1905

D.P. Johnston
Notary Public.

---

Choc New Born 586
Joe Mitchell Folsom b. 11-17-04

Choctaw 3712.

Muskogee, Indian Territory, April 6, 1905.

Joseph H. Folsom,
Matoy, Indian Territory.

Dear Sir:

Receipt is hereby acknowledged of the affidavits of Sissie Folsom and W. T. Lindsey to the birth of Joe Mitchell Folsom, son of Joseph H. and Sissie Folsom, November 17, 1904, and the same have been filed with our records as an application for the enrollment of said child.

Respectfully,

Commissioner in Charge.

# Applications for Enrollment of Choctaw Newborn
## Act of 1905 Volume IX

BIRTH AFFIDAVIT.

### DEPARTMENT OF THE INTERIOR.
### COMMISSION TO THE FIVE CIVILIZED TRIBES.

IN RE APPLICATION FOR ENROLLMENT, as a citizen of the Choctaw Nation, of Joe Mitchell Folsom, born on the 17 day of Nov, 1904

Name of Father: Joseph H Folsom     a citizen of the Choctaw Nation.
Name of Mother: Sissie Folsom     a citizen of the Choctaw Nation.

Postoffice Matoy I.T.

### AFFIDAVIT OF MOTHER.

UNITED STATES OF AMERICA, Indian Territory,
Central     DISTRICT.

I, Sissie Folsom, on oath state that I am 28 years of age and a citizen by Blood, of the Choctaw Nation; that I am the lawful wife of Joseph H Folsom, who is a citizen, by Blood of the Choctaw Nation; that a Male child was born to me on 17 day of Nov, 1904; that said child has been named Joe Mitchell Folsom, and was living March 4, 1905.

Sissie Folsom

Witnesses To Mark:

Subscribed and sworn to before me this 29 day of Mch, 1905

J.H.P. Smith
Notary Public.

### AFFIDAVIT OF ATTENDING PHYSICIAN OR MID-WIFE.

UNITED STATES OF AMERICA, Indian Territory,
Central     DISTRICT.

I, W.T. Lindsey, a Doctor, on oath state that I attended on Mrs. Sissie Folsom, wife of Joseph H Folsom on the 17 day of Nov, 1904; that there was born to her on said date a male child; that said child was living March 4, 1905, and is said to have been named Joe Mitchell Folsom

Dr. W.T. Lindsey

Witnesses To Mark:

## Applications for Enrollment of Choctaw Newborn
## Act of 1905  Volume IX

Subscribed and sworn to before me this  29  day of     Mch     , 1905

J.H.P. Smith
Notary Public.

---

Choc New Born 587
    Gilbert Tennent[sic] Braine   b. 12-25-04

Choctaw 4570.

Muskogee, Indian Territory, April 6, 1905.

Clarence Braine,
    McAlester, Indian Territory.

Dear Sir:

    Receipt is hereby acknowledged of the affidavits of Carrie E. Tennant Braine and M. W. Cowan to the birth of Gilbert Tennant Braine, son of Clarence and Carrie E. Tennant Braine, December 25, 1904, and the same have been filed with our records as an application for the enrollment of said child.

Respectfully,

Commissioner in Charge.

7 NB 587

**COPY**

Muskogee, Indian Territory, April 26, 1905.

Carrie E. Tennant Braine,
    1404 Forest Avenue,
        Parsons, Kansas.

Dear Madam:

    Receipt is hereby acknowledged of your letter of April 18, 1905, stating that you have forwarded papers in the matter of the enrollment of your child Gilbert Tennant Braine and you ask if the same have been received.

## Applications for Enrollment of Choctaw Newborn
## Act of 1905   Volume IX

In reply to your letter you are advised that the affidavits heretofore forwarded to the birth of your child Gilbert Tennant Braine have been filed with our records as an application for the enrollment of said child.

Respectfully,

SIGNED   *Tams Bixby*
Chairman.

---

**BIRTH AFFIDAVIT.**

### DEPARTMENT OF THE INTERIOR.
### COMMISSION TO THE FIVE CIVILIZED TRIBES.

---

**IN RE APPLICATION FOR ENROLLMENT,** as a citizen of the   Choctaw   Nation, of Gilbert Tennant Braine   , born on the   25   day of   Dec   , 1904

Name of Father: Clarence Braine   a citizen of the ............................ Nation.
Name of Mother: Carrie E Tennent[sic] Braine   a citizen of the   Choctaw   Nation.

Postoffice   M$^c$Alester I.T.

---

**AFFIDAVIT OF MOTHER.**

UNITED STATES OF AMERICA, Indian Territory,
............................................................. DISTRICT.

I,   Carrie E. Tennent Braine   , on oath state that I am   31   years of age and a citizen by   blood   , of the   Choctaw   Nation; that I am the lawful wife of Clarence Braine   , who is a citizen, by ........................ of the ........................ Nation; that a   Male   child was born to me on   25   day of   Dec   , 1904; that said child has been named   Gilbert Tennent Braine   , and was living March 4, 1905.

Carrie E. Tennent Braine
Witnesses To Mark:
{

Subscribed and sworn to before me this   24"   day of   March   , 1905

My com. expires   Aso[sic] Smith
Feb 23 1907   Notary Public.

---

## Applications for Enrollment of Choctaw Newborn
## Act of 1905  Volume IX

### AFFIDAVIT OF ATTENDING PHYSICIAN OR MID-WIFE.

UNITED STATES OF AMERICA, Indian Territory,
.................................................... DISTRICT.

I, MW Cowan , a Physician , on oath state that I attended on Mrs. Carrie E T Braine , wife of Clarence Braine on the 25$^{th}$ day of Dec , 1904; that there was born to her on said date a male child; that said child was living March 4, 1905, and is said to have been named Gilbert Tennant Braine

MW Cowan M.D.

Witnesses To Mark:
{

Subscribed and sworn to before me this 24" day of March , 1905

Aso[sic] Smith
Notary Public.

My com. expires Feb 23 1907

---

Choc New Born 588
Lowell C. Shoemake  b. 8-17-04

———

7-N.B. 588.

Muskogee, Indian Territory, June 5, 1905.

Estella Shumake[sic],
Bennington, Indian Territory.

Dear Madam:

Receipt is hereby acknowledged of your letter of May 27, relative to the application for the enrollment of your son, Lowell C. Shoemake.

In reply to your letter you are advised that the affidavits heretofore forwarded to the birth of this child have been filed with our records as an application for his enrollment, and you will be notified when is enrollment is approved by the Secretary of the Interior.

# Applications for Enrollment of Choctaw Newborn
## Act of 1905  Volume IX

Respectfully,

Commissioner in Charge.

---

BIRTH AFFIDAVIT.

### DEPARTMENT OF THE INTERIOR.
### COMMISSION TO THE FIVE CIVILIZED TRIBES.

---

IN RE APPLICATION FOR ENROLLMENT, as a citizen of the Choctaw Nation, of Lowell C. Shoemake, born on the 17$^{th}$ day of August, 1904

Name of Father: J.E. Shoemake    a citizen of the   U. S.   Nation.
Name of Mother: Estella Shoemake    a citizen of the   Choctaw   Nation.

Postoffice   Bennington I.T.

---

AFFIDAVIT OF MOTHER.

UNITED STATES OF AMERICA, Indian Territory, }
 Central                DISTRICT.

I, Estella Shoemake, on oath state that I am 20 years of age and a citizen by Blood, of the Choctaw Nation; that I am the lawful wife of J. E. Shoemake, who is a citizen, by marriage of the Choctaw Nation; that a male child was born to me on 17$^{th}$ day of August, 1904; that said child has been named Lowell C. Shoemake, and was living March 4, 1905.

Estella Shoemake

Witnesses To Mark:

Subscribed and sworn to before me this 29$^{th}$ day of March, 1905

C.C. M$^c$Clard
Notary Public.

---

AFFIDAVIT OF ATTENDING PHYSICIAN OR MID-WIFE.

UNITED STATES OF AMERICA, Indian Territory, }
 Central                DISTRICT.

I, Pollie Shoemake, a midwife, on oath state that I attended on Mrs. Estella Shoemake, wife of J.E. Shoemake on the 17$^{th}$ day of

## Applications for Enrollment of Choctaw Newborn
## Act of 1905   Volume IX

August    , 1904; that there was born to her on said date a    male    child; that said child was living March 4, 1905, and is said to have been named Lowell C. Shoemake

Pollie Shoemake

Witnesses To Mark:
{

Subscribed and sworn to before me this 29$^{th}$ day of March   , 1905

C.C. M$^c$Clard
Notary Public.

---

Choc New Born 589
    Lawrence Graham   b. 6-17-03

7-NB-589
7-NB-1260

Muskogee, Indian Territory, July 25, 1905.

Mary J. F. Graham,
    Bengal, Indian Territory.

Dear Madam:

    Replying to that portion of your letter of July 18, 1905, in which you ask the status of the enrollment of Lawrence Graham and Grace Ella, Marion Francis and Benjamin C. Merryman, you are advised that the enrollment of Benjamin C. and Marion Francis Merryman as citizens by blood of the Choctaw Nation was on June 30, 1905, approved by the Secretary of the Interior.

    The names of Lawrence Graham and Grace Ella Merryman has been placed upon a schedule of citizens by blood of the Choctaw Nation which has been forwarded the Secretary of the Interior, and you will be notified when their enrollment is approved.

Respectfully,

Commissioner.

Applications for Enrollment of Choctaw Newborn
Act of 1905 Volume IX

## Affidavit of Attending Physician or Midwife

UNITED STATES OF AMERICA,
INDIAN TERRITORY,
Central DISTRICT

I, Rutha Millus a midwife on oath state that I attended on Mrs. Mary J.F. Graham (nee Merryman) wife of Vano Graham on the 17 day of June , 190 3, that there was born to her on said date a male child, that said child is now living, and is said to have been named Lawrence Graham

Rutha Millus *Midwife* M. D.

Subscribed and sworn to before me this the 18 day of March 1905

B F Johnson
My Commission Expires Jan 25-1907    Notary Public.

WITNESSETH:
Must be two witnesses who are citizens and know the child. { Abraham Merryman
Jefferson Yorn }

We hereby certify that we are well acquainted with Rutha Millus a Midwife and know her to be reputable and of good standing in the community.

Must be two citizen witnesses. { Abraham Merryman
Jefferson Yorn }

# NEW BORN AFFIDAVIT

No

## CHOCTAW ENROLLING COMMISSION

IN THE MATTER OF THE APPLICATION FOR ENROLLMENT as a citizen of the Choctaw Nation, of Lawrence Graham born on the 17 day of June 190 3

Name of father Vano Graham a citizen of non Nation, final enrollment No... *D.C. Merryman*
Name of mother Mary J.F. Graham a citizen of Choctaw Nation, final enrollment No. 8454

295

## Applications for Enrollment of Choctaw Newborn
## Act of 1905   Volume IX

Bengal I.T.   Postoffice.

### AFFIDAVIT OF MOTHER

UNITED STATES OF AMERICA  
INDIAN TERRITORY  
DISTRICT   Central

I   Mary J.F. Graham  [*Merryman* nee]  , on oath state that I am   18   years of age and a citizen by   blood   of the   Choctaw   Nation, and as such have been placed upon the final roll of the   Choctaw   Nation, by the Honorable Secretary of the Interior my final enrollment number being   8457   ; that I am the lawful wife of   Vano Graham   , who is a citizen of the   ~~Choctaw~~ *non*   Nation, and as such has been placed upon the final roll of said Nation by the Honorable Secretary of the Interior, his final enrollment number being   —   and that a   male   child was born to me on the   17   day of   June   190 3; that said child has been named   Lawrence Graham   , and is now living.

WITNESSETH:   Mary Graham

Must be two witnesses who are citizens { Abraham Merryman  
Jefferson Yorn

Subscribed and sworn to before me this, the   17   day of   February   , 190 5

James Bower  
Notary Public.

My Commission Expires:  
Sept 23 - 1907

*Final Enrollment No 8457*

**BIRTH AFFIDAVIT.**

## DEPARTMENT OF THE INTERIOR,
### COMMISSION TO THE FIVE CIVILIZED TRIBES.

**IN RE Application for Enrollment,** as a citizen of the   Choctaw   Nation, of   Lawrence Graham   , born on the   17   day of   June   , 1903

Name of Father: Vano Graham      a citizen *none* ~~of the~~ Choctaw   Nation.  
Name of Mother: Mary J.F. Graham      a citizen of the   Choctaw   Nation.

Post-Office:   Bengal I.T.

# Applications for Enrollment of Choctaw Newborn
# Act of 1905   Volume IX

**AFFIDAVIT OF MOTHER.**

UNITED STATES OF AMERICA, }
   INDIAN TERRITORY.
   Central    District.

I, Mary J.F. Graham (Merryman), on oath state that I am 18 years of age and a citizen by blood, of the Choctaw Nation; that I am the lawful wife of Vano Graham, ~~who is a citizen~~, none by of the —— Nation; that a male child was born to me on 17 day of June, 1903, that said child has been named Lawrence Graham, and is now living. March 4 1905

                                    Mary J.F. Graham

WITNESSES TO MARK:
   { Ida Isaacs
     M E Johnson

*Subscribed and sworn to before me this* 18 *day of* March, 1905.

                                      B F Johnson
                                        NOTARY PUBLIC.

**AFFIDAVIT OF ATTENDING PHYSICIAN OR MID-WIFE.**

UNITED STATES OF AMERICA, }
   INDIAN TERRITORY.
   Central    District.

I, Rutha Millus, a Midwife, on oath state that I attended on Mrs. Mary J F Graham, wife of Vano Graham on the 17 day of June, 1903; that there was born to her on said date a male child; that said child is now living and is said to have been named Lawrence Graham

                                     her
                          Rutha Millus  x
WITNESSES TO MARK:                  mark
   { L S Millus
     S.E. Graham

*Subscribed and sworn to before me this* 18 *day of* March, 1905.

                                    B F Johnson
                                    NOTARY PUBLIC.

My Commission Expires Jan 28 - 1909

## Applications for Enrollment of Choctaw Newborn
## Act of 1905   Volume IX

Choc New Born 590
> Roy Hill Shuler   b. 1-6-04

Choctaw 4873.

Muskogee, Indian Territory, April 6, 1905.

William Robert Shuler,
> Newberg, Indian Territory.

Dear Sir:

    Receipt is hereby acknowledged of the affidavits of Maggie Shuler (Andrews) and N. J. Johnson to the birth of Roy Hill Shuler, son of William R. and Maggie Shuler, January 6, 1904, and the same have been filed with our records as an application for the enrollment of said child.

Respectfully,

Commissioner in Charge.

7-4873

Muskogee, Indian Territory, April 6, 1905.

L. H. Riter,
> Newburg, Indian Territory.

Dear Sir:

    Receipt is hereby acknowledged of your letter of March 29, 1905, in which you ask that the birth certificate of Roy Hill Shuler be returned to you in order that you may place thereon the date your commission as Notary Public expires which is March 11, 1909.

    In reply to your letter you are advised that the Commission does not require that the date the expiration of the Notary's commission be placed upon the affidavits and it is impracticable to comply with your request that the affidavits to the birth of Roy Hill shuler[sic] be returned to you.

Respectfully,

Commissioner in Charge.

## Applications for Enrollment of Choctaw Newborn
## Act of 1905   Volume IX

BIRTH AFFIDAVIT.

### DEPARTMENT OF THE INTERIOR.
### COMMISSION TO THE FIVE CIVILIZED TRIBES.

IN RE APPLICATION FOR ENROLLMENT, as a citizen of the   Choctaw   Nation, of   Roy Hill Shuler   , born on the 6$^{th}$ day of Jan , 1904

Name of Father: William Robert Shuler   ~~a citizen of the   C~~   Nation.
Name of Mother: Maggie Shuler (nee Andrews) a citizen of the Choctaw Nation.

Postoffice   Newberg, I.T.

### AFFIDAVIT OF MOTHER.

UNITED STATES OF AMERICA, Indian Territory,
Central   DISTRICT.

I, Maggie Shuler , on oath state that I am 35 years of age and a citizen by Blood , of the Choctaw Nation; that I am the lawful wife of William Robert Shuler , who is a citizen, by _____ of the _____ Nation; that a male child was born to me on 6th day of January , 1904; that said child has been named Roy Hill Shuler , and was living March 4, 1905.

Maggie Shuler

Witnesses To Mark:
{

Subscribed and sworn to before me this 28th day of March , 1905

L. H. Ritter
Notary Public.

### AFFIDAVIT OF ATTENDING PHYSICIAN OR MID-WIFE.

UNITED STATES OF AMERICA, Indian Territory,
Central   DISTRICT.

I, N. J. Johnson , a Physician , on oath state that I attended on Mrs. Maggie Shuler , wife of William R Shuler on the 6th day of January , 1904; that there was born to her on said date a male child; that said child was living March 4, 1905, and is said to have been named Roy Hill Shuler

N. J. Johnson M.D.

Witnesses To Mark:
{

# Applications for Enrollment of Choctaw Newborn
## Act of 1905 Volume IX

Subscribed and sworn to before me this 28th day of March, 1905

L. H. Ritter
Notary Public.

---

Choc New Born 591
Hester V. Fisher  b. 11-24-02

Choctaw 183.

Muskogee, Indian Territory, April 6, 1905.

Elizabeth Ellen Fisher,
Naples, Indian Territory.

Dear Madam:

Receipt is hereby acknowledged of the affidavits of Elizziebeth[sic] Ellen Fisher and Emily Fisher to the birth of Hester V. Fisher, daughter of J. A. and Elizabeth Ellen Fisher, November 24, 1902, and the same have been filed with our records as an application for the enrollment of said child.

Respectfully,

Commissioner in Charge.

**COPY**

7 N. B. 591

Muskogee, Indian Territory, April 11, 1905.

J. A. Fisher,
Naples, Indian Territory.

Dear Sir:

There is inclosed you herewith for execution application for the enrollment of your infant child, Hester V. Fisher, born November 24, 1902.

In having these affidavits executed care should be exercised to see that all names are written in full, as they appear in the body of the affidavit, and in the event that either

## Applications for Enrollment of Choctaw Newborn
## Act of 1905   Volume IX

of the persons signing the affidavit are unable to write, signatures by mark must be attested by two witnesses. Each affidavit must be executed before a Notary Public and the notarial seal and signature of the officer must be attached to each separate affidavit.

Respectfully,

SIGNED

LM 11-23

*T. B. Needles.*
Commissioner in Charge.

7 NB 591
**COPY**
Muskogee, Indian Territory, April 26, 1905.

J. A. Fisher,
    Naples, Indian Territory.

Dear Sir:

    Receipt is hereby acknowledged of the affidavits of Elizabeth Ellen Fisher and Emily A. Fisher to the birth of Hester V. Fisher, daughter of J. A. and Elizabeth Ellen Fisher, November 24, 1902, and the same have been filed with our records in the matter of the enrollment of said child.

Respectfully,
SIGNED

*Tams Bixby*
Chairman.

BIRTH AFFIDAVIT.

**DEPARTMENT OF THE INTERIOR.**
**COMMISSION TO THE FIVE CIVILIZED TRIBES.**

**IN RE APPLICATION FOR ENROLLMENT,** as a citizen of the       Choctaw       Nation, of Hester V. Fisher         , born on the 24" day of November  , 1902

Name of Father:  J.A. Fisher                    a citizen of the    U. S.    Nation.
Name of Mother:  Elizabeth Ellen Fisher         a citizen of the   Choctaw   Nation.

Postoffice    Naples Ind Ter.

# Applications for Enrollment of Choctaw Newborn
## Act of 1905   Volume IX

### AFFIDAVIT OF MOTHER.

UNITED STATES OF AMERICA, Indian Territory,
.................................................... DISTRICT.

I,  Elizabeth Ellen Fisher  , on oath state that I am  21  years of age and a citizen by  Blood  , of the  Choctaw  Nation; that I am the lawful wife of  J A Fisher  , who is a citizen, ~~by~~ ———— of the  United States  Nation; that a  Female  child was born to me on  24"  day of  November  , 1902; that said child has been named  Hester V. Fisher  , and was living March 4, 1905.

Elizabeth Ellen Fisher

Witnesses To Mark:
{

Subscribed and sworn to before me this  20  day of  April  , 1905

James M Gordon
My term of office expires March 1907         Notary Public.

---

### AFFIDAVIT OF ATTENDING PHYSICIAN OR MID-WIFE.

UNITED STATES OF AMERICA, Indian Territory,
   Southern               DISTRICT.

I,  Emily A Fisher  , a  Mid Wife  , on oath state that I attended on Mrs.  Elizabeth Ellen Fisher  , wife of  J A Fisher  on the  24"  day of  November  , 1902; that there was born to her on said date a  Female  child; that said child was living March 4, 1905, and is said to have been named  Hester V Fisher

emily a fisher[sic]

Witnesses To Mark:
{

Subscribed and sworn to before me this  20$^{th}$  day of  April  , 1905

James M Gordon
My term of office expires March 1907         Notary Public.

---

BIRTH AFFIDAVIT.

**IN RE-APPLICATION FOR ENROLLMENT**, as a citizen of the  Choctaw  Nation, of  Hester V Fisher , born on the  24$^{th}$  day of  November  , 190 2

Name of Father:  J. A. Fisher         a citizen of the  ————  Nation.
Name of Mother:  Elizziebeth Ellen Fisher    a citizen of the  Choctaw  Nation.

## Applications for Enrollment of Choctaw Newborn
## Act of 1905  Volume IX

Postoffice   Naples I.T.

### AFFIDAVIT OF MOTHER.

UNITED STATES OF AMERICA, INDIAN TERRITORY,  
Southern          District.

I, ℰLizzie~~beth~~ Ellen Fisher, on oath state that I am 21 years of age and a citizen by blood, of the Choctaw Nation; that I am the lawful wife of J. A. Fisher, who is a citizen, by —— of the —— Nation; that a female child was born to me on 24<sup>th</sup> day of November, 1902, that said child has been named Hester V Fisher, and is now living.

ℰLizzie~~beth~~ Ellen Fisher

Witnesses To Mark:

Subscribed and sworn to before me this 13<sup>th</sup> day of March, 1905.

My commission expires          F. E. Rice  
Dec 4-1907                     Notary Public.

### AFFIDAVIT OF ATTENDING PHYSICIAN OR MID-WIFE.

UNITED STATES OF AMERICA, INDIAN TERRITORY,  
Southern          District.

I, Emley[sic] Fisher, a midwife, on oath state that I attended on Mrs. ℰLizzie~~beth~~ Ellen Fisher, wife of J A Fisher on the 24<sup>th</sup> day of November, 1902; that there was born to her on said date a female child; that said child is now living and is said to have been named Hester V Fisher

emley fisher

Witnesses To Mark:

Subscribed and sworn to before me this 16 day of Mch, 1905.

J M Gordon  
Notary Public.

My Com expires Mch 1907

## Applications for Enrollment of Choctaw Newborn
## Act of 1905   Volume IX

<u>Choc New Born 592</u>
    Mary Elizabeth Motes   b. 12-22-04

---

7-3306

Muskogee, Indian Territory, April 6, 1905.

John A. Motes,
    Allen, Indian Territory.

Dear Sir:

    Receipt is hereby acknowledged of the affidavits of Levina Motes and W. C. Threlkeld to the birth of Mary Elizabeth motes, daughter of John A. and Levina Motes, December 22, 1904, and the same have been filed with our records as an application for the enrollment of said child.

    Respectfully,

    Commissioner in Charge.

---

**COPY**

7-N. B. 592

Muskogee, Indian Territory, April 11, 1905.

Wirt Franklin,
    Idabel, Indian Territory.

Dear Sir:

    Inclosed herewith you will find birth affidavit executed before you as a Notary Public, as to the birth of Mary Elizabeth Motes, infant child of John A. and Levina Motes, which does not bear the imprint of your notarial seal. Please attach same in proper place and return the affidavit to the Commission.

    Respectfully,

    SIGNED

    *T. B. Needles.*

LM 11-22    Commissioner in Charge.

---

## Applications for Enrollment of Choctaw Newborn
## Act of 1905   Volume IX

BIRTH AFFIDAVIT.

### DEPARTMENT OF THE INTERIOR.
### COMMISSION TO THE FIVE CIVILIZED TRIBES.

IN RE APPLICATION FOR ENROLLMENT, as a citizen of the Choctaw Nation, of Mary Elizabeth Motes, born on the 22th[sic] day of December, 1904

Name of Father: John A Motes     a citizen of the Choctaw Nation.
Name of Mother: Levina Motes     a citizen of the Choctaw Nation.

Postoffice   Allen, Ind. Ter.

### AFFIDAVIT OF MOTHER.

UNITED STATES OF AMERICA, Indian Territory,
Central   DISTRICT.

I, Levina Motes, on oath state that I am 25 years of age and a citizen by blood, of the Choctaw Nation; that I am the lawful wife of John A Motes, who is a citizen, by marriage of the Choctaw Nation; that a female child was born to me on 22th day of December, 1904; that said child has been named Mary Elizabeth Motes, and was living March 4, 1905.

                         her
                Levina x Motes
Witnesses To Mark:       mark
   { Peter Maytubby Jr
   { Victor M Locke JR

Subscribed and sworn to before me this 27th day of March, 1905

                 Wirt Franklin
                 Notary Public.

### AFFIDAVIT OF ATTENDING PHYSICIAN OR MID-WIFE.

UNITED STATES OF AMERICA, Indian Territory,
Central   DISTRICT.

I, W. C. Threlkeld, a physician, on oath state that I attended on Mrs. Levina Motes, wife of John A Motes on the 22 day of December, 1904; that there was born to her on said date a female child; that said child was living March 4, 1905, and is said to have been named Mary Elizabeth Motes

                 W.C. Threlkeld M.D.

# Applications for Enrollment of Choctaw Newborn
## Act of 1905    Volume IX

Witnesses To Mark:

{

Subscribed and sworn to before me this 30 day of March, 1905

My commission expires    J. L. Cart
June 7-1908              Notary Public.

---

Choc New Born 593
    Joseph Mansfield Garland   b. 1-10-03

7-2440

Muskogee, Indian Territory, April 6, 1905.

Frank Garland,
    Stigler, Indian Territory.

Dear Sir:

    Receipt is hereby acknowledged of your letter of April 1, 1905, enclosing the affidavits of Jahnie[sic] Garland and C. C. Jones to the birth of Joseph Mansfield Garland, Indian Territory son of Frank and Jannie[sic] Garland, Indian Territory January 10, 1903, and the same have been filed with our records as an application for the enrollment of said child.

    Respectfully,

Commissioner in Charge.

---

**BIRTH AFFIDAVIT.**

## DEPARTMENT OF THE INTERIOR.
## COMMISSION TO THE FIVE CIVILIZED TRIBES.

    **IN RE APPLICATION FOR ENROLLMENT**, as a citizen of the   Choctaw   Nation, of Joseph Mansfield Garland   , born on the 10th day of January , 1903

Name of Father: Frank Garland         a citizen of the Choctaw Nation.
Name of Mother: Jannie[sic] Garland   a citizen of the Choctaw Nation.

Postoffice   Garland, Ind. Ter.

# Applications for Enrollment of Choctaw Newborn
## Act of 1905 Volume IX

### AFFIDAVIT OF MOTHER.

UNITED STATES OF AMERICA, Indian Territory,
Central DISTRICT.

I, Jannie Garland, on oath state that I am 22 years of age and a citizen by blood, of the Choctaw Nation; that I am the lawful wife of Frank Garland, who is a citizen, by blood of the Choctaw Nation; that a male child was born to me on 10th day of January, 1903; that said child has been named Joseph Mansfield Garland, and was living March 4, 1905.

Jannie Garland

Witnesses To Mark:

Subscribed and sworn to before me this 30$^{th}$ day of March, 1905

C.C. Jones
Notary Public.

---

### AFFIDAVIT OF ATTENDING PHYSICIAN OR MID-WIFE.

UNITED STATES OF AMERICA, Indian Territory,
Central DISTRICT.

I, C. C. Jones, a physician, on oath state that I attended on Mrs. Jannie Garland, wife of Frank Garland on the 10th day of January, 1903; that there was born to her on said date a male child; that said child was living March 4, 1905, and is said to have been named Joseph Mansfield Garland

C C Jones

Witnesses To Mark:

Subscribed and sworn to before me this 30 day of March, 1905

J. N. Jones
Notary Public.

## Applications for Enrollment of Choctaw Newborn
## Act of 1905 Volume IX

**NEW-BORN AFFIDAVIT.**

Number..............

### ...Choctaw Enrolling Commission...

IN THE MATTER OF THE APPLICATION FOR ENROLLMENT, as a citizen of the Choctaw Nation, of Joseph Mansfield Garland

born on the 10$^{th}$ day of __January__ 190 3

Name of father    Frank Garland    a citizen of    Choctaw
Nation final enrollment No.  7064
Name of mother    Janie Garland    a citizen of    Choctaw
Nation final enrollment No.  7065

Postoffice    Garland, I.T.

### AFFIDAVIT OF MOTHER.

UNITED STATES OF AMERICA
INDIAN TERRITORY
Central    DISTRICT

I    Janie Garland    , on oath state that I am 22    years of age and a citizen by  Blood  of the  Choctaw    Nation, and as such have been placed upon the final roll of the  Choctaw  Nation, by the Honorable Secretary of the Interior my final enrollment number being    7065  ; that I am the lawful wife of  Frank Garland    , who is a citizen of the    Choctaw    Nation, and as such has been placed upon the final roll of said Nation by the Honorable Secretary of the Interior, his final enrollment number being    7064    and that a    Male    child was born to me on the 10$^{th}$    day of    January    190 3; that said child has been named    Joseph Mansfield Garland    , and is now living.

Janie Garland

Witnesseth.
Must be two Witnesses who are Citizens. } Ward Garland Jr

W.N. Franklin

Subscribed and sworn to before me this    6$^{th}$    day of  Jan    190 5

C. C. Jones
Notary Public.

My commission expires:  March 3$^{d}$ 1907

# Applications for Enrollment of Choctaw Newborn
## Act of 1905 Volume IX

## AFFIDAVIT OF ATTENDING PHYSICIAN OR MIDWIFE

UNITED STATES OF AMERICA
INDIAN TERRITORY
................................ DISTRICT

I, C. C. Jones a Physician on oath state that I attended on Mrs. Janie Garland wife of Frank Garland on the 10$^{th}$ day of January, 190 3, that there was born to her on said date a male child, that said child is now living, and is said to have been named Joseph Mansfield Garland

C. C. Jones

Subscribed and sworn to before me this, the ........................................... day of Jan 7$^{th}$ 190 5

C.C. Jones     Notary Public.

WITNESSETH:
Must be two witnesses ⎰ Ward Garland Jr
who are citizens    ⎱ W.N. Franklin

We hereby certify that we are well acquainted with C. C. Jones a Physician and know him to be reputable and of good standing in the community.

Ward Garland Jr.

W.N. Franklin

---

Choc New Born 594
    Wesley Anderson Cole b. 11-12-04

BIRTH AFFIDAVIT.

### DEPARTMENT OF THE INTERIOR.
### COMMISSION TO THE FIVE CIVILIZED TRIBES.

IN RE APPLICATION FOR ENROLLMENT, as a citizen of the Choctaw Nation, of Wesley Anderson Cole, born on the 12 day of November, 1904

Name of Father: George W Cole     a citizen of the white Nation.
Name of Mother: Emily F Cole      a citizen of the Choctaw Nation.

Postoffice Stigler

## Applications for Enrollment of Choctaw Newborn
## Act of 1905 Volume IX

### AFFIDAVIT OF MOTHER.

UNITED STATES OF AMERICA, Indian Territory, }
Central DISTRICT. }

I, Emily F Cole, on oath state that I am 23 years of age and a citizen by blood, of the Choctaw Nation; that I am the lawful wife of George W Cole, who is a citizen, by ~~of the~~ white Nation; that a male child was born to me on 12 day of November, 1904; that said child has been named Wesley Anderson Cole, and was living March 4, 1905.

Witnesses To Mark:
{

Emily F Cole

Subscribed and sworn to before me this 30th day of March, 1905

E M Dalton
Notary Public.
My commission expires Oct 20-1908

### AFFIDAVIT OF ATTENDING PHYSICIAN OR MID-WIFE.

UNITED STATES OF AMERICA, Indian Territory, }
Central DISTRICT. }

I, A. F. Ferrell, a physician, on oath state that I attended on Mrs. Emily F Cole, wife of George W Cole on the $12^{th}$ day of Nov, 1904; that there was born to her on said date a male child; that said child was living March 4, 1905, and is said to have been named Wesley Anderson Cole

R. F. Ferrell, M.D.
Witnesses To Mark:
{

Subscribed and sworn to before me this 31 day of March, 1905

E M Dalton
Notary Public.
My commission expires Oct 20-1908

# Applications for Enrollment of Choctaw Newborn
# Act of 1905   Volume IX

Choc New Born 595
   Luther Bowers   b. 11-3-04

---

Choctaw 4788.

Muskogee, Indian Territory, April 7, 1905.

Ray Bowers,
   Tuttle, Indian Territory.

Dear Sir:

Receipt is hereby acknowledged of the affidavits of Susan Bowers and Katie Newton to the birth of Luther Bowers, son of Ray and Susan Bowers, November 3, 1904, and the same have been filed with our records as an application for the enrollment of said child.

Respectfully,

Commissioner in Charge.

---

## AFFIDAVIT OF ATTENDING PHYSICIAN OR MIDWIFE

UNITED STATES OF AMERICA
INDIAN TERRITORY
   Central   DISTRICT

I,   Mrs Katie Newton   a   midwife on oath state that I attended on Mrs. Susie Bowers   wife of   Ray Bowers on the 3$^{rd}$   day of November  , 190 4 , that there was born to her on said date a   Male child, that said child is now living, and is said to have been named   Luther Bowers

Katie Newton   *Midwife*.

Subscribed and sworn to before me this, the   16"   day of Jan   190 5

WITNESSETH:   J H Elliott   Notary Public.
Must be two witnesses
who are citizens   { Samuel L Wooley
                    { Mrs J H Bruce

311

# Applications for Enrollment of Choctaw Newborn
## Act of 1905   Volume IX

We hereby certify that we are well acquainted with Katie Newton a midwife and know her to be reputable and of good standing in the community.

    Mrs J H Bruce                        Stuart I.T.

    Samuel L Wooley                Stuart I T

    My com exp July 8" 1908

---

BIRTH AFFIDAVIT.

### DEPARTMENT OF THE INTERIOR.
### COMMISSION TO THE FIVE CIVILIZED TRIBES.

**IN RE APPLICATION FOR ENROLLMENT**, as a citizen of the Chocktaw[sic] Nation, of Luther Bowers, born on the 3rd day of Nov, 1904

Name of Father: Ray Bowers        a citizen of the US ~~Nation~~.
Name of Mother: Susan Bowers    a citizen of the Choctaw Nation.

                     Postoffice     Tuttle I.T.

### AFFIDAVIT OF MOTHER.

UNITED STATES OF AMERICA, Indian Territory,
Southern           DISTRICT.

I, Susan Bowers, on oath state that I am 25 years of age and a citizen by Blood, of the Choctaw Nation; that I am the lawful wife of Ray Bowers, who is a citizen, ~~by~~ —— of the U.S. Nation; that a male child was born to me on 3$^{rd}$ day of Nov, 1904; that said child has been named Luther Bowers, and was living March 4, 1905.

                             Susan Bowers

Witnesses To Mark:
    H Bruce

Subscribed and sworn to before me this 23$^{rd}$ day of Mar, 1905

                       J.H. Carlisle
My Com ex. Jan 26$^{th}$ 1907         Notary Public.

## Applications for Enrollment of Choctaw Newborn
## Act of 1905 Volume IX

**AFFIDAVIT OF ATTENDING PHYSICIAN OR MID-WIFE.**

UNITED STATES OF AMERICA, Indian Territory,
Central                    DISTRICT.

I, Mrs Katie Newton , a Midwife , on oath state that I attended on Mrs. Mrs Susan Bowers , wife of Roy[sic] Bowers on the 3rd day of ~~March~~ Nov , 1905[sic]; that there was born to her on said date a male child; that said child was living March 4, 1905, and is said to have been named Luther Bowers

                                            Katie Newton
Witnesses To Mark:
 { J H Bruce
   W L Wooley

Subscribed and sworn to before me this 30th day of March , 1905

                            J.H. Elliott
                                  Notary Public.

---

**NEW-BORN AFFIDAVIT.**

        Number..............

### ...Choctaw Enrolling Commission...

---

IN THE MATTER OF THE APPLICATION FOR ENROLLMENT, as a citizen of the Choctaw Nation, of Luther Bowers

born on the 3rd day of __November__ 190 4

Name of father    Ray Bowers            a citizen of    United States
Nation final enrollment No. —
Name of mother    Susie Bowers          a citizen of    Choctaw
Nation final enrollment No. 13216

                                        Postoffice    Stuart I.T.

**AFFIDAVIT OF MOTHER.**

UNITED STATES OF AMERICA
INDIAN TERRITORY
    Central    DISTRICT

           I    Susie Bowers                    , on oath state that I am 25 years of age and a citizen by Birth of the Choctaw Nation, and as such have been placed upon the final roll of the Choctaw Nation, by the Honorable

313

# Applications for Enrollment of Choctaw Newborn
## Act of 1905  Volume IX

Secretary of the Interior my final enrollment number being   13216  ; that I am the lawful wife of   Ray Bowers   , who is a citizen of the   United States   Nation, and as such has been placed upon the final roll of said Nation by the Honorable Secretary of the Interior, his final enrollment number being ............... and that a   Male   child was born to me on the 3$^{rd}$   day of   November   190 4; that said child has been named   Luther Bowers   , and is now living.

Susan Bowers

Witnesseth.

Must be two Witnesses who are Citizens.   Samuel L Wooley

Mrs J H Bruce

Subscribed and sworn to before me this   16$^{th}$   day of  Jan     190 5

J H Elliott
Notary Public.

My commission expires: July 8" 1908

---

Choc New Born 596
    Sarah L Roberson   b.  1-10-03

Choctaw 4569.

Muskogee, Indian Territory, April 7, 1905.

James W. Roberson,
    Kiowa, Indian Territory.

Dear Sir:

Receipt is hereby acknowledged of the affidavits of Reola Roberson and Sarah T. Baker to the birth of Sarah L. Roberson, daughter of James W. and Reola Roberson, January 10, 1903, and the same have been filed with our records as an application for the enrollment of said child.

Respectfully,

Commissioner in Charge.

## Applications for Enrollment of Choctaw Newborn
## Act of 1905   Volume IX

## AFFIDAVIT OF ATTENDING PHYSICIAN OR MIDWIFE

UNITED STATES OF AMERICA
INDIAN TERRITORY
Western   DISTRICT

I, Sarah T Baker   a   Mid wife on oath state that I attended on Mrs. Reola Robertson[sic]   wife of   James W. Robertson[sic] on the 10 day of January, 190 3, that there was born to her on said date a Female child, that said child is now living, and is said to have been named Sarah L Robertson

Sarah T Baker   M.D.

Subscribed and sworn to before me this, the ............................ day of March 22   190 5

*My commission expires Nov 27 1907*   John M Lenz   Notary Public.

WITNESSETH:
Must be two witnesses { Enoc F McCasson   Howe IT
who are citizens        { Watson Billy      Howe IT

We hereby certify that we are well acquainted with Sarah T Baker a midwife and know her to be reputable and of good standing in the community.

J M Lenz                           Enterprise IT

Noah E Mouser                      Enterprise I.T.

---

**NEW-BORN AFFIDAVIT.**

Number..............

## ...Choctaw Enrolling Commission...

IN THE MATTER OF THE APPLICATION FOR ENROLLMENT, as a citizen of the Choctaw   Nation, of   Sarah L Roberson

born on the 10 day of ___January___ 190 3

Name of father   James W Roberson   a citizen of   Choctaw Nation final enrollment No. 680
Name of mother   Reola Roberson   a citizen of   Choctaw Nation final enrollment No. 12657

## Applications for Enrollment of Choctaw Newborn
## Act of 1905  Volume IX

Postoffice   Kiowa I.T.

### AFFIDAVIT OF MOTHER.

UNITED STATES OF AMERICA
INDIAN TERRITORY
Central   DISTRICT

I   Reola Roberson   , on oath state that I am 25 years of age and a citizen by Blood of the Choctaw Nation, and as such have been placed upon the final roll of the Choctaw Nation, by the Honorable Secretary of the Interior my final enrollment number being 12657 ; that I am the lawful wife of James W Roberson , who is a citizen of the Choctaw Nation, and as such has been placed upon the final roll of said Nation by the Honorable Secretary of the Interior, his final enrollment number being 680 and that a Female child was born to me on the 10 day of January 190 3; that said child has been named Sarah L Roberson , and is now living.

          her
Reola x Roberson
          mark

Witnesseth.
Must be two Witnesses who are Citizens.   A.F. Stover
   Mattie Howe

Subscribed and sworn to before me this 1st day of Apl 190 5

HB Rowley
Notary Public.

My commission expires:
Nov 22nd 1905

---

Choc New Born 597
   Clarence Jefferson Underwood  b. 12-3-03

**COPY**

7 N. B. 597

Muskogee, Indian Territory, April 11, 1905.

Thomas Underwood,
   Tussy, Indian Territory.

Dear Sir:

    There is inclosed you herewith for execution application for the enrollment of your infant child, Clarence Jefferson Underwood, born December 3, 1903.

## Applications for Enrollment of Choctaw Newborn
## Act of 1905  Volume IX

In the affidavits heretofore filed with the Commission, the one of the mother shows the child was living on March 30, 1903. It is necessary that her affidavit show he was living on March 4, 1905.

The affidavits also show the child claims through you. It is, therefore, necessary that you furnish either the original or a certified copy of the license and certificate of your marriage to his mother, Fannie Underwood, forwarding same with the return of the inclosed application.

In having these affidavits executed care should be exercised to see that all names are written in full, as they appear in the body of the affidavit, and in the event that either of the persons signing the affidavit are unable to write, signatures by mark must be attested by two witnesses. Each affidavit must be executed before a Notary Public and the notarial seal and signature of the officer must be attached to each separate affidavit.

Respectfully,
SIGNED
*T. B. Needles.*
Commissioner in Charge.

LM 11-20

BIRTH AFFIDAVIT.

### DEPARTMENT OF THE INTERIOR.
### COMMISSION TO THE FIVE CIVILIZED TRIBES.

IN RE APPLICATION FOR ENROLLMENT, as a citizen of the Choctaw Nation, of Clarence Jefferson Underwood, born on the 3" day of December, 1903

Name of Father: Thomas Underwood   a citizen of the Choctaw Nation.
Name of Mother: Fannie Underwood   a citizen of the U. S. Nation.

Postoffice   Tussy, Ind. Ter.

AFFIDAVIT OF MOTHER.

UNITED STATES OF AMERICA, Indian Territory, } DISTRICT.

I, Fannie Underwood, on oath state that I am 22 years of age and a citizen by ———, of the United States Nation; that I am the lawful wife of Thomas Underwood, who is a citizen, by Blood of the Choctaw Nation; that a male child was born to me on 3" day of December, 1903; that said child has been named Clarence Jefferson Underwood, and was living March 4, 1905.

Fannie Underwood

## Applications for Enrollment of Choctaw Newborn
## Act of 1905   Volume IX

Witnesses To Mark:

    Subscribed and sworn to before me this 21 day of    Apr    , 1905

                              H.G. Liston
                              Notary Public.

**AFFIDAVIT OF ATTENDING PHYSICIAN OR MID-WIFE.**

UNITED STATES OF AMERICA, Indian Territory,
   Southern         DISTRICT.

    I,  J. I. Taylor    , a  Physician    , on oath state that I attended on Mrs.  Fannie Underwood    , wife of  Thomas Underwood    on the 3" day of December  , 1903; that there was born to her on said date a    male    child; that said child was living March 4, 1905, and is said to have been named Clarence Jefferson Underwood

                              J.I. Taylor M.D.

Witnesses To Mark:

    Subscribed and sworn to before me this 21 day of    Apr    , 1905

                              H.G. Liston
                              Notary Public.

                              Choctaw N.B. 597.

                Muskogee, Indian Territory, May 1, 1905.

Thomas Underwood,
    Tussey[sic], Indian Territory.

Dear Sir:

    Receipt is hereby acknowledged of the affidavits of Fannie Underwood and J. I. Taylor to the birth of Clarence Jefferson Underwood, son of Thomas and Fannie Underwood, December 3, 1903; also the marriage license and certificate between Thomas Underwood and Fannie Cox, and the same have been filed in the matter of the enrollment of said child.

                    Respectfully,

                                    Chairman.

Applications for Enrollment of Choctaw Newborn
Act of 1905 Volume IX

## Certificate of Record of Marriage

United States of America,  
   Indian Territory, } sct.  
   Southern District.

DEPARTMENT OF THE INTERIOR,
Commission to the Five Civilized Tribes.

**FILED**
APR 29 1905
*Tams Bixby* CHAIRMAN

I, C. M. CAMPBELL, Clerk of the United States Court, in the Territory and District aforesaid DO HEREBY CERTIFY, that the License for and Certificate of Marriage of

MR     Thomas Underwood,     and
M     Fanny Cox.

FILED

Feb 17 1902 8AM

C. M. CAMPBELL, Clerk.
Southern Dist. Ind. Ter.

were filed in my office in said Territory and District the    17"    day of    February A.D., 190 3    and duly recorded in Book    G of Marriage Record, Page    166

    WITNESS my hand and Seal of said Court, at Ardmore, Indian Territory
    this    17"    day of February    A.D. 190 3

    C. M. Campbell
                  CLERK.

Return this License to the United States Clerk at Ardmore, Indian Territory that it may be recorded, when it will be mailed to the proper address.

Ardmoreite Steam Print.

Applications for Enrollment of Choctaw Newborn
Act of 1905   Volume IX

 | **MARRIAGE LICENSE** |

UNITED STATES OF AMERICA,  
INDIAN TERRITORY,   ss:   To Any Person Authorized by Law to Solemnize Marriage, Greeting:  
SOUTHERN DISTRICT.

You are hereby commanded to solemnize the Rite and publish the Banns of Matrimony between Mr. Thomas Underwood of Wynnewood in the Indian Territory, aged 21 years, and M Fanny Cox of Wynnewood in the Indian Territory, aged 21 years, according to law; and do you officially sign and return this License to the parties therein named.

Witness my hand and official Seal, this 14" day of FCbruary[sic] A. D. 190 3

**C. M. CAMPBELL**
Clerk of the United States Court.

**Certificate of Marriage.**

UNITED STATES OF AMERICA,  
INDIAN TERRITORY,   ss:  
SOUTHERN DISTRICT.         I,      C M Campbell

Clerk U S Court So Dist I.T. do hereby certify that on the 14 day of Feby , A. D. 190 3 , I did duly according to law, as commanded in the foregoing License, solemnize the Rite and publish the Banns of Matrimony between the parties therein named.

Witness my hand this 14 day of Feby A. D. 190 3

My credentials are recorded in the office of the Clerk of the United States Court, Indian Territory, Southern District, at Ardmore, Book____, Page___

(NOTE-The person officiating should fill in the spaces for book and page and sign here.)

C.M. Campbell  
a      Clerk US Court  
So Dist Ind Ter

Applications for Enrollment of Choctaw Newborn
Act of 1905 Volume IX

BIRTH AFFIDAVIT.

## DEPARTMENT OF THE INTERIOR,
### COMMISSION TO THE FIVE CIVILIZED TRIBES.

IN RE Application for Enrollment, as a citizen of the Chickasaw[sic] Nation, of Tussy I. T. [sic] , born on the 3 day of Dec , 1903

Name of Father: Thomas J Underwood     a citizen of the Chocktaw[sic] Nation.
Name of Mother: Fanny Underwood     a citizen of the Chocktaw Nation.

Post-Office: Tussy, I.T.

### AFFIDAVIT OF MOTHER.

UNITED STATES OF AMERICA,
    INDIAN TERRITORY.
Southern District.

I, Fanny Underwood , on oath state that I am 22 years of age and a citizen by Intermarriage , of the Chocktaw Nation; that I am the lawful wife of Thomas J Underwood , who is a citizen, by Blood of the Chocktaw Nation; that a male child was born to me on 3$^{rd}$ day of Dec , 190 3, that said child has been named Clarence Jefferson Underwood , and is now living.

Fannie Under Wood[sic]

WITNESSES TO MARK:

Subscribed and sworn to before me this 30 day of March , 1903

H.G. Liston
NOTARY PUBLIC.

### AFFIDAVIT OF ATTENDING PHYSICIAN OR MID-WIFE.

UNITED STATES OF AMERICA,
    INDIAN TERRITORY.
Southern District.

I, J I Taylor , a Physician , on oath state that I attended on Mrs. Fannie Underwood , wife of Thomas J Underwood on the 3 day of Dec , 190 3; that there was born to her on said date a male child; that said child is now living and is said to have been named Clarence Jefferson Underwood

## Applications for Enrollment of Choctaw Newborn
### Act of 1905 Volume IX

WITNESSES TO MAKE:

J.I. Taylor M.D.

{

Subscribed and sworn to before me this 31 day of March, 1903

H.G. Liston
NOTARY PUBLIC.

---

Choc New Born 598
    William H. Riddle  b. 10-8-03

598

# NEW BORN
## CHOCTAW
ENROLLMENT

WILLIAM H. RIDDLE

(BORN OCTOBER 8, 1903)

As Citizen of the
CHOCTAW NATION
Act of Congress
Approved March 3, 1905

598

## Applications for Enrollment of Choctaw Newborn
## Act of 1905 Volume IX

BIRTH AFFIDAVIT.

### DEPARTMENT OF THE INTERIOR.
## COMMISSION TO THE FIVE CIVILIZED TRIBES.

IN RE APPLICATION FOR ENROLLMENT, as a citizen of the Choctaw Nation, of William H. Riddle, born on the 8th day of October, 1903

Name of Father: William Riddle — a citizen of the Chocktaw[sic] Nation.
Name of Mother: Henrietta Riddle — a citizen of the Chocktaw Nation.

Postoffice Wynnewood, I.T.

### AFFIDAVIT OF MOTHER.

UNITED STATES OF AMERICA, Indian Territory,
Southern DISTRICT.

I, Henrietta Riddle, on oath state that I am forty two years of age and a citizen by intermarriage, of the Chocktaw Nation; that I am the lawful wife of William Riddle, who is a citizen, by blood of the Chocktaw Nation; that a male child was born to me on 8th day of October, 1903; that said child has been named William H. Riddle, and was living March 4, 1905.

         her
      Henrietta x Riddle
Witnesses To Mark:   mark
 Frank C. Robinson
 W.E. Sittle

Subscribed and sworn to before me this 28th day of March, 1905

      Frank C. Robinson
      Notary Public.

### AFFIDAVIT OF ATTENDING PHYSICIAN OR MID-WIFE.

UNITED STATES OF AMERICA, Indian Territory,
Southern DISTRICT.

I, J. I. Taylor, a Physician, on oath state that I attended on Mrs. Henrietta Riddle, wife of William Riddle on the 8th day of October, 1903; that there was born to her on said date a male child; that said child was living March 4, 1905, and is said to have been named William H. Riddle.

      J. I. Taylor M.D.

# Applications for Enrollment of Choctaw Newborn
## Act of 1905   Volume IX

Witnesses To Mark:
{ Dan Stephens

Subscribed and sworn to before me this 30 day of March , 1905

H.G. Liston
Notary Public.

---

Choc New Born 599
Archie Lee Perkins   b. 11-10-03

**BIRTH AFFIDAVIT.**

**DEPARTMENT OF THE INTERIOR.**
**COMMISSION TO THE FIVE CIVILIZED TRIBES.**

**IN RE APPLICATION FOR ENROLLMENT,** as a citizen of the  Chocktaw[sic]   Nation, of Archie Lee Perkins   , born on the  10$^{th}$  day of  December  , 1903

Name of Father: Charlie A Perkins      a citizen of the United States Nation.
Name of Mother: Ella Riddle Perkins    a citizen of the  Chocktaw  Nation.

Postoffice   Robberson, I.T.

**AFFIDAVIT OF MOTHER.**

UNITED STATES OF AMERICA, Indian Territory, }
Southern              DISTRICT.

I, Ella Riddle Perkins   , on oath state that I am  nineteen  years of age and a citizen by   blood  , of the   Chocktaw   Nation; that I am the lawful wife of Charlie A. Perkins   , who is a citizen, by —— of the  United States  ~~Nation~~; that a   male   child was born to me on  10$^{th}$  day of  December  , 1903; that said child has been named  Archie Lee Perkins   , and was living March 4, 1905.

Ella Riddle Perkins

Witnesses To Mark:
{

# Applications for Enrollment of Choctaw Newborn
## Act of 1905   Volume IX

Subscribed and sworn to before me this  30   day of     March        , 1905

Clarence E Moreland
Notary Public.

---

**AFFIDAVIT OF ATTENDING PHYSICIAN OR MID-WIFE.**

UNITED STATES OF AMERICA, Indian Territory,  
Southern           DISTRICT.

I,   J. I. Taylor          , a  Physician         , on oath state that I attended on Mrs.   Ella Riddle Perkins       , wife of   Charlie A Perkins    on the   $10^{th}$ day of December   , 1903; that there was born to her on said date a    male    child; that said child was living March 4, 1905, and is said to have been named Archie Lee Perkins

J. I. Taylor M.D.

Witnesses To Mark:

Subscribed and sworn to before me this  31   day of     March        , 1905

Clarence E Moreland
Notary Public.

# Index

ABNERSON
  Mary .................................................. 235
ADAIR
  Babe ................................................ 28,34
ADAMS
  J Frank ............................................. 280
ALBRIGHT
  Mrs R E ............................................. 66
  R E .................................................... 67
ALLEN
  Eva Lena ............................. 100,101,102
  Evalina ................................ 100,103,104
  Laura ............................................ 102,103
  Laura Gray ........................ 100,101,102
  Lena .............................................. 102,103
  Rufus ............... 100,101,102,103,104
ANDREWS
  Maggie .................................... 298,299
ANGELL
  W H ................. 93,107,164,166,256
ARCHER
  Arthur O ........................................ 256
ARMSTRONG
  J R ......................... 34,35,36,37,125
AUSTIN
  W A ................................................. 181
BACON
  Alfred ............................................. 251
  S L .......................................... 245,247
BAKER
  Sarah T ................................. 314,315
BALDWIN
  Minnie ........................................... 179
BASCOM
  Alice ......................... 19,22,23,24,25
  Allice ........................................ 20,21
  Arthur ............. 19,20,21,22,23,24,25
  John ................ 19,20,21,22,23,24,25
BATES
  Samuel R ............................. 114,115
  Samuel R, MD .......................... 115
BAXTER
  Daisy ......................................... 98,99
  Mrs M E ....................................... 165
  Wallace M ................................... 165
BEALEY
  W H ........................................ 168,169

BEARDELEY
  Pearl .............................................. 199
BELL
  T M ........................................ 219,220
BENNETT
  A L ......................................... 216,217
BENTLEY
  J C ............................... 199,200,202
  J C, MD ..................................... 200
BENTON
  E W ............................................... 217
  A W ............................................... 216
BERRY
  Dena ................................... 56,57,58
  John ............................. 56,57,58,59
  Ray .............................. 56,57,58,59
BETTS
  Bettie .................................... 164,165
  David C .......... 162,163,164,165,166
  Emma ............. 162,163,164,165,166
  Ida Florence ................. 161,162,163
  Wallace M .................................. 164
  Wallace Mitchell .......... 161,162,166
BEVILL
  Alice E ................................ 186,187
  Roy ..................................... 186,187
BICKERS
  A L ................................................. 11
BILLS
  R C ....................................... 246,248
BILLY
  Austin ........................... 210,211,212
  Watson ......................................... 315
BIXBY
  Tams
  2,20,29,49,58,61,62,69,72,80,81,82,8
  5,101,119,127,128,131,149,161,163,
  185,190,192,207,208,221,228,230,24
  0,241,250,257,259,281,286,291,301,
  319
BLACKWELL
  A T ................................................. 84
BLAKELY
  F C ............................................... 101
BLAYLOCK
  Thos A ......................... 280,282,284
  Thos A, MD ........................ 282,284

# Index

BOATRIGHT
  Mattie ................................266,267
  Mrs J S.......................................266
BOBO
  Lacey P ...............................174,175
BOHANAN
  Silway ..................................238,239
  Steven .................................238,239
BOND
  Alice ..............................37,38,39,40
  E H ..............................................40
  Readmond...........................38,39,40
  Redmond .............................37,38,39
  Richard S .............................37,38,39
  Sallie ..............................37,38,39,40
BOND & MELTON ....................1,197
BOOTH
  T S ..............................................5,6
  T S, MD........................................ 6
BOWER
  James
    33,137,139,142,143,145,146,176,182
    ,184,296
BOWERMAN
  Edie A..........................................39
BOWERS
  J H .............................................115
  Luther ...................311,312,313,314
  Ray .......................311,312,313,314
  Roy .............................................313
  Susan ....................311,312,313,314
  Susie ..................................311,313
BOX
  Geo ..............................................54
  M J ...............................................54
BRAINE
  Carrie E T .................................292
  Carrie E Tennant........................290
  Carrie E Tennent........................291
  Clarence......................290,291,292
  Gilbert Tennant....................291,292
  Gilbert Tennent..........................290
BRIAN
  C F ...............................................15
BRIGGS
  I A, MD ..............................162,166
BROADWAY

Eva................................................69
BROWDER
  Bell .....................................228,230
BROWN
  (Illegible) ............................101,104
  H H ......................76,77,78,82,87,88
  Henrietta .........150,151,152,154,155
  Henrietta Hodges ..........149,153,154
  J R.......................................154,155
  John R 148,149,150,151,152,153,154
  John R, Jr
    ....... 148,149,150,151,152,154,155
  John T ..................................32,33
BROWN & MARSH.......................74
BROWN & TURNER ......................85
BRUCE
  H................................................312
  J H .............................................313
  Mrs J H ........................311,312,314
BUCHANAN
  Mattie ................................25,26,28
BUCK
  E 49
BULLARD
  Andre L .....................................269
  Andrew C .............269,270,271,272
  Andrew L....................270,271,272
  Villa M ...............................271,272
  Villey...................................269,270
  Villey M .............................271,272
BURTON
  E W............................................216
  Frederick Arthur ...........272,273,274
  H E ......................................273,274
  Lela M ................................273,274
BUTLER
  S H..........................................79,87
BYINGTON
  Henry.......................................98,99
CALLAWAY
  A B ............................................... 9
CALLOWAY
  A B .................................13,14,15,17
  A B, MD...............................14,17
CAMPBELL
  C M .. 72,73,74,159,192,193,319,320
  E M............................................158

328

# Index

J B ............................................... 271
Minnie ....................................... 199
Susan Frances ........................... 199
CARK
J L ............................................. 170
CARLISLE
J H ..................................... 199,312
CARNES
Lewis ........................................ 267
CARNEY
M D ................................... 133,134
CARR
Wm O ..................................... 14,17
CART
J L ............................................. 306
CAUDILL
W C ............................................ 47
CHARLESTON
Susan ..................................... 38,40
CHASTAIN
J D ..................................... 262,263
CHILTON
Alma Lee ............................ 1,2,3,4
Blake ................................... 1,2,3,4
Jim ..................................... 1,2,3,4
CLARK
Dr J L ........................................ 168
James L .................................... 170
Perry M ...................................... 32
CLARKSON
J D ............................................ 272
J D, MD .................................... 272
CLECKLER
W H ..................................... 262,265
W H, MD .................................. 265
W M ........................................... 263
CLINE
A J .............................................. 94
COLE
Emily F ............................... 309,310
George W .......................... 309,310
Wesley Anderson .............. 309,310
COLEMAN
R B ..................................... 186,187
COLEY
David ................................. 270,271
COLLINS

E L ....................................... 274,277
E L, MD .............................. 274,275
COLWELL
W M ........................................... 260
CONLEY
William J .................................... 207
COON
Albert .................................. 245,247
James ................................. 245,247
Jimmey .............................. 246,248
Viney ................................. 245,247
COONE
Albert ........................................ 247
Jimmey ......................... 245,246,249
Viney ................................. 246,248
Vinie ......................................... 249
COOPER
J T .............................................. 84
COPELAND
J J ............................................... 57
COWAN
M W .................................... 290,292
M W, MD .................................. 292
COX
Fannie ....................................... 318
Fanny .................................. 319,320
CRAIG
J R ......................................... 57,58
J R, MD ...................................... 57
CRAWFORD
Jno P ......................................... 205
CROSBY
Bessie ....................................... 267
CROSS
John H ........................ 111,112,113
M E ............................................ 113
CULBERTSON
J 13
J, MD .......................................... 13
James ...................................... 9,10
CUMMINGS
Minnie Lee ......................... 282,283
CUNNINGHAM
Bettie .................................. 130,131
CURRY
Guy A ................................. 269,271
DALTON

# Index

E M..........310
DANIEL
  Beatrice..........212,213,214
  Betrice..........215
  Eliza Jane..........212,213,215
  J F..........212,213,214,215
  Walter Monroe..........212,213,214,215
DARLING
  W A..........195,196,197
DAVIS
  S C..........204,206
  S C, MD..........206
  W L..........285,286
  W L, MD..........287
DAWSON
  E L..........1,2,3,4
  E L, MD..........3,4
DEAN
  Dr S C..........216
  S C..........216,218
  Sam'L C, MD..........218
  Samuel C..........215
  Samuel C, MD..........216
  T R..........53
  W N..........279,280
  W N, MD..........280
DEBILLY
  H L..........194
DILBECK
  S M..........95,96
DOBYNS
  Annie Belle..........284,285,286,287
  Ethel..........284,285,287,288
  Joanna..........284,285,286,287,288
  Oscar..........284,285,286,287,288
DONNELLY
  W C..........260
DORNELL
  T W..........116
DOWNING
  J H..........50,51,52
  S H..........126
DRISKILL
  Frank..........77
DUKES
  G W..........210
DURANT
  John..........43,45
DWIGHT
  E T..........126,127,129
  Edwin..........125
  Emma..........125
EDWARDS
  M S..........55,56
ELDER
  J L..........27
ELLIOTT
  J H..........311,313,314
ESTON
  W N..........218
EVERETT
  Willard N..........41
EVINS
  E L..........257
  E L, MD..........261
EWING
  C H..........99,150,152,153,224,227
FALCONER
  Henry..........274,275,276,277
  Ida L..........274,275,276,277
  John Henry..........274,275,276,277
FALKNER
  J W..........63
FANNER
  W S..........167
FANNIN
  E J..........260
FARMER
  B F..........47,48,51,52,53
  Benj F..........49,50
  Fannie..........48,52,53
  Fannie L..........47,49,50,51
  J L..........49,52
  Nancy..........47,51
  Nannie..........48,49,53
  Samuel Arnold 47,48,49,50,51,52,53
FARRILL
  Bernice..........15,16,17
  Bernice Emery..........18
  Emery..........15,16,17,18
  Harriet..........15,16,17,18
  Sue Constance..........9,11,13,14,15
  Theodosia..........9,10,11,12,14,15
  Walter..........9,10,11,12,14,15

330

# Index

Walter E ........................................... 12
Walter Edwin ............................. 9,10
FEATHERSTON
   L C ............................................... 266
   Lucius C ......... 265,266,267,268,269
   Mittie A ......... 265,266,267,268,269
   William A ....... 265,266,267,268,269
FERRELL
   R F ................................................ 310
   R F, MD ........................................ 310
FISHER
   Elizabeth ...................................... 300
   Elizabeth Ellen .............. 300,301,302
   Elizziebeth Ellen ........... 300,302,303
   Emily ............................................ 300
   Emily A ................................ 301,302
   Emley ........................................... 303
   Hester V ................. 300,301,302,303
   J A ......................... 300,301,302,303
FOLSOM
   A E ............................ 91,98,165,252
   Israel ............................. 176,177,178
   Joe Mitchell ......................... 288,289
   Joseph H .............................. 288,289
   Julia A .......................................... 273
   A R ............................................... 253
   Sissie ................................... 288,289
FORT
   Brooks ................................... 98,100
FOWLER
   D A ........................................ 26,27
FRANCIS
   Flora E ......................................... 158
   Flora Ellen .................... 157,159,161
FRANKLIN
   W N ..................................... 308,309
   Wirt
      10,15,16,116,122,135,136,137,140,1
      41,144,145,147,148,183,188,202,218
      ,277,278,305
FRAZIER
   Johnson ............................... 200,201
   Mary ........................................ 46,47
   Miriam ..................................... 37,39
   Winnie ..................................... 37,39
FREEMAN
   George ................................. 176,177

FREENEY
   Henry C .................................. 262,263
FULTON
   Dr J S .............................................. 91
   J S ............................................... 91,93
   J S, MD .......................................... 91
   W B ............................................... 194
GARDNER
   E J ............................................. 27,28
   Flora Ellen ................... 155,156,161
   Helena Lawsyann ...................... 161
   Hellena Lansyann ............... 155,156
   Hellena Lausyann ...................... 160
   J A ............................... 157,158,160
   James Adolphus ........... 157,158,161
   James Dolphin
      .............. 155,156,157,158,160,161
   James M .................................... 161
   James W ................................... 157
   Mr J A ................................ 158,159
   R A ........................................ 64,65
GARLAND
   Frank ..................... 306,307,308,309
   J M ............................................... 54
   Jahnie ........................................ 306
   Janie .................................... 308,309
   Jannie ................................. 306,307
   Joseph Mansfield ... 306,307,308,309
   Sarah ........................................... 54
   Ward, Jr .............................. 308,309
GAZAWAY
   Cornelia E .................................. 5,6
   Jessie Jerome ............................ 5,6
   Samuel C ....................................... 5
GILL
   Dr J J .......................................... 242
   Dr John J .................................... 242
   Jno J, MD ........................... 242,244
   John J ................................. 241,244
GILLIAN
   (Illegible) .................................. 270
   Mary F ...................................... 269
GOBEN
   H G ................ 149,150,152,154,155
   H G, MD ............... 150,152,154,155
GOODING
   H L ..................................... 245,247

Jno H ..................................... 275
GOODNIGHT
  E G ..................................... 275
GORDON
  J M ....................................... 303
  James M ............................... 302
  R J .......................... 100,102,103
  R J, MD ...................... 102,103,104
GRAHAM
  Lawrence ............... 294,295,296,297
  Mary ..................................... 296
  Mary J F ................ 294,295,296,297
  S E ....................................... 297
  Vano ......................... 295,296,297
GRAY
  Laura ..................................... 102
  Lawla ..................................... 101
GRAY-ALLEN
  Laura .......................... 101,103,104
GRIST
  J M ....................................... 111
GRUBBS
  J O ....................................... 185
  John O ................................... 186
GRUGGS
  J O ....................................... 188
  J O, MD ............................. 186,188
GYER
  L L ......................................... 79
  Lee L ................................ 75,76,79
HACKSON
  Henry ..................................... 175
HALLOWAY
  Ola ......................................... 196
HAMLIN
  Israel ............... 172,173,176,177,178
  Isreael .............................. 175,176
  Isreal ..................... 174,175,178,179
  Sallie
    172,173,174,175,176,177,178,179
  Sally ..................................... 175
  William
    172,173,174,175,176,177,178,179
HAMPTON
  Watson ............................. 132,133
  Watt ..................................... 133
HANCOCK

Jincey ............................ 132,133,135
Jincy ..................................... 133
Josephine ........ 131,132,133,134,135
Juicey ..................................... 135
A L ........................................ 267
Willie ..................................... 132
Willis 132,133,134,135,136,242,243
HARLAN
  Sarah A .............................. 213,214
HARRELL
  H B .......................... 200,201,202
  W E ....................................... 276
HARRIS
  Aaron ................................ 176,177
  Elias .................................. 252,253
  Mrs S A ................................. 139
  S A ....................................... 139
HARRISON
  M W ......... 116,118,119,121,122,123
  M W, MD ....... 116,118,121,122,123
  W ........................................ 274
  W H ..................................... 274
HART
  J J ........................................ 206
HARTSHORNE
  W O ....................... 137,138,278
  W O, MD ............................... 137
HAYES
  J C ................................. 189,194
  J L ....................................... 190
  Josephus .. 189,190,191,193,194,195
  Josephus C ............................ 197
  Nancy L 189,190,191,194,195,196,197
  Nannie L ............................... 193
  Pearl Luetta Gertrude
    ............. 188,190,193,194,195,196
  Pearlie Luella Gertrude ............. 189
  Perlie Luella Gertrude
    ............. 189,190,191,194,195,197
HAYS
  J C ....................................... 192
  Josephus C ............................ 196
  Nancy L ................................. 196
  Perlie Luella Gertrude ............. 196
  S E ....................................... 156
HENDRIX
  Edgar ........................ 204,205,206

# Index

Evelina ..........................204,205,206
William ..........................204,205,206
HENRY
   Pat .....................................230,231
HENSHAW
   Geo A ...............................................62
HERNDON
   E B .....................................................26
   Edgar B ..........................25,26,27,28
   Lucy ................................25,26,27,28
   Maude ............................25,26,27,28
HERRON
   Jo h L .............................................271
   John ................................................270
   John L ............................................270
HICKMAN
   E H .................................................276
   E L ......................... 137,138,142,143
HIGGINS
   R W .................................................262
   Robert W ................................264,265
HIGH
   Dr M C ............................................77
HODGED
   Henrietta ........................................149
HODGES
   Henrietta ................ 151,152,154,155
HOLLOWAY
   Ola ..........................................193,194
HOLT
   Sue ...............................................61,63
HOMER
   Ellen .........................................94,95,96
   Enoch ......................................94,95,96
   Saler ........................................94,95,96
HOOVER
   Andrew J, MD ............................156
   A J .................................................156
   J T ...................................105,108,109
HOWE
   Mattie .............................................316
HUBERT
   J C ..................................................266
HULSEY
   Wm J .............................................263
HUNTER
   George ............ 124,125,127,128,129
   Minnie ................. 124,125,127,129
   Thomas .... 124,125,126,127,128,129
   Thomas W ............................126,129
   Thos W ..................................36,127
ISAACS
   Ida ...................................................297
ISH
   W W ........................................133,134
IZARD
   S B ......................................... 108,109
JACKSON
   David ..............................................266
   H G ..................................................179
   Mary ............................208,209,210
JACOBS
   Isaac A ......................... 113,114,115
   Lizzie M ....................... 113,114,115
   Nita .............................. 113,114,115
JAMES
   Abner ..................... 206,208,209,210
   Arabel ....................................206,207
   Henry ...........................206,207,211
   Katie .....................................200,201
   Mary ........ 206,207,208,209,210,211
   Silas ......... 206,207,208,209,210,211
   A W ................................................236
   W C ................................................150
JETER
   Alonzo ...........................................235
JOHNSON
   B F .........................................295,297
   Isabell ...................................253,256
   M E .................................................297
   N J ..........................................298,299
   N J, MD ........................................299
JOHNSTON
   D P ..............................286,287,288
JONES
   Amanda .......................253,254,255
   Amandy .......................................254
   Annie ............................................199
   C C ...................... 306,307,308,309
   Charles ................................. 182,183
   Charley ........................ 181,183,184
   Francis M .....................................105
   Frank .............................................197
   Frank H ....................... 197,198,199

## Index

Gladys ........................... 197,198,199
H N ................................................ 105
Hiram N ......................................... 107
Ida M ............................................. 105
J N .................................................. 307
Joseph ..................................... 182,184
Juston H ................................. 105,107
Lela .......................................... 181,184
Lena ......................................... 182,183
Lenora M .............. 105,107,108,109
Louina ..................................... 182,183
Luena .............................. 181,183,184
Maggie ........................... 197,198,199
Mandy .................................... 252,253
Mike .............................. 19,22,24,25
Minnie .................................... 124,127
Sena ................................................ 181
T W ................................................ 111
W E .......................................... 181,182
W E, MD ........................................ 181
Wilson ........................................... 254
KIMBRELL
   Dell ............................................. 196
KINCADE
   Lela M ....................................... 273
KING
   Charley ............... 11,12,13,14,17,18
KISTLER
   J C .............................................. 261
KUYKENDALL
   L A ............................................... 84
LAIN & SHEEGOG ...................... 220
LARECY
   W E ....................................... 246,247
LARICY
   W E ....................................... 248,249
LEE
   Robert E ............................... 189,190
LEFLORE
   Allen 28,29,30,31,32,33,34,35,36,37
   Ella ................. 28,29,30,34,35,36,37
   Ellen ...................................... 32,33
   Forbis ............................. 20,21,23,24
   Louie ...................... 136,143,144
   Louie Fudge ................. 142,143,144
   Louis ........................................... 142
   Luther ............................ 30,31,32,33

Mary B .................................. 142,143
Mayme B ....................................... 144
Ruthie ........ 28,29,30,31,34,35,36,37
LENZ
   John M ....................................... 315
LEWIS
   Charley Allen ........ 262,263,264,265
   E F ....................................... 284,288
   Hallicha ........................................ 94
   Hallisha ........................................ 96
   Mrs T B ...................................... 262
   Ruthie .................... 262,263,264,265
   Thomas ....................................... 262
   Thomas B .............. 262,263,264,265
LINDSAY
   James Murray ............... 219,220,221
   Juanita .................... 219,220,221,222
   Lewis ............................ 220,221,222
   Lewis E ......................... 219,220,221
   Lewis Murray ........ 219,220,221,222
   Mrs .............................................. 222
LINDSEY
   Dr W T ........................................ 289
   Nina ...................................... 130,131
   Selden T ...................................... 130
   W A .............................................. 206
   W T ....................................... 288,289
   Waldo .................................. 130,131
LINKER
   N L ................. 109,110,111,112,113
LISTON
   H G ....................... 318,321,322,324
LOCKE
   Victor M, Jr .................. 135,183,305
LONG
   Le Roy ............................... 96,98,99
   LeRoy ......................................... 100
   LeRoy, MD ................................... 98
LOVING
   Carl Logan ............. 199,200,201,202
   Eva B ..................... 199,200,201,202
   M A ....................... 199,200,201,202
LOWE
   Alvin H .................................. 6,7,8,9
   B M ......................................... 7,8,9
   Boyd M ........................................... 7
   Ella I ....................................... 7,8,9

# Index

LOWERY
  G L ............................................... 6
LUDLOW
  Austen...............................236
  Austin ...... 235,236,237,238,239,240
  Ester Samuel..............................236
  Josephene...........................236,238
  Josephine ...............235,237,238,239
  Lemsay ...............................236,239
  Lemsy .......................................236
  Magdalene ................................236
  Magdaline 235,237,238,239,240,241
  Nellie Samuel ............................236
  Silward ......................................236
LUNSFORD
  T B...................................42,43,44
LUNTS
  Henry................................103,104
LYNCH
  C S..............................................32
  Chas S...........................29,30,32,37
  Chas S, MD .........................32,36
LYNN
  Adley Vy ...............281,282,283,284
  Adly Vy .....................................280
  Henry Lee........280,281,282,283,284
  J Y ..............................................62
  Minnie Lee ............280,282,283,284
MCCAIN
  C E........................................95,96
  J L...............................................22
  Joe ...................................22,24,25
MCCALL
  W A ..............................189,190,193
  William......................................193
MCCANN
  Joe ..............................................19
MCCARTNEY
  Charles.........................215,217,218
  Chas E ................................216,217
  Elsie......................215,216,217,218
  Ruth ............................215,217,218
  Rutha ..................................216,217
MCCASSON
  Enoc F .....................................315
MCCAUGHEY
  Emmett.....................................220

MCCLARD
  C C ....................................293,294
MCCLELLAN
  Ora M .......................................222
  Stelma.......................................222
  Velma.......................................222
MCCLISH
  Durie......................241,242,243,244
  Lorden ..................241,242,243,244
  Minnie ...................257,258,260,261
  Mrs ...........................................242
  Ross ...........257,258,259,260,261
  Sissie.........................................243
  Sissy ..................................241,244
  Zelma.............256,257,258,260,261
MCCLURE
  Alfred Wade .......................120,121
  I N...................................170,171
MCCOY
  N H.............................................74
  N S C ..........................................73
MCCURTAIN
  Ida N.........................................146
MCDANIEL
  Amy...............167,168,169,170,171
  Lucetta...........167,168,169,170,171
  M ................................................50
  William.................168,169,170,171
  Wm ............................167,168,169
MCELHANNAN
  M K ......................................43,44
MCGAHEY
  A J ........................................91,92
  J H ........................................91,92
MCGINNIS
  W P..........................................261
MCINTOSH
  Alex..........................................209
MCKENNON & DEAN .................265
MACKEY
  Forbis.........................................176
MCLELLAN
  Belle .........................................223
MCLELLAN
  Belle ..................................224,225
MCLELLAN
  Belle .........................................226

# Index

MCLELLAN
  Belle .......................... 227,228,229
MCLELLAN
  Belle .......................................... 231
MCLELLAN
  Belle .......................................... 232
MCLELLAN
  Belle .......................................... 232
MCLELLAN
  Belle .......................................... 233
  E B ...................................... 228,230
MCLELLAN
  Edmund ..................................... 223
MCLELLAN
  Edmund ............................... 224,225
MCLELLAN
  Edmund ..................................... 226
MCLELLAN
  Edmund ......................... 227,228,229
MCLELLAN
  Edmund ............................... 231,232
MCLELLAN
  Edmund ............................... 232,233
  Ora M ........................................ 225
MCLELLAN
  Ora M ........................................ 226
MCLELLAN
  Ora M ........................... 227,228,229
  Stelma .............................. 225,228,229
MCLELLAN
  Stelma ................................. 231,232
MCLELLAN
  Stelma ......................................... 232
MCLELLAN
  Stelma ......................................... 232
MCLELLAN
  Stelma ......................................... 233
MCLELLAN
  Velma .......................................... 223
MCLELLAN
  Velma ..................... 224,225,228,229
MCMULLAN
  W B ............................................ 268
MCMURTREY
  Clyde .................................. 117,118
MAHAR
  C H ...................................... 142,145

C H, MD ............................... 142,145
Charles H ............................. 144,147
Charles H, MD ..................... 144,147
MANN
  Jewel .......................................... 180
  Jewell .................................. 180,181
  Jewwll ........................................ 180
  John Leo ....................... 179,180,181
  Stella ................................... 180,181
MANSFIELD, MCMURRAY &
  CORNISH ................... 62,83,128,241
MARKHAM
  S S ...................................... 246,248
MARTIN
  C B ...................................... 203,204
  C B, MD ..................................... 204
  W H ............................... 236,237,238
  Wm L .......................................... 237
MASSEY
  W W ................................... 213,214
MATHEWS
  Alma Lee .................................. 2,3,4
  A N ............................................. 151
MATTHEWS
  Alma Lee ..................................... 1,2
MAXEY
  J F ....................................... 242,243
MAY
  Robt ............................................ 222
MAYTUBBY
  Peter, Jr ....................................... 305
MELTON
  Ado ............................................ 3,4
  Alger ............................................... 3
  W J ................. 223,225,228,232,233
  W J, MD .............................. 223,232
MERRICK
  Edward ...................................... 273
MERRYMAN
  Abraham ............................ 295,296
  Benjamin C ............................... 294
  Carl O ................................. 137,138
  Carl Ocey ........................... 136,137
  D C ............................................. 295
  Grace Ella .................................. 294
  Leonidas ............................ 136,137
  Leonidas E ......................... 137,138

# Index

Marion Francis .......................... 294
Mary J F ....................... 295,296,297
Sarah ................................... 136,137
Sarah E ............................... 137,138
MILLER
   H C .............................................. 167
MILLS
   James ........................................... 183
MILLUS
   L S ................................................ 297
   Rutha ..................................... 295,297
MITCHELL
   Hattie ........................... 72,73,85,87
   M L .................................................. 75
MONROE
   Milton ........................................... 178
MONTGOMERY
   D M .............................................. 7,9
   D M, MD ......................................... 9
   Mrs ................................................ 267
MOON
   Nancy L ....................................... 192
MOORE
   E A ................. 136,137,138,145,146
   Ethan Allen ................... 145,146,147
   Ida N ............................. 145,146,147
   Lyman R ....................... 145,146,147
   Mary J ................................... 279,280
   Nancy L ................................ 189,192
   Nancy M ...................................... 279
   Thomas D ................................... 279
   William .................................... 15,17
MORAN
   D S ......................................... 108,109
MORELAND
   Clarence E ................................... 325
MORGAN
   Hiram M ............................... 105,106
   Hiram N ........................ 107,108,109
   J M .................................................. 105
   J M, MD ....................................... 105
   Justin H ......................... 105,108,109
   Juston H ........................ 105,106,107
   Lenora M ............... 106,107,108,109
   Thos M ..................................... 107,108
   Thos M, MD ................................ 107
MORRIS

   H ............................................ 234,235
MOSES
   Chas ............................................. 254
MOSTELLER
   Minnie ................................. 257,259
MOTES
   John A ................................. 304,305
   Levina .................................. 304,305
   Mary Elizabeth ................... 304,305
MOUSER
   Noah E .......................................... 315
MULKEY
   Jas H .............................................. 131
MURRAY
   Lewis E ......................................... 219
NAIL
   Nicholas ........................................ 266
NAWLIN
   N R ....................................... 265,269
NEEDLES
   T B
     1,19,29,45,48,68,85,119,148,161,171
     ,173,229,251,258,281,285,301,317
NEWMAN
   E A ............................................... 254
   M W ..................... 20,21,22,23,24,25
NEWTON
   Katie ............................. 311,312,313
NICHOLS
   C B .................................................. 15
   T J ............................................. 70,71
NICHOLSON
   Lawrence W ........... 96,97,98,99,100
   Mamie E ...................... 97,98,99,100
   Mayme E ....................................... 98
   Minnie E ........................................ 96
   Omer R .................. 96,97,98,99,100
NOEL
   Elsie .............................................. 183
   Luena ........................... 181,183,184
NOLAN
   M A ............................................... 274
NORRIS
   C W ................................................ 17
NUNNELLY
   A L ................................................. 27
OAKES

# Index

Daniel W ..........................234
Mary A .............................234
Mary Margarite .................234
OWENS
   Clarence .......... 184,185,186,187,188
   Ed ....................... 185,186,187,188
   Susie ............................. 185,187,188
   Susie Bevill .......................186,187
PARSONS
   J M .............................................245
   J M, MD ....................................245
   John M ...............................246,249
PATTERSON
   Isaac D .......................................263
PAXTON
   Eli ..........................................43,44
PAYTE
   A J ........................109,110,111,112
   Nettie W ................109,110,111,112
   Roy K .............109,110,111,112,113
   Roy T ........................................110
PERKINS
   Archie Lee ..........................324,325
   Charlie A .............................324,325
   Ella Riddle ..........................324,325
PERRY
   Albert ...................................170,171
   Clifford .......................................261
PETER
   Barnabas .............................182,184
PILGREEN
   Hasrod
     116,117,118,120,121,122,123,124
   J B ..............................................122
PLUMMER
   Wallis G .....................................151
POWELL
   Earnest .................................216,217
   Mary .............................................55
PRICE
   John R ..........................223,226,232
PRIDDY
   J R ................................................40
RABON
   Boyd ..............................202,203,204
   Cora A .......................................203
   Cora E .................................203,204

Robert .........................................203
Robert L ......................................203
Robt L ..................................203,204
RALSTON
   Benj W .......................................220
   Benj W, MD ...............................222
   Benj. W, MD ..............................220
   Benjamin W ...............................221
RANDELL
   A C .............................................113
RAPPOLEE
   H E .............................225,226,228
   H E, MD ....................................226
   J L .................. 224,225,227,228,233
REDFIELD
   Orrin M ......................................130
REIDT
   Gerald .................................262,264
REXROAT
   U T ................................................ 6
REYNOLDS
   Isabell .........................................235
   J T .......................................117,118
RICE
   F E ..............................................303
   S A .......................................180,181
RICHERSON
   Maggie F .....................................68
RIDDLE
   Henrietta ....................................323
   William ......................................323
   William H ...........................322,323
RIGGS
   J J .........................176,177,178,179
RILEY
   Chilion ...............................81,86,88
RITER
   L H ............................................298
RITTER
   L H .....................................299,300
ROBERSON
   James W .......................314,315,316
   Reola .............................314,315,316
   Sarah L .........................314,315,316
ROBERT
   Watkin .........................................44
ROBERTS

# Index

Sam T, Jr ..... 41,42,209,210,211,212
Watkin ........................................... 45
ROBERTSON
   James W ................................. 315
   Reola ........................................ 315
   Sarah L .................................... 315
ROBINSON
   Cora ........................................... 66
   Denver Madison ..................... 66,67
   Frank C .................................... 323
   Parlee ................................... 207,211
   Samuel P .................................... 66
ROGERS
   B F ............................................. 91
   Dwight C ................................ 91,93
   Dwight Charles .......................... 91
   Geo D ........................................ 90
   Kittie C ...................................... 93
   Kittie D ............................... 91,92,93
   W F ............................................ 92
   William F ............................ 91,92,93
ROSE
   *(Illegible)* F ............................. 170
   Jane ....................... 173,176,177,178
ROWLEY
   H B .......................................... 316
RUSHING
   Frank W .................................. 269
RUSSELL
   Dora ............................. 139,140,141
   Robert ............. 139,140,141,142,143
   Stella ........................... 139,140,141
SANNER
   Charley ................................. 67,69
   Charlie ............................... 67,68,69
   Eva Broadway ................... 67,68,71
   Ira .............................................. 69
   J J ...................................... 67,68,69
   Jessie James ............................. 68
   Maggie F .................................. 68
   William ..................................... 69
   William A ................................. 68
   William Ira ............................ 67,70
SEE
   Geo ......................................... 222
SEETON
   J W ............................ 157,159,160

SHANAFELT
   Richard .................................... 256
SHANNON
   R B ........................................... 101
SHOEMAKE
   Estella ...................................... 293
   J E ............................................ 293
   Lowell C ..................... 292,293,294
   Pollie ................................. 293,294
SHONEY
   W A ............................. 151,245,248
SHULER
   Maggie ............................... 298,299
   Roy Hill .............................. 298,299
   William R ........................... 298,299
   William Robert ................... 298,299
SHUMAKE
   Estella ...................................... 292
SIMPSON
   Joe ........................................ 64,65
   M C ............................................ 64
   Mary .......................................... 65
SITDHAM
   Marion ....................................... 90
SITTLE
   W E .......................................... 323
SMITH
   Aso ..................................... 291,292
   J H P ................................. 289,290
SOCKEY
   Ben ..................................133,134
SONNER
   Charlie ................................. 69,70
   Eva Broadway .................. 69,70,71
   J J ...................................... 69,70,71
   Mrs ....................................... 70,71
   William Ira ................................ 71
SPEARS
   W S .................................. 67,70,71
   W S, MD ............................... 70,71
SPENCE
   G R .......................................... 196
SPENCER
   D O ....................................... 25,27
STANLEY
   W M ...................................... 26,27
STANTON

# Index

W H .................49
STEED
  Dayton B ..............64,65
STEPHENS
  Dan ..............324
STIDHAM
  Harold
    72,75,76,78,79,80,81,82,83,84,86,87,
    88,89,90,91
  Harrie M .................75
  Hattie
    74,77,78,79,80,81,83,84,85,86,87,88,
    89,90
  Hattie M ..............75,76,86
  Herold ...............86
  Marion
    72,73,74,75,76,77,78,79,80,83,84,85,
    87,88
  Marion Z ...............86
  Meron ...............86
  Merron ...............85
STIDHAM HAROLD .............77
STONE
  C L ................133
STOVER
  A F ................316
STOWERS
  Frances ...............61
  Laura Frances ...............62
  Laura Francis ..............63,64,65
  Laura Winnie ..........59,60,63,64
  Wesley ........59,60,61,62,63,64,65
  William M ................60
  William Monroe .........61,63,64,65
SULLIVAN
  C L ................17
SUMTER
  R O ...............164,165
  Robt O ...............165
SWINK
  William W ...............26
SWISHER
  O P .............213,214,215
TAYLOR
  J I ...........318,321,323,325
  J I, MD .............318,322,323,325
  John ........11,12,13,14,17,18,276

THOMAS
  C M .................279,280
  D ..............210,211,212
  Jno J ................41
  Loise .............278,279,280
  Mary J .............279,280
  Mary J Moore .............279
THOMPSON
  Amanda ........251,253,254,255,256
  Amandy ................254
  Calvin
    249,250,251,252,253,254,255,256
  Ellen ...............242,243
  G W ................193
  Green ................50
  J M ................206
  Mandy ...............252,253
  A P ................140
  R A ................102
  Simpson ...............177
  Wallace ...............252,253
  Wilburn 250,251,252,253,254,255,256
THRELKELD
  W C ................304,305
  W C, MD ...............305
TIDMORE
  Dr John ..........189,190,195,197
  John ...............195,197
TOBLER
  Albert ...............277,278
  Annie E ...............277,278
  Emmet ...............277,278
TRAHAN
  Rena ................275
TUCKER
  Atha E ..........115,116,117,118
  Clarence J 118,119,120,121,122,123
  Joseph B ...............119,122
  Joseph S ..........115,116,117,118
  Martha B ............120,121,122
  Martha Belle .............119,123
  Martha M .........115,116,117,118
  Oscar. 116,118,119,120,121,122,123
UNDERWOOD
  Clarence Jefferson . 316,317,318,321
  Fannie ..............317,318,321
  Fanny ................321

# Index

Thomas ............ 316,317,318,319,320
Thomas J ....................................321
VINSON
    Belle .................................125,129
WADE
    Alex .......................................32,33
WALKER
    Dellar ....................................53,54
    Hortey ...................................53,55
    Laura ..................................120,121
    Mary ..........................................55
    May .......................................53,54
    Willie .................................53,54,55
WALLIS
    Watson .........................20,21,23,24
WALTON
    E M .................................12,13,18
WAX
    S H ..........................................205
WEAVE
    L T ............................................40
WELCH
    B A ..........................................242
WELLS
    Henry .................................230,231
WENNER
    S W .......................................95,96
WEST
    A T .............................153,154,155
WHEELER
    J T .........................156,157,158,160
WHITE
    J M ..........................................272
WILKEN
    Josephine .................................238
WILKIN
    Josephine ............................237,239
WILLIAMS
    Daniel ........................................46
    Francis ...................................46,47
    J E .......................................6,103
    Joseph .......................................42
    Martha ...................................46,47
    Travis .................................139,141
WILLINGHAM
    Dollie ....................................64,65
WILLIS

Alin ..........................................41,44
Cillen ....................................42,43,45
Cillin .........................................43,44
James .......................41,42,43,44,45
Levy .........................41,42,43,44,45
WILLIS JAMES ..............................45
WILSON
    Bicy .........................................251
    W A ...........................................84
WIMLUSH
    Robt ...................................169,172
WINSTEAD
    L A ............................................84
    L A, MD .....................................84
WISE
    George N .................................135
WMS .............................................101
WOOLEY
    Samuel L .....................311,312,314
    W L ..........................................313
WOOTTON
    S H ..........................................159
YANDELL
    J D ....................................244,245
YORN
    Jefferson ............................295,296

www.ingramcontent.com/pod-product-compliance
Lightning Source LLC
Chambersburg PA
CBHW020241030426
42336CB00010B/572